Annuity Markets and Pension Reform

This book treats two vital but neglected public policy issues: how should distributions from individual accounts be regulated, and how can the market for private annuities function better? It provides a comprehensive survey of the issues that arise when contributors to individual accounts become eligible for distributions. In particular, the book also addresses the question of whether annuitization or other restrictions on distributions should be mandatory, and if so, whether the provision of annuities should be privatized? Given the diminishing importance of public pensions around the world, the growing number of the elderly, and the increasing importance of defined contributions plans, the voluntary demand for private annuities will continue to grow. Since it is vital that annuities be reasonably priced and that annuity markets be effectively regulated, the book proposes some reforms to enhance the efficiency of the annuity market. Its analytical framework is applicable to a broad range of countries.

George A. (Sandy) Mackenzie is an assistant director, Research Department, International Monetary Fund (IMF) in Washington, DC. He was born in Halifax, Nova Scotia, and educated at Dalhousie University and Oxford, which he attended on a Rhodes Scholarship. Mr. Mackenzie has been a member of the economic staff of the IMF for more than 27 years. His interest in pension issues is longstanding, and his work in the area includes advising South American governments on individual accounts reform, and a number of papers on related issues. He has published in *Finanzarchiv*, *Public Finance/Finances Publiques*, the *Journal of Budgeting and Finance*, and *Staff Papers, International Monetary Fund*.

Annuity Markets and Pension Reform

George A. (Sandy) Mackenzie
International Monetary Fund

CAMBRIDGE
UNIVERSITY PRESS

CAMBRIDGE
UNIVERSITY PRESS

32 Avenue of the Americas, New York NY 10013-2473, USA

Cambridge University Press is part of the University of Cambridge.

It furthers the University's mission by disseminating knowledge in the pursuit of education, learning and research at the highest international levels of excellence.

www.cambridge.org
Information on this title: www.cambridge.org/9780521846325

© George A. (Sandy) Mackenzie 2006

First published 2006
First paperback edition 2012

A catalogue record for this publication is available from the British Library

Library of Congress Cataloguing in Publication data

Mackenzie, G. A. (George A.), 1950
Annuity markets and pension reform / George A. (Sandy)
Mackenzie.
p.   cm.
Includes bibliographical references and index.
ISBN-13: 978-0-521-84632-5 (hardback)
ISBN-10: 0-521-84632-3 (hardback)
1. Pensiontrusts. 2. Lifeannuities. 3. Retirementincome.
I. Title.
HD7105.4.M22 2006
331.25´24–dc22   2006011483

ISBN 978-0-521-84632-5 Hardback

To the memory of Paul Hoeberechts and the memory of Leslie Schaffer
Physicians and Healers Both

At present we want to encourage prudence in the sense of distributing income through a man's life. When that time comes all sorts of fancy devices possibly with a counter-insurance element in it, e.g., annuities on joint lives ...

From the notes of Lord Keynes for the National Debt Enquiry, 1945

***

"Father, I have often thought that life is very short." — This was so distinctly one of his subjects that he interposed.

"It is short, no doubt, my dear. Still, the average duration of human life is proved to have increased of late years. The calculations of various life assurance and annuity offices, among other figures which cannot go wrong, have established the fact."

"I speak of my own life, father."

"O indeed? Still," said Mr. Gradgrind, "I need not point out to you, Louisa, that it is governed by the laws which govern lives in the aggregate."

From *Hard Times*, by Charles Dickens

***

In the strange universe of *King Lear*, nothing but precipitous ruin lies on the other side of retirement.

From *Will in the World: How Shakespeare Became Shakespeare*, by Stephen Greenblatt

Contents

List of Tables   *page* xi

Acknowledgments   xiii

Introduction   1
  Annuities ancient and modern   1
  Renaissance   6
  A guide to the book   12
  Chapter outline   14

PART ONE

1. The Demand Side of the Annuity Market   21
  Introduction   21
  Private annuity markets: an international comparison   21
  Why the demand for annuities is limited   28
  Annuity pricing   43
  The insurance value of annuities   48
  Annuities and alternative investment strategies   50
  Conclusions   55

2. The Supply Side of the Annuity Market   58
  Introduction   58
  Major risks of the annuity business   59
  A simple model of funding   61
  Relaxing the assumptions of the simple model   62
  Other aspects of annuity pricing   72
  Conclusions   78

3. The Regulation of Annuity Providers   81
  Introduction   81

The rationale for regulation   82
Approaches to regulation   85
The regulation of investments   87
Regulation of reserves   93
Protection of annuitants in the event of the failure of
the provider   103
Regulatory implications of the growth of annuity
markets: conclusions   104

4. Experience with Individual Account Reforms   106
   Introduction   106
   The Chilean reform   106
   Other Latin American systems   119
   Eastern and Central Europe   124
   Similarities and differences between Latin America and Europe   128

PART TWO

5. Individual Liberty versus Security in Retirement, and the
   Government's Role   133
   Introduction   133
   The case for restrictions on withdrawals and mandatory
   annuitization   134
   Regulation of withdrawals from defined contribution plans   138
   Public sector versus private sector provision   141

6. Policy Issues with Both Public and Private Sector
   Provision of Mandatory Annuities   144
   Introduction   144
   The scope for respecting individual preferences   144
   Rules to determine the extent of annuitization   146
   The case for exemptions   147
   The form of the annuity   149
   Safety net issues   154

7. Policy Issues with Privatization of the Provision of Annuities   163
   Introduction   163
   The level and variability of premiums   163
   Premium differentiation   167
   Guarantees for annuity payments   170
   Taxation of annuities   172
   Administrative aspects of private provision   175

8. Conclusions and Recommendations   177
   Policy issues with either public or private provision of
   mandatory annuities   177
   Issues with private provision of mandatory annuities   181
   Public versus private provision: a summing up   184
   Making the voluntary private annuity market
   more efficient and reliable   187

   Appendix 1: The Economics and Financing of Annuities   194
   Introduction   194
   A two-period model   194
   Bequests, lumpy expenditure, and other complications   198
   The cost and funding of annuities   210
   Relaxing the assumptions   214
   Adverse selection   219
   An aside on the timing of annuitization   221
   The insurance value of annuities   222

   Appendix 2: Aging and Its Impact on Pension Systems   225
   A parable   225
   Real-world aging problems   228
   Macroeconomic aspects of an individual accounts reform   229

   Glosssary   231
   References   235
   Index   244

List of Tables

I.1 Elderly dependency ratios of the world's population
and major regions   *page* 7

1.1 Principal forms annuities can take   22

1.2 Money's worth ratio values for a group of
countries: nominal annuities   46

2.1 Period life table, New Zealand, male
population   74

4.1 Chile: share of life annuities and programmed
withdrawals by class of pension as of March 2004
(in percent except where indicated)   113

4.2 Basic features of Latin American systems
(emphasizing the distributional phase)   120

4.3 Basic features of Eastern and Central
European systems (emphasizing the distributional phase) 126

Acknowledgments

The basis for this work was a sabbatical at the Urban Institute in 2001—2002, where I wrote two papers covering or touching on many of the issues I deal with here. I want to thank my UI colleagues, in particular Rudy Penner, for providing me with such a hospitable and stimulating environment. I owe a particular debt to Mike Orszag for encouraging me to develop the sabbatical papers into a book. Many colleagues and friends made valuable comments on earlier drafts or helped in other ways, notably: Mike Orszag, Peter Heller, Eduardo Ley, Juan Yermo, Allison Schrager, Linda Mallon, John Mueller, Robert Holzmann, Gordon Funt, and Alain Joustain. My earlier work at the UI benefited from the comments of participants in seminars held there, at the International Finance Corporation, and the International Monetary Fund. I would also like to thank Mark Johannes, Roberto Rocha, Jacob Schaad, and Istvan Szekely for their help on particular country matters. My colleagues in the IMF's research department, Raghu Rajan and David Robinson, contributed with their indulgence of the "book leave" I took at odd times during the year.

Before embarking on this enterprise, I had always been a bit skeptical of the ritual apologies and thanks authors gave their families. Now I understand. Carolyn and Marjorie Mackenzie were wonderfully tolerant of the demands this work made on my time.

Finally, despite all the help and assistance I have received, any errors of any kind that remain in this work are my responsibility, and mine alone. None of the views expressed here should necessarily be taken to represent the views of the IMF, or IMF policy.

Introduction

ANNUITIES ANCIENT AND MODERN

The annuity is a financial investment that entitles the investor — the annuitant — to a series of regular payments, usually monthly, over a period defined in the annuity contract. In the case of a simple life annuity, the payments stop upon the annuitant's death, although some life annuities provide for payments over a minimum specified period, like five or ten years, or until the death of the annuitant, whichever is longer.

The life annuity has the special property of entitling the annuitant to a regular income over the rest of the annuitant's life, regardless of how long he or she lives. It thus provides insurance to retired people against living for so long that they outlast their means, while generating substantially higher income than fixed interest investments, and obviating the need to skimp and hoard in old age. The life annuity also imposes discipline on spending in retirement, because it prevents retired people from spending their nest egg all at once. Unlike a bond, or a more conventional financial investment, an annuity normally cannot be resold. In the United States, and most other countries where there is a market for them, life insurance companies are responsible for funding life annuities, although other financial institutions or intermediaries may market them.

Annuities have an ancient lineage. The word annuity is derived from *annulus*, Latin for annual, and annuities figured in the financial affairs of the ancient Romans. In third century AD Rome, the law regarding wills and estates held that the lawful heirs to an estate should not receive an inheritance that was less than one-fourth of the value of the estate. Wealthy Romans would sometimes grant annuities to persons other than the lawful heirs. This stratagem might have served to dodge inheritance tax and to spite an unlucky relative. Some things never change.

1

In order to calculate the minimum share of an estate due to the lawful heir as well as liability to inheritance tax, Roman law needed some means of capitalizing the value of an annuity's income stream. The law relied on the following rule: if the recipient of the annuity was aged 30 or less, multiply the annual payment by 30; if the annuitant was aged 31 to 60, multiply the annual payment by the difference between 60 and the annuitant's age. This rule implied that a life annuity providing an annual income in the equivalent of 100 denarii (plural of *denarius*, a silver coin) had a maximum value of 3000 *denarii*, which obtained when the annuitant was aged 30 or less. Its value declined by 100 *denarii* for each additional year of age above 30, until it reached zero for an annuitant aged 60, an age few Romans would have attained.

Roman law did at least recognize that the value of a life annuity should decline with the initial age of the annuitant. Then and now, an annuity's value is determined in large part by the life expectancy of the annuitant. Life expectancy declines with age: the older an annuitant is, the smaller the number of payments he will receive. However, the rule that Roman law used to capitalize a life annuity resulted in a very rapid decline in the value of the annuity as the age of the annuitant increased. The capitalized value of a given annual income for life in the case of a 52-year-old would be twice that of a 56-year-old. The life expectancy of a 56-year-old, even in third century AD Rome, was probably not that much less than that of a 52-year-old, however, and a 60-year-old would not have had a life expectancy of zero years!

In the third century AD, the Roman jurist Ulpian proposed to modify the way annuities were valued. His innovation resulted in a more sensible relationship between the value of the annuity and the age of the annuitant. Specifically, Ulpian proposed that the ratio of premium to annual income should decline more smoothly, from 30 at age 20, to 20 at age 40, to 9 at age 50, 7 at age 55, and 5 at age 60.[1]

As Bernstein observes in *Against the gods: The remarkable story of risk* (1996), about 1400 years were to pass before the pricing of annuities became more sophisticated. A rigorous basis for the pricing of annuities required advances in applied probability theory and in the production of demographic statistics as well as the development of financial markets. An annuity provider needs reliable data on the life expectancy of potential annuitants of a given age and sex, and on how the number of

---

[1] This account of annuities in Roman times is drawn mainly from Greenwood (1940). Other sources are Marquis James (1947), Jack (1912), and Poterba (2001, 2005).

years of additional life varies among individuals of a given age. In 1693, Edmond Halley, discoverer of the comet that bears his name, constructed a table based on data from a German town giving life expectancies by age: the additional number of years a person aged 40, 45, 50, and so on could expect to live. The French mathematician De Moivre used Halley's table in his work on the mathematics of annuities.

Even before these advances, life annuities were being used in pre-Renaissance Europe by the Church and assorted annuity dealers to raise funds (Marquis James, 1947). Shakespeare invested a large part of his wealth near the end of his career in an annuity-like arrangement (Greenblatt, 2004). However, the provision of annuities was far from being confined to churches or individuals. The governments of both England and Holland had been using the sale of life annuities to raise money, in Holland's case as early as 1540 (Bernstein, 1996). Adam Smith notes the use of both "annuities on lives" and annuities for terms of years (certain annuities) by England in the time of William and Mary (Smith, 1789, pp. 992–93). Smith also refers to annuities with a term as long as 99 years, pointing out that their value should be very close to the value of a perpetual bond. Annuities with so long a term would have been inheritable. Life annuities were the largest part of the debt of the *ancien régime* on the eve of the French Revolution (Ferguson, 2001, p. 172). However, not until the late eighteenth century were annuities priced based on life expectancy. In the late seventeenth century, both Dutch and British governments were offering annuities at premiums that did not apparently vary with the age of the purchaser (Hacker, 1976). The terms they did offer imply that their exchequers did not have a good idea of the cost of the average annuity contract to their governments, and may also have reflected some default risk.

By the nineteenth century, insurance companies in England and other European countries, armed with more reliable data on mortality rates and the statistical techniques necessary to exploit them, were able to offer both life annuities and term certain annuities, the latter making payments for a specified period whether or not the annuitant survived. Hacker (1976) reports that tables devised in 1780 by Richard Price, who worked from parish registers in Northampton, were the standard source for both British and American insurance companies until well into the second half of the nineteenth century.

References to annuities are common in nineteenth century fiction. The novels of Jane Austen and Charles Dickens are replete with them: one wonderful example is found in *Nicholas Nickleby*: "At every small deprivation or discomfort which presented itself in the course of the four-and-twenty hours to remind her of her straitened and altered circumstances, peevish visions of her dower of one thousand pounds had arisen before Mrs. Nickleby's mind, until at last she had come to persuade herself that of all her late husband's creditors she was the worst used ... And yet she had loved him for many years.... Such is the irritability of sudden poverty. A decent annuity would have restored her thoughts to their old train at once" (1839, p. 126). In *Hard Times*, Dickens caricatures utilitarian philosophy when he has Mr. Gradgrind speak of the calculations of "various life insurance and annuity offices, among other figures which cannot go wrong," which have established that life expectancy has increased. Balzac's *Père Goriot* also includes several references to annuities, including a transaction where old Goriot sells a life annuity in exchange for an annuity with a smaller regular payment to raise money for his daughters. References to annuities in Victorian times would have included annuities funded by private estates and individuals as well as annuities provided by insurance companies.

As the annuities business grew, life insurers developed databases on the mortality of annuitants. They were able to verify what intuition and common sense had already told them. People who buy annuities have longer life expectancies than the population at large of the same age. The average 65-year-old who purchases an annuity will live longer than the average 65-year-old who does not. A line from Jane Austen's *Sense and Sensibility*, well known to both Janites and students of annuities, puts it with her characteristic brevity: "... people always live forever when there is any annuity to be paid them" (1811, p. 10). As the book's subsequent chapters will explain, this difference between the life expectancies of annuitants and nonannuitants, between individuals who purchase annuities and those who do not, is a key to understanding how annuity markets work. Part of it may simply reflect the facts that the demand for annuities depends on income, and that income is related to longevity. However, even when income differences are taken into account, the life expectancy of annuitants appears to be longer than the population at large. This phenomenon is what is meant by adverse selection.

Concern over the consequences of adverse selection explains why many economists have thought that it would be a mistake to rely on the voluntary purchase of private annuities to provide a large share of retirement income. Lawrence Thompson (1998, p. 31) notes that where the market for private annuities is entirely voluntary, adverse selection can be a serious enough problem to limit the market's effectiveness. Diamond and Orszag (2004, pp. 72–3) voice similar concerns.

With the growth of the welfare state leviathan in most industrial and some emerging market economies in the second half of the twentieth century, governments assumed a major responsibility for the provision of income in retirement. This is particularly true of the countries of Western and Northern Europe. The retirement benefit that social security pays in the United States is less generous than the benefits bestowed by the large continental European systems, but it plays a very important role in alleviating poverty among the elderly in America.

Public pension systems normally provide a benefit to retired people in the form of a life annuity with a regular monthly payment. In most countries, the benefit is indexed to the cost of living, and is increased once a year in line with the increase in the consumer price index. In some countries, it has been indexed to wages, with the result that its purchasing power varies with the real wage. The public pension or the annuity that the public pension system provides thus provides both longevity insurance and inflation insurance.[2] Given the importance attached to protecting family members in the event of the death or disability of a contributor to social security, the American social security benefit package also includes a disability pension, a benefit for the spouse of the contributor whether or not she has worked outside the home, as well as a benefit in the event of the contributor's death or the dissolution of the marriage, and survivors' benefits for other family members. The same is true of most OECD public pension systems, although these benefits can take many forms.

The life annuities sold by life insurance companies — the book will refer to them as private annuities when it is important to distinguish them from the annuity that the public pension system provides — are not very popular these days. Apart from a few countries where the purchase of annuities is required or strongly encouraged, no country has a large market for private annuities. This lack of demand stems in part from the public pension system's provision of a close substitute. The sponsors of the defined benefit pension plans that American corporations have established for their employees do purchase annuities on a group basis for retiring employees,

---

[2] Full inflation insurance requires that the lag in the adjustment of the benefit to increases in the price level be short, or that inflation remain low. The combination of large jumps in the price level and a substantial adjustment lag can entail huge swings in the real value of the benefit. The experience of Argentina during the hyperinflation of 1989–90 is a sobering example. Even monthly adjustments with a lag of one month could not prevent large gyrations in the real value of pensions from month to month (Mackenzie, 1995).

but the market for individual annuities, particularly that for life annuities, is small. The market for what are known as variable annuities is quite large, but these instruments lack the basic features of a life annuity. They are more like a mutual fund, with an option to buy an annuity with a regular fixed payment or one with a payment that varies with the value of portfolio of financial assets in which the variable annuity has been invested.

RENAISSANCE

Despite the small size of private annuity markets in most countries, private annuities should come back into vogue. Some basic demographic and economic trends are increasing the size of annuity markets. In particular, population aging around the world has strained the finances of the world's public pension systems, which has encouraged or prompted calls for reforms to these systems that will diminish the role of the public pension in the provision of retirement income and enhance that of annuities and similar financial instruments. At the same time, the demand for annuities has been boosted by a decline in the importance of traditional defined benefit employer pension plans, and the related rise in defined contribution plans (these terms are explained below and defined in the glossary). Finally, the growing share in the total population of older people must have a direct effect on annuity markets, because demand for annuities increases with age.

A global demographic transition. The world is undergoing a momentous demographic transition. Until well into the nineteenth century, even the industrialized nations of Europe had young populations. Few of their citizens lived to see their 70th birthday, and population growth was gradual. With the combination of advances in public health, and notably the revolution in the approach to infectious diseases, improved sanitation and personal hygiene, and a general improvement in living standards, infant mortality dropped and the life expectancy of adults increased (Lee, 2003; IMF, 2004b).

The aging of the world's population continued in the twentieth century under the impetus of declining fertility rates and increased longevity. Between 1950 and 2000, the median age in the more developed regions of the world, as classified by the United Nations, grew from 28.6 years to 37.3 years.[3] The share of the population aged 65 years or over grew from 8 percent to 14 percent. The population was also aging in other regions,

---

[3] The UN classification includes Canada, United States, Japan, Australia, New Zealand, and the countries of western Europe in the more developed regions category.

Table I.1. *Elderly dependency ratios of the world's population and major regions estimates and medium variant from WPP, The 2002 Revision*

	Elderly dependency ratio[a]		
	1950	2000	2050
World	9	11	25
More developed regions	12	21	44
Less developed regions	7	8	22
Africa	6	6	10
Asia	7	9	26
Europe	13	22	49
Eastern Europe	10	19	48
Northern Europe	16	24	41
Southern Europe	12	24	60
Western Europe	15	24	48
Latin America and the Carribean	7	9	29
North America	13	19	33
Oceania	12	15	30

[a] The elderly dependency ratio is the ratio of the number of persons aged 65 or over to the number of persons aged 15–64
Source: United Nations 2003b

although demographically speaking, it remained young. At the same time, falling birth rates and increasing life expectancies of older persons were causing a decline in the child dependency ratio – the ratio of the number of children aged 0–14 to the number of persons of working age – 15–64 and an increase in the elderly dependency ratio – the ratio of the number of persons aged 65 and over to the number of persons of working age.

The aging of the world's population will continue. In its medium variant, which is based on conservative demographic assumptions, the Population Division of the United Nations Department of Economic and Social Affairs projects that the elderly dependency ratio for the more developed regions will increase from 21 percent in 2000 to 44 percent by 2050 (see Table I.1). The aging of the populations of Eastern Europe is particularly pronounced, but population aging in Northern and Western Europe leaves that region with an elderly dependency ratio that is noticeably higher than that of North America.

The sheer increase in the numbers of older persons is striking. The number of persons aged 60 or more is projected to grow from 606 million in 2000 to 1.9 billion in 2050. The increase in the less developed areas is particularly marked, although the numbers of persons in this age group who live in the developed areas is projected to increase from 232 million in 2000 to 394 million in 2050. More striking still is the projected growth in the number of persons aged 80 years or more. In 2000, the world was home to an estimated 69 million octogenarians. By 2050, their number is projected to grow to 377 million (UN, 2003b, p. 16–17). This more than fivefold increase boosts their share of the world's population from 1.1 percent in 2000 to 4.2 percent in 2050. No less than 21 countries, including France, Germany, Italy, and Japan are projected to have an octogenarian population that equals at least 10 percent of total population. China alone is projected to have 98 million persons in this age group, and India 47 million. Despite the large margin of error to which any demographic projections are subject, the conclusion that the share of the elderly in the world's population will increase greatly is inescapable.

Population aging and pension reform. Population aging and reforms to public pension systems that address the fiscal pressures that aging entails will increase the demand for private annuities. The increase in demand will result from both changes in the terms of conventional public pension plans and more radical reforms to public plans that change their structure. The typical public pension plan is financed on what is known as a pay as you go basis. The payroll taxes levied on the wages and salaries earned by active labor force participants pay for the pensions of retired people.

Population aging strains the finances of public pension systems. The number of retired people increases faster than the number of labor force participants, with the result that pension benefits increase faster than the payroll tax revenues that finance them. The conventional solution to this financial imbalance is some combination of increases in payroll tax rates and a reduction in average pensions. This reduction can be accomplished in any number of ways: for example, by indexing pensions, once granted, to consumer prices instead of wages (wages normally grow faster than prices); by indexing the contribution of past wages to the pensionable base to consumer prices rather than wages; or by increasing the minimum age at which a worker can retire.

The financial difficulties of public pension systems have increased the attractiveness of the more radical solution that takes the form of the partial or complete privatization of pension plans. Pension privatization establishes an individual or personal account for each person currently contributing to public pension plans (the book will refer to privatization as an individual accounts reform). In the United States, individual accounts reform proposals typically take one of two forms. In the first, known as a "carve-out," several percentage points of the payroll tax that finances social security are simply diverted to an account established in the contributor's name. In the second, known as an "add-on," the contribution to the individual account is added on top of the payroll tax, and levied on the same base. In some add-on proposals, the additional money for the accounts comes in whole or in part from the general revenues of the budget; in others, it comes directly from the participants. Since the coverage of social security in the United State and public pension plans in other countries is in principle universal or near universal, a public pension system with an individual accounts component is tantamount to a universal compulsory savings plan.

In the typical individual accounts reform proposal, the account holder exercises some discretion over how the monies in her account are invested during the contributory period. The income that an account will generate for the account holder in retirement will depend on the total value of the contributions she makes, and the average return they earn. However, whether the funds that accumulate in the account will generate a steady flow of income that will last through retirement will depend on how the funds are invested at retirement and the form that distributions (withdrawals) from the account actually take.

One of the basic issues this book will address is the amount of discretion the account holder should have over distributions from her account at retirement. In Chile, which pioneered the individual accounts reform, the account holder who is eligible for retirement typically uses most if not all of the funds that have accumulated in his account either to purchase an annuity from a private annuity provider or to finance a series of programmed withdrawals. If the account holder has enough money to fund an annuity with a regular payment that achieves both a minimum level and a specified replacement ratio, the residual balance in the account is at the account holder's disposal. Similar arrangements can be found in other countries that have adopted a variant of the Chilean system. This requirement must increase the demand for private annuities and might increase it greatly.

It is not necessary that private insurance companies (or other private financial institutions) administer distributions from individual accounts. Instead, the annuity could be provided directly by the state, through a specialized agency or public financial institution, or even the agency responsible for administering what remains of the public pension system. Indeed, the question of whether the distribution phase of an individual account pension should be privatized as it was in Chile is another basic issue that the designers of reform need to confront.

An individual accounts reform is bound to diminish the role of the public pension in the provision of retirement income. In Chile, for workers just entering the labor force or older workers who chose to transfer to the new system, the public pension was completely replaced by the annuity funded by accumulated contributions plus earnings. The payroll tax that financed the public pension was simply eliminated. The public pension is now a minimum pension paid only to those Chileans with too little in their accounts to purchase an annuity with a regular payment above the minimum that the law requires. The typical individual accounts reform proposal for the United States would have the income from the individual account replace only part of the benefit that social security would normally pay. But the role that the social security benefit plays in supporting Americans in retirement will be diminished.

An increase in the demand for private annuities can be expected even if governments do not require their citizens to purchase them. Even without an individual accounts reform, population aging will require a change in the terms of public pension systems to prevent their collapse. The average age at which people retire will increase, and pensions will be lower than what they otherwise would have been. The pressures on public pension systems mean that retired people will need to find alternative sources of income in retirement. They will have to save more while they work or work longer, and they will need to make a decision about what to do with these additional savings when they retire.[4] The issue of the adequacy of private saving is particularly important in the United Kingdom, where the public pension is not particularly generous (UK Pensions Commission, 2004).

The demise of employer-provided defined-benefit pension plans. A defined benefit plan is so termed because the plan defines the way the benefit is calculated. A typical defined benefit plan makes the pension vary with the average salary earned in the last few years before retirement (the pensionable base) and the number of years of contributions. For example,

---

[4] A declining public pension, other things being equal, raises the amount of savings (the retirement nest egg) people will need to achieve a given standard of living in retirement. Working longer has the opposite effect, since it lowers the saving rate needed to achieve a given amount of savings upon retirement. Nonetheless, unless life expectancy in retirement declines, the increase in the working period does not reduce the demand for annuities.

a participant might receive 2 percent of the pensionable base salary for each year of participation up to twenty years, and 1.5 percent thereafter, up to a maximum pension of 70 percent of his average salary during his last years of work. Employers are expected to fund defined benefit plans, and it is they, not their employees, who are to bear the risk of a disappointing financial market performance.

For a variety of reasons, including changes to the tax laws which favor defined-contribution plans, the administrative complexity of defined benefit plans, and perhaps an increased aversion to the risk they entail, many American corporations no longer offer defined benefit plans in their benefit packages (Gale and Orszag, 2003). The recent well-publicized problems of a number of large defined benefit plans of financially troubled American corporations as well as a decline in the prevalence of long spells of employment with a single employer (sometimes referred to as the end of lifetime employment) have made these plans less attractive to employees. In place of defined benefit plans, employers are offering their employees defined contributions plans. Whereas some 30 years ago, about two-thirds of employees with an employer-provided plan were contributing to a defined benefit plan, today their coverage has shrunk to about one-third. Moreover, many defined benefit plans have been converted to cash balance or hybrid plans, which remain defined benefit plans legally, but share characteristics of defined benefit and defined contributions plans. In particular, the employer continues to assume investment risk, but the benefit is specified in terms of the contributor's account balance, which earns a specified rate of return and is credited periodically with new contributions, usually made by the employer (R. Clark, 2003).

A pronounced shift from defined benefit to defined contributions plans has also taken place in the United Kingdom, and there have been similar shifts in Australia and Canada. The United Kingdom Pensions Commission has estimated that active membership of open private sector defined benefit schemes has fallen by 60 percent since 1995 (UK Pensions Commission, 2004 p. 85). Employer-provided defined contributions plans typically specify that the employee contribute some fixed percentage of his salary up to some ceiling to the plan. Income in retirement will depend on the total value of contributions and the average rate of return they earn, which is just what happens with an individual accounts reform. Usually, no minimum rate of return is guaranteed.

From the point of view of financial security in retirement, there is a critical difference between the two types of plans. With defined benefits plans, the employer, not the employee, bears the risks of poor financial market performance. If the employer is financially troubled, the employee can end up bearing part of the risk, but otherwise the employer is expected to make good any shortfall in plan reserves, whatever its cause. Another important difference, of particular concern for the book, is that the contributor will typically have more discretion over distributions from the plan upon retirement under a defined contributions plan. It is reasonable to suppose that the demand for individual annuities would increase with the shift to DC plans. That said, in the United States, the annuitization of the balances of employer-sponsored 401k plans is very uncommon. Reno et al. (2005, p. 54) report that less than one plan in five offers an annuity option, and that only two percent of plan participants chose that option.

Growth in the natural market for private annuities. The market for private annuities could be expected to grow even if, by some miracle, a painless solution could be found to the financial woes of public pension plans. Since the elderly are the natural market for private annuities, their growing demographic clout is bound to increase the market's size. Not only do they represent a large share of the population, they are living longer, a development that poses a challenge to the institutions that will fund annuities for them.

One way or another, many countries will experience a marked increase in the demand for private annuities in the coming decades. A part, or perhaps most of that growth, will result from the establishment of an individual accounts system that requires account holders to buy an annuity from an insurance company when they retire, but some part will result directly from increases in the number of potential annuitants, the decline in importance of the traditional public pension, and changes in the form taken by employer-provided pensions. If private annuities do come to provide a much larger share of income in retirement than they do now, then society has a stake in ensuring that annuities markets function as efficiently as possible, and that they are effectively regulated.

A GUIDE TO THE BOOK

This book has two main aims. The first is to provide a guide to the policies that should govern and regulate distributions from the individual accounts that would be established by an individual accounts reform of a public pension system. The second is to consider the adequacy of the regulation and supervision of the annuity business, and how private annuity markets might function more efficiently. The book's discussion of experience with individual accounts systems and private annuity markets pays a good deal of attention to developments in the United States, the United Kingdom, and Chile, because experience with the annuity markets in these countries has been the most studied. However, it also pays attention to developments elsewhere. Its discussion of policy issues is meant to be applicable to both industrial and emerging market countries. In fact, it is this latter group that has taken most enthusiastically to individual accounts reforms.

The book will not treat every aspect of an individual accounts reform of a public pension system. The literature devoted to that subject is vast and still growing. The book is concerned specifically with the rules that would govern distributions from individual accounts, and in particular with the feasibility and desirability of relying on private financial institutions to provide annuities in the event of mandatory annuitization. It is also concerned with the regulatory implications of an enlarged private annuities market. It will give an overview of what an individual accounts reform entails for a public pension system, but will not address in any detail the issues that arise with what has been called the accumulation phase of individual accounts. In other words, it does not discuss how the accounts function during the contributory period, or address such issues as the impact of an individual accounts reform on household or national savings rates.

The design of economic policies usually starts from the premise that the government should not interfere with individual choice or the operations of markets unless it is possible to demonstrate an obvious problem (what economists call market failure) with this policy of laissez-faire. In the case of distributions from individual accounts, for example, this premise requires us to justify restrictions on them based on good evidence of people's shortsightedness or financial incompetence. If the private sector is denied a role in the provision of annuities (assuming that restrictions on withdrawals from individual accounts do apply), that conclusion needs to be based on solid evidence of failures in the annuity market, or similar problems. Similarly, a requirement of group purchase of annuities might be justified on the grounds that this will overcome the adverse selection to which annuities markets are subject.

These basic issues regarding freedom of choice and the role of the public sector in the annuities market after an individual accounts reform cannot be adequately addressed without considering a host of technical issues and matters of design. Some of these issues arise whether or not the provision of annuities is privatized. One example is the precise form the annuity should take. There are many varieties among which to choose. Another is the appropriateness of discrimination between men and women in the pricing of annuities, or the appropriateness of discrimination based on other personal or socio-economic characteristics (health, race, etc.). Other issues arise only when the provision of annuities is privatized; for example, the adequacy of the existing regulatory and supervisory framework for insurance companies.

The growth in the market for private annuities that will take place even if there is no individual accounts reform raises policy issues of its own. Apart from the basic issue of the adequacy of the regulatory and supervisory framework, there is the issue of how the growth in demand for annuities may affect the market itself; the cost and variety of the annuities the market will offer. Could a market for indexed annuities develop in the United States, as it has in the United Kingdom, or would that development depend on a requirement that the accumulated balance in an individual account be invested in these instruments upon retirement?

CHAPTER OUTLINE

The introduction has given the reader a foretaste of the book's arguments, which are developed and elaborated in the two parts, of four chapters each, that follow. The first part introduces and develops the subject of annuities, and then provides the necessary background to the ensuing discussions of policy. The second part addresses policy toward distributions from individual accounts, and the regulatory and policy implications of the increased demand for annuities that can be expected to materialize over the next few decades.

Chapter 1 begins by giving the flavor of the diverse forms annuities can take. It then conducts a quick tour of the international scene, describing the market for annuities as it has developed in a group of countries with annuity markets of varying sizes. The chapter then turns to deal with the economics of annuities, and an analysis of what determines the demand for them, and the influences that have tended to keep annuity markets small. Chapter 1 also compares annuities as an investment with other financial instruments. Chapter 1 and the other three chapters of part one are intended to be intelligible to the informed layperson. They draw from a more technical and mathematical presentation in Appendix 1.

Chapter 2 complements Chapter 1. It considers the supply side of the market for private annuities, and explains how life insurers price and fund life annuities. It lays particular emphasis on the risks inherent in the private provision of annuities. Chapter 3 describes the supervisory and regulatory framework in countries with established annuity markets. The main goal of Chapter 3 is to pinpoint the weaknesses in the regulatory framework that might make private annuities an unreliable source of income in retirement. It also addresses the pros and cons of the two major regulatory models.

Chapter 4 surveys the individual accounts reforms that have taken place around the world, starting with a detailed account of the Chilean reform, and then summarizing the key features of reforms elsewhere in Latin America, and in eastern and central Europe. It emphasizes reforms (the great majority) where participation in the individual accounts component of the public pension system is compulsory and focuses on the distributional phase. A good understanding of how an individual accounts system works is necessary for a proper appreciation of the issues that arise with distributions from individual accounts. Chapter 4 also looks at the regulatory issues that have arisen in Chile and other emerging market countries that have added an individual accounts component to their pension system.

Chapter 5 opens Part 2, the book's policy section, by addressing two fundamental issues of political philosophy that arise with distributions from individual accounts. The first is the justification for any restrictions on individual account distributions. The chapter gives short shrift to the laissez-faire solution of complete liberalization, because this would defeat one of the basic purposes of a public pension system. It makes a general case for a policy of only limited exceptions to full annuitization. The second issue Chapter 5 addresses is the rationale, assuming that there is mandatory annuitization, for private sector provision. Chapter 5 raises the question, and considers what general criteria should be applied to determine whether privatization was good public policy. These general criteria are intended to guide the more detailed technical discussions that follow. Chapter 5 also addresses the issue of whether restrictions should be imposed on withdrawals from employer-provided defined contributions plans.

Chapter 6 turns to the issues of design that would arise with mandatory annuitization regardless of whether or not the provision of annuities was privatized. The chapter addresses such issues as the form the annuity should take; the rule that should be applied to determine the share of the funds in an individual account that will be subject to mandatory annuitization; the feasibility of allowing specific exceptions to a policy of general mandatory annuitization; and the need for and potential hazards of a guarantee on the account balance. Chapter 6 also addresses the distributive impact of an individual accounts reform and its implications for the social safety net.

Chapter 7 deals with the issues that would arise with if annuity provision were privatized. Two vital issues are whether private annuities are on average good value for money, and how stable annuity premiums would be. The chapter will draw on the discussion in Part 1 of the impact of adverse selection and interest rates on annuity pricing. Unpredictable premiums are a potentially important source of risk to annuitants, and one that is distinct from the risk involved in investing the funds in individual accounts in the financial markets.

The privatization of annuity provision raises the contentious issue of the need to guarantee the annuity contract. Guarantees are a mixed blessing, because they can encourage unsound investments by the annuity provider. The institution of deposit insurance is thought to have contributed to the U.S. savings and loans crisis of the 1980s, because it reduced the incentive for the depositors of savings and loan institutions to monitor their financial health and shift deposits out of poorly managed institutions. An ill-designed guarantee policy for annuities could have similar consequences. The move to private annuities also raises the question of how they should be taxed. The United States is not alone in giving social security benefits a tax treatment that differs from other income. Finally, the chapter surveys the range of administrative issues that the adoption of an individual accounts system would entail if annuity provision were to be privatized.

Chapter 8 pulls together the arguments of the preceding chapters to propose conclusions on the three key issues that book explores: the desirable scope of mandatory annuitization and related design issues, the desirability of privatizing the provision of annuities, and the scope for making the voluntary annuity market more efficient and reliable. On the contentious issue of privatization, Chapter 8 does not propose a "one size fits all countries" solution. Nonetheless, the failures that affect the annuities market mean that if some degree of annuitization is mandatory, confiding some or all of the functions involved in the provision of annuities to the state may be more efficient than private sector provision. Despite the popularity of private sector provision – it was the preferred mode of provision in virtually all the individual accounts reforms that have been or are being implemented in Central and South America and Eastern and Central Europe – complete privatization of the distribution phase will not be a good idea for every country, whatever its circumstances and state of development. Public sector provision of annuities implies that some part of the funds that accumulate in individual accounts would be used to acquire an annuity from the government, which could be combined with what was left of the public pension.

The book has two appendices. Appendix 1 provides a formal and mathematical treatment of the economics of annuities and the funding practices of insurance companies that serves to underpin the more informal arguments that the chapters of part one will present. Appendix 2 sets out the basic macroeconomic effects of aging and sketches the kinds of policies that can be implemented to mitigate these effects. It explains why both conventional reforms of the public pension system and radical reforms will need to raise the rate of saving and the rate of economic growth if they are not simply exercises in sharing a given level of consumption across generations. The book also includes a glossary of technical terms.

PART ONE

1

The Demand Side of the Annuity Market

INTRODUCTION

Annuities come in many shapes and sizes (see Table 1.1 for a taxonomy). They differ as regards the duration of the distribution phase, and as regards rights of survivorship — i.e. whether an annuity continues to be paid at some rate to a surviving spouse or some other party when the annuitant dies. Annuities also differ according to the timing and number of the premium payments made before distributions begin, and according to the form the distributions take (fixed or variable). Variable payment annuities may assume a number of forms, and may be classified according to whether the payment has a fixed component or not. Typically, it does. Annuities with a fixed payment may be further classified according to whether the payment is fixed in nominal or in real terms. The single premium immediate life annuity (SPIA) tells us by its name the timing and number of premium payments, the timing of the start of annuity payments, and the period over which they are paid. In addition, the SPIA is fixed in nominal terms, and may or may not have rights of survivorship.

The life annuity is not the only form of annuity — nor are annuities the only financial instrument — that can provide or contribute to a secure retirement. However, it is unique in providing insurance against the consequences of living an unexpectedly long life and either exhausting one's savings before life ends, or being obliged to live in privation to forestall that contingency.

PRIVATE ANNUITY MARKETS: AN INTERNATIONAL COMPARISON

The private annuity market is very small in most countries, if it exists at all. Chile, the Netherlands, Switzerland, and the United Kingdom are

21

Table 1.1. *Principal forms annuities can take*

Duration of distribution phase

Life only or whole annuity — the annuitant's post-annuitization lifetime

Certain annuity — a fixed period, whether or not the annuitant lives to the end of it

Temporary annuity — the shorter of a specified period and the annuitant's post-annuitization lifetime

Form of regular payment

Level (fixed in nominal terms)

Fixed initially in nominal terms, with periodic step increases at a predetermined rate (tilted, escalating, or rising)

Variable

Minimum payment guaranteed

Minimum payment guaranteed with increases irreversible

Variable payment depending on performance of underlying assets (investment risk borne entirely by annuitant)

With profit

Indexed

Indexed with cap on increase in percentage terms (limited price indexed)

Fully indexed (index-linked)

Premium payment arrangements

Immediate single payment

Regular payments (for a deferred annuity)

Timing of income payments

Immediate (payments commence at the end of the first period after annuitization, usually a month)

Deferred (payments begin some time after annuitization)

Right of survivorship

Single life (where payments cease upon the annuitant's death)

Joint-life annuity (where payments cease when one of the lives covered dies)

Joint-survivor annuity (payments (usually reduced) continue until the death of the second life; with symmetric joint-life annuity, payment is the same regardless of which spouse survives; with contingent annuity, payment to one may be lower than to the other)

Guarantee features

Certain and life (period-certain) annuity — payments are made for a minimum specified period, even if the annuitant dies before the period ends

Refund of premium annuity — payments are made until their sum equals the value of the premium

Other

Impaired lives

Sources: Blake (1999); Stark and Curry (2002); Atkinson and Dallas 2000; Reno et al. (2005)

Note: Table 1.1 shows the principal forms annuities can take; it is not exhaustive exceptions to this rule. Canada and the United States may be partial exceptions, although in neither country is the annuity market large in comparison with markets for other financial instruments. Annuity markets are also developing in Argentina, Peru, and the other South American countries where individual accounts reforms were implemented in the early to mid 1990s, and can be expected to develop in Hungary and the other Eastern and Central European countries that have implemented similar reforms more recently.[1]

The annuity market in the *United States* offers many different kinds of annuities. The premium income of life insurance companies from the sale of both individual and group annuities grew by about 6 percent annually on average between 1989 and 1999, or roughly in line with GDP (Poterba 2001, p. 29). In 1999, premium income amounted to about 2.8 percent of GDP. Premium income for group contracts — which are taken out by the sponsors of defined-benefit pension plans for their employees — amounted to about 1.6 percent of GDP.

Premiums for individual annuities amounted to about 1.2 percent of GDP. However, the market for individual annuities is dominated by variable annuities. The deferred or variable annuity, although it has both an accumulation phase and a distribution phase, is essentially a tax-favored investment vehicle similar to a mutual fund. Typically, the policy holder may choose a lump-sum withdrawal option after the policy has reached a specific maturity date, so that an investment in a variable annuity entails no obligation to annuitize. Many variable annuities offer the holder a guaranteed minimum payment, although payments vary with the return on the investments that fund the annuity. Sales of variable annuities in 1999 are estimated to have amounted to about 1.1 percent of GDP. The share of holders who choose to annuitize appears to be low. Reno et al. (2005, p. 78) report that some $10 billion of premium income is generated annually by the conversion of deferred variable annuities into life annuities. However, annual premium income from the direct sale of individual life annuity

[1] The Swedish pension system has a notional defined contribution component (the "first pillar") and a compulsory individual account component. The balances of both accounts are converted into an annuity, which the state supplies. Private pension companies manage and invest the contributions to the individual accounts component, and private asset managers are involved at the distribution stage with variable annuities. However, the state monopolizes the provision of fixed annuities (Palmer, 2000).

contracts amounts to only about $5 billion, or less than 0.1 percent of GDP.[2]

The annuity market in the *United Kingdom* is much larger relative to the size of the UK economy than the American annuity market is to the U.S. economy, and the relative importance of the life annuity is greater. Sales of individual immediate annuities amounted to £7.5 billion (0.6 percent of GDP) in 2004. Some £7.2 billion were conventional (i.e. with a regular payment fixed in nominal terms). The origins of this comparatively greater role lie with the pension reforms of the Thatcher government in the early 1980s. These reforms introduced an individual accounts component into the public pension system by allowing contributors to the public system to opt out of the earnings-related component of the plan (now known as the State Second Pension) in favor of either an occupational (employer-provided) defined-benefit plan or a defined-contribution plan (money purchase plan, in British parlance). The possibility of opting out in favor of a personal pension — something like a U.S. IRA — was introduced in 1988 (UK Pensions Commission 2004, p. 73).

Contributors to the public plan who opt out of it to participate in a private money purchase scheme are obliged, when they retire, to use all of the funds that would otherwise have gone to finance the earnings-related component of the public pension to buy an indexed annuity. The annuity is to be purchased between the ages of 60 and 75, and is priced using unisex mortality rates, to mirror the unisex annuity the state system would have provided. Of any additional funds that an employee contributes to a defined-contributions plan, at least 75 percent must be used to buy an annuity, whose purchase is to be made between the ages of 50 and 75. (In 2006, the requirement of annuitization by age 75 will be dropped.) The remainder may be taken as a tax-free lump sum. The UK annuity market can be expected to grow as more and more individuals with defined-contributions plans reach retirement age (Banks and Emerson (1999)). Other aspects of the UK annuity market are addressed in Chapter 2.

Life annuities have become common in *Chile* with the growth in the number of Chileans retiring under the system of individual accounts that

---

[2] Variable annuities can include hefty surrender charges over some minimum holding period, making them inappropriate investments for older people who wish to liquidate the proceeds without penalty, or avoid imposing a penalty on their heirs. See the article "Who's Preying on Your Grandparents?" in the May 15, 2005 edition of the New York Times. The article prompted a letter from a retired actuary who complained that the negative publicity given to variable annuities could discourage retired people from investing in immediate life annuities, which might benefit them.

was introduced in 1981. This development reflects the restrictions the law imposes on the form that withdrawals from individual accounts may take, the restrictions being intended to ensure that account holders have sufficient funds to acquire an annuity or finance a series of withdrawals that will allow them a reasonable standard of living in retirement. The accumulated funds in individual accounts typically finance either an indexed life annuity or a series of programmed withdrawals. The normal retirement age is 65 years for men, and 60 for women. However, early retirement is permissible provided the funds in the individual account are sufficient to finance an annuity or programmed withdrawal that achieves a specified minimum replacement rate and real value. The Chilean system is described in some detail in Chapter 4.

In *Switzerland*, the law and regulations governing the mandatory employer-provided pension system, which was introduced in 1985, result in what Cardinale et al. (2002) have termed the quasi-compulsory annuitization of pension benefits. About 80 percent of employer-provided plans are defined contributions plans. For the most part, pension funds convert the accumulated savings into annuities or buy nominal annuities from life insurers at group rates. The law requires a minimum conversion factor for the mandatory part of the occupational pension system. There is also a voluntary annuity market that is fed by voluntary saving (Cardinale et al., 2002, pp. 78−83). In consequence, the Swiss annuity market is quite large.

Singapore has a small market for life annuities. Kristensen and Yew-Lee (2002) report that, as of 2000, life insurance companies in Singapore had issued about 23,000 life annuity contracts (about 6 percent of the population of both sexes aged 60 and older). The regulations governing withdrawals from the Central Provident Fund, a publicly-run defined-contributions scheme do not require annuitization, although they do limit the alternatives. At age 55, an account holder is required to set aside a specified minimum of the funds accumulated in his account (the Minimum Sum) to finance a basic level of income in retirement at age 62. (The rest may be withdrawn.) These funds may be used to purchase a deferred life annuity with payments to begin at age 62; withdrawn to make a deposit at a bank, or left with the CPF, where they would earn a minimum nominal rate of 4 percent. At retirement, funds left with the CPF or deposited with a bank are paid out monthly until the balance is exhausted. This choice means that, strictly speaking, Singaporeans are not obliged to annuitize any part of the balance of their account.

Some concern has been expressed that in light of the modest level of the minimum sum (S$ 80,000 or about $52,000) and the lack of a strong interest in annuitization, Singaporeans will be vulnerable to outlasting their resources. Recently, the interest of life insurers in the market may have declined because of changes to their capital requirements that effectively increase the cost of provisioning. The supply of life annuities has also been inhibited by a shortage of long-dated bonds (this point will be taken up more generally in Chapter 2).

One special feature of Singapore's system is that contributors may withdraw funds before retirement to finance the purchase of a house or apartment, and for other social benefits such as education and health care. This liberal withdrawals policy is possible because the fund's contribution rate, which is split between employer and employee, is very high – before the Asian crisis of 1977 it was 40 percent, but was subsequently reduced to 33 percent for those contributors aged 50 or below, and 30 percent for those aged 50–55 years (Doyle, Mitchell, and Piggott, 2001; Cardinale et al., 2002). However, the structure of the CPF together with other policies creates a strong incentive to invest in housing, raising the possibility, as McCarthy et al. (2002) discuss, that many retired Singaporeans will be asset rich and cash poor.

Australia's pension system has a privately managed individual accounts component, known as the Superannuation Guarantee, which applies to most workers. Employers are required to remit a contribution of 9 percent of salary to complying superannuation funds. These funds are often industry based (OECD, 2001). At age 55, the "preservation age," the account holder may elect to receive either a lump sum withdrawal or an income stream. The standard age (i.e. old age) pension is subject to a minimum retirement age of 65 years for men ($61\frac{1}{2}$ for women) and to a means test that applies to both income and wealth. (The capitalized value of life annuities is not subject to the wealth test, but their income is included in the income subject to the means test.) These conditions create an incentive for account holders to elect the lump sum withdrawal option under the Superannuation Guarantee program and spend the money quickly in order to increase the size of their age pension. Partly because of this disincentive to annuitization, and partly because of a shortage of long-term bonds for insurance companies to hold to finance payments to annuitants who survive a long time after annuitization, the Australian annuity market remains comparatively small. Most annuities are so-called allocated annuities, where the balance of the funds is gradually drawn down; they do not make a regular payment for life. Concern over the disincentive to annuitize has led to a change in the law that will increase the preservation age from 55 to 60 by 2025 (Sass, 2004) as well as the enactment of tax incentives for annuitization.[3]

Annuities markets in *France, Germany, Italy,* and *Japan* are small, mainly because of the relative generosity of the state pension system and the important complementary role played by occupational pensions. In Italy's case, its inflationary past may also play a role. The Netherlands has a flourishing voluntary market for annuities, and is thus an exception to the continental pattern of small voluntary markets. This reflects the fact that, although tax-advantaged saving schemes are voluntary, benefiting from the tax break requires that the accumulated balance be entirely annuitized (Cardinale et al., 2002, pp. 58–60).

As Chapter 2 will discuss, a flourishing market for indexed life annuities depends on the existence of indexed government securities. Markets for these instruments have been functioning for some time in the *United Kingdom, Chile,* and *Israel.* They are popular in Chile and Israel, two countries with low inflation rates today but with an inflationary past. A market for indexed annuities exists in the United Kingdom as well, but is not very large, perhaps because the initial payments are substantially lower than those of nominal or level annuities. In the United States, as Reno et al. (2005, p. 51) note, the market for indexed annuities barely exists. Part of the reason for this may be that although the U.S. Treasury has been issuing indexed debt (Treasury inflation-protected securities or TIPS) since 1997, the total stock of these instruments remains small. As of June 2004, TIPS of all maturities amounted to about $200 billion, or slightly less than 2 percent of GDP (Reno et al., 2005, 86).

Markets for indexed annuity, albeit very small ones, are also found in those South American countries, where the individual account reforms implemented in the second half of the 1990s include provisions requiring account holders to either buy an indexed life annuity or engage in a series of programmed withdrawals when they retire. Hungary and other Eastern and Central European countries that have implemented individual accounts reforms in recent years also require account holders to obtain an indexed annuity. These reforms are so recent that no account holder has yet drawn a pension.

This brief review of the international experience shows that annuity markets are larger, or are growing at a faster pace, in those countries that

[3] The retirement age for women is being gradually increased to 65 (Doyle, Mitchell and Piggott, 2001; OECD 1999, 2001).

have public pension systems with an important defined-contributions component and that encourage or require the annuitization of the funds accumulated in an individual account upon retirement. The annuity markets of countries where individual annuitization is voluntary can and do differ in their relative size. Nonetheless, even among countries with sophisticated financial systems and an established record for financial stability, individual annuity markets are small. Group annuity markets can be substantial, but this usually requires employer-provided pension plans that cover a large share of the working population. In addition, even if employer-provided plans are not defined-benefit, the demand for group annuities may be increased, as it is in Switzerland, by a regulation requiring the annuitization of the balances of employees' defined contribution plans upon retirement.

As the next section will discuss, there is a potentially large voluntary demand for annuities, despite various inhibiting influences on the size of the market. There are good reasons to believe that annuity markets should flourish even without the artificial stimulus to demand that is created when the state requires the annuitization of the balances of individual accounts or defined contributions plans, or provides tax incentives for the purchase of annuities.

WHY THE DEMAND FOR ANNUITIES IS LIMITED

That the private *voluntary* annuity market is small in most countries is not in dispute. Why this should be so is less obvious. Some economists regard the limited demand for annuities as a paradox. That view derives from an influential paper by Yaari (1965), which showed that under some special assumptions, not only would people want to invest at least a part of their wealth in annuities, they would invest in nothing else. This chapter explains informally how this result, that annuities might rule the financial world, is derived. Its discussion is based on the more rigorous mathematical presentation of Appendix 1, to which the chapter will often refer. This chapter will concentrate on the SPIA, referred to simply as a life annuity — because of this instrument's unique insurance feature and its (comparative) simplicity.

The Potential Attraction of Annuities

To see what makes a life annuity attractive, it is helpful to think of it as a fixed-interest security, like a Treasury bill or bond, but with the special feature that payment of interest and principal is contingent upon the holder's survival. Temporary annuities (i.e. annuities that are paid until the end of a specified period or until the annuitant dies, whichever comes sooner) are not common, and are definitely not issued for periods as short as one year. Nonetheless, it is instructive to assume that one-year temporary annuities exist, and specifically, that they pay a fixed return plus return of capital if and only if the annuitant is alive at the end of one year. A one-year temporary annuity like this is identical to a fixed-interest security or bill with a maturity of one year, except that payment is contingent on the annuitant's survival.

The one-year annuity *must* be worth less than the one-year bill, since the bill pays a return whether its holder is alive or dead. The difference in value, which depends on the annuitant's life expectancy, among other factors, is highly consequential. Specifically, the annuitant, if he lives, will be able to enjoy a higher level of income and consumption in the year after purchase than he would if he purchased the bond. Put another way, the contingent rate of return of the annuity, the rate of return conditional on the annuitant's survival is higher than the (unconditional) rate of return on the bill.

A second and more realistic example involves a 65-year-old woman contemplating the choice between investing in 30-year bonds and buying a life annuity to finance consumption over a period of what she assumes will be at most 30 years.[4] She considers investing in the bonds, and works out how much money she could spend each year without exhausting her capital. When she prices life annuities, she should find that she could finance the same annual expenditure level for a smaller outlay. The basic reason is again that a life annuity is a contingent security. The bond can generate a stream of income over a 30-year period that is payable to whomever owns the bond, including the holder's estate, should she die before the bonds mature. The life annuity's payments stop when the annuitant dies.

In this second example, we have assumed that the potential annuitant knows that her maximum life span at age 65 will be 30 years. In practice, people cannot be certain how many years of life remain to them. Faced with this uncertainty, a retired person who lacks a sizeable pension and is not

---

[4] The exposition assumes that the investment in bonds is divisible, so that the capital may be encroached upon gradually, without the need for reinvesting the proceeds of periodic sales at rates of interest that may differ from the rate of interest prevailing when the investment was made.

planning to return to the labor market, confronts the problem of maintaining an average rate of expenditure that will not exhaust the savings she accumulated during her working life before she dies. The second example contrasts two strategies of dealing with longevity risk. The first is to make a very conservative assumption about life expectancy, invest in fixed-interest securities and carefully program the level of expenditure so that capital will not be exhausted before death. With this strategy, the retired person self-insures against the risk of outliving her resources.

The second strategy is to buy a life annuity. It is arguably the superior strategy. In principle, a life annuity with a premium no greater than the cost of the bonds should finance a higher level of consumption than the self-insurance strategy will, and if the annuitant has underestimated her longevity, she will not have to curtail her consumption. A life annuity also provides insurance against the risk of overestimating longevity. An annuity can thus protect its holder from both an excess of caution, causing excessive expenditure economies during the retirement period, and the consequences of overspending.[5] More fundamentally, even if a retired person could knowledgeably predict her maximum lifespan, an annuity with a maximum term equal to that lifespan should allow her higher expenditure than a bond of the same remaining maturity.

The higher consumption that an annuitant enjoys comes at a cost. The purchase of a life annuity entails an irrevocable and irreversible transfer of capital from the purchaser to the annuity provider. Since payments cease upon the annuitant's death, her premature demise would entail a substantial loss, for her heirs if not for her. Another cost of annuitization is loss of liquidity. Annuities are not a liquid asset, and normally it is not possible to borrow against the stream of expected payments. Bonds may be sold — although that may entail a loss if interest rates have risen — since bond markets are normally liquid in countries with sophisticated financial systems. Bank deposits and other financial instruments are also liquid, although liquidation before term may entail a penalty.

We now sketch a derivation of Yaari's famous result about the superiority of annuities over other investments. In addition to the

---

[5] In Dante's *Inferno*, one class of sinners, those condemned for hoarding or squandering, are consigned to the fourth circle of hell, where, burdened by heavy weights, they spend all eternity running at and colliding with each other. As Virgil relates to Dante: "Each one of the shades here massed/In the first life had a mind so squinty-eyed/That in his spending he heeded no proportion" (Pinsky 1994, p. 69). Although it is unlikely that Dante was writing an allegory about a world without annuities, a regular life-long income might save many older persons from a hellish post-retirement.

assumption of no bequest motive, Yaari assumed that annuity premiums were actuarially fair, which guaranteed that the contingent rate of return on an annuity would exceed the rate of return on a bond of the same maturity. In the case of a life annuity, the premium should be less than the price of any bond with a term to maturity that equals the maximum possible lifespan of the annuitant.[6] He also assumed, as Appendix 1 does, that the only uncertainty impinging on an annuitant's decision was the date of his death. In addition, there is no need for liquidity. Given these assumptions, a person will maximize lifetime consumption by investing in annuities rather than bonds or other fixed-term instruments. There is no need to hold bonds, because there are no unforeseen large expenditures to finance, and annuities finance a higher regular stream of expenditure than bonds.

Davidoff, Brown, and Diamond (2005) derive results similar to Yaari's, but with less restrictive assumptions. In particular, they find that provided any financial asset, including risky ones, can be annuitized, and there is no bequest motive, annuitization of at least a part/all of a person's wealth will be optimal. Actuarial fairness is a sufficient but not a necessary condition for this result, since the conditional return to the annuity can exceed the return on a conventional fixed interest instrument without the assumption of actuarial fairness holding. The basic idea is that a market could develop for an asset that would have exactly the same return − the same interest, dividend, or capital gain income − as a conventional asset, provided the holder remained alive. For example, a financial institution might annuitize a certificate of deposit by marketing instruments that were identical to conventional certificates of deposit, except that upon the death of the holder, they would be valueless. This provision would in principle allow the institution to offer a rate of return on the annuity-form of the CD that was higher than the rate on the conventional instrument.

Bequests and Precautionary Expenditure

Economic theory implies that markets for life annuities should be thriving, but as the earlier cross-country survey of annuity markets revealed, markets where annuities are purchased voluntarily without tax incentives to boost the demand for them are small worldwide. Much, if not all, of the gap

---

[6] If the rate of interest is r and the regular payment is A, the price of a perpetual bond is A/r. The price of a 30-year bond (B) with annual coupon of A is $B = A/r(1 - 1/(1 + r)^{30})$. The higher the rate of interest r, the less is the difference.

between fact and theory is attributable to the strong assumptions that underlie the theory.

By assuming away a bequest motive, Yaari's model could pinpoint a crucial feature of annuities. Nonetheless, a desire to leave bequests is a basic motive for saving. Adding a bequest motive as a separable argument to a two-period (working life–retirement) model of intertemporal choice implies that a person allocates his wealth across consumption in working life, expected consumption in retirement, and a bequest, comparing the satisfaction he would get from leaving a bequest to the satisfaction from consumption in the two periods. As Appendix 1 demonstrates, the bequest motive should reduce both actual consumption in the first period and planned consumption in the second (see the Section, Bequests, Lumpy Expenditure, and Other Complications). Consequently, the size of the annuity that the person will buy will decline, and the demand for other assets will increase, because these assets, unlike annuities, can be bequeathed.

A question that might arise is why someone who desires to leave a bequest should annuitize any part of his wealth (particularly if a potential heir is posing the question). The standard model assumes that the extra or marginal satisfaction that a person gets from the legacy he bestows diminishes as its amount grows. At the margin, he will compare the expected utility or satisfaction he will gain from an extra dollar of bequest, with the utility gained from an extra dollar of consumption. The larger the planned bequest, the less he leaves for himself and the more he values his consumption at the margin. As Appendix 1 explains, the standard model assumes that wealth holders are concerned not with maximizing the value of the estate they might leave if they died relatively young — a strategy that would make annuities unattractive — nor with maximizing the expected value of their estate (roughly speaking, the value of the estate they would leave if their life span proved to be average). Both of these strategies could entail the wealth holder leaving little or nothing to his heirs, if he lives a very long life. Instead, the standard model assumes that a retired person would plan to leave a specific amount (a certain bequest).

The literature on bequests distinguishes between accidental and deliberate bequests (Gale and Slemrod, 2001). Accidental bequests occur when a person who accumulates assets to finance consumption in retirement and to provide for the possibility of large expenditures caused by medical or other emergencies dies before the end of his planning horizon. (The accidental bequest motive assumes that these assets are not invested in annuities.) The discussion of motives for deliberate bequests distinguishes between altruistic bequests and so-called exchange bequests. Exchange bequests are intended to provide children or other heirs with strong incentives to perform various services (for example, looking after the parents if they are unable to look after themselves), or simply be compliant (choose a socially suitable spouse or career, take over responsibility for the family business, and so forth). When King Lear eschews this approach and instead deeds his kingdom to his two elder daughters while still alive, they quickly renege on their promise to look after the old man in the style and with the retinue he expected.

The literature on the bequest motive is inconclusive. Gale and Slemrod (2001), in a survey of the issue, conclude that the evidence does not support any one of the motives that economists have proposed, suggesting that a mixture of motives may underlie bequests. In the United States, bequests of some amount are very common — although their average size is not very large — but what is less clear is whether most of them have been intended or not. Dynan, Skinner, and Zeldes (2002) argue that it is in fact difficult to distinguish between accidental and deliberate bequests, arguing that the same funds can do double duty: they can finance unlikely but still possible emergency-related expenditures, and they can be inherited. In effect, a person may plan to leave an estate with a given *expected* value — with the actual value exceeding the expected value if he dies relatively young, and vice versa — rather than set aside a part of his wealth for his heirs, making no plans to encroach upon it regardless of how long he lives. In effect, the possibility of a larger than expected bequest makes up for the possibility of leaving little or nothing.

Among the wealthiest families of any country, some part of bequests must be deliberate. The size of the typical estate of the well-to-do is much larger than could be justified by any precautionary motive. The considerable sums that some families spend on estate planning where inheritance taxes are imposed would be entirely wasted if the families had no bequest motive. The purchase or maintenance of life insurance when there is no need for a family to ensure against the loss of a primary earner and deliberate *inter vivos* transfers are further evidence for deliberate bequests (Gale and Slemrod, 2001). What can be said with some assurance is that bequests, accidental or deliberate, must reduce the demand for life annuities to some extent, but how much is uncertain.

As the discussion of accidental bequests implies, the need to finance large and unexpected expenditures would reduce the demand for annuities, particularly given the current limited range of annuity product design. A market for short-term annuities would reduce the need to hold money in savings accounts or in fixed interest investments to defray exceptional expenditure. The shorter the term of the annuity, the more liquid it would be. As in the earlier example, an annuity might have a term of one year, but with the original premium plus interest being paid in 12 monthly installments contingent on the annuitant's survival through the end of the year, with the monthly payments being saved. If the need for the exceptional expenditure did not arise, the one-year annuity could simply be rolled over. If there is a moderate amount of leeway in the financing of unforeseen expenditure, people could hold a life annuity to finance regular expenditure, and an annuity like the one just described to finance a part of exceptional expenditure.

In many countries, a market does exist for annuities with a term as short as five years. Terms shorter than this would entail frequent rollovers, which would have a prohibitive effect on transactions costs and hence on the premium per dollar.[7] Given the limits on terms, someone who annuitized too large a share of his wealth might be risking serious liquidity problems. The risk to the elderly of such problems can be reduced if they obtain health and long-term care insurance. This step would obviate the need to maintain a large precautionary balance to defray the heavy bills that an unexpected illness might bring in its wake, and reduce the risk that investing in an annuity would entail serious liquidity problems.[8] It follows that the demand for annuities should in principle increase as insurance for the contingencies against which precautionary balances are maintained becomes less expensive and more widely available.

Tax-favored Competing Assets

The tax systems of many countries reduce the demand for annuities by treating other assets more favorably. The preferential tax treatment of housing and certain savings vehicles in the United States and other countries undoubtedly reduces the demand for annuities. The typical American on the verge of retirement holds a large share of her assets in

---

[7] Suppose there was a lump-sum element to the cost of a one year annuity equal to one percent of the premium. Comparing the cost of five successive one-year annuities to a five-year term annuity (itself very short), the flexibility of the one-year arrangements would cost approximately an additional four percent of the initial capital.

[8] A life annuity can be combined with disability insurance by incorporating an uplift feature, under which the regular payment is increased by some specified amount upon the onset (and determination) of disability. Annuities with this feature have been issued in the UK.

residential housing — the house or apartment she lives in and owns. This is particularly true of the less well off, although not of the very poor, for whom social security wealth — the capitalized value of expected social security benefits — can account for nearly all of their wealth (Gustman et al., 1997, p. 75). Homeownership rates are quite high in other industrialized countries as well.

The owner-occupier who is retiring could conceivably sell her house and use some or all of the proceeds to acquire an annuity, and then rent a similar property. As Appendix 1 discusses at greater length (see the Sub-section, Competing Assets: Residential Investment), the tax treatment of owner-occupied housing means that owning will in fact dominate renting.[9] In most countries, the owner-occupier, unlike a rental property company, pays no tax on the imputed rent she is deemed to earn on her property. The conditional rate of return to an annuity would have to be very high to make selling a home, buying an annuity and renting the preferred strategy. In any case, tax considerations are only one influence on the decision to own rather than rent a home.

The favorable tax treatment of retirement savings vehicles like the IRA and the 401(k) plan in the United States, and the Registered Retirement Savings Plan in Canada may have an indirect impact on annuity demand. The funds that accumulate in these accounts typically must be withdrawn within a few years of the normal retirement age. To the extent that they actually increase retirement savings, they could be expected to increase the demand for annuities. In the United States, the purchase of an annuity does not reduce the account holder's liability to tax upon withdrawal of the funds in the account. In Canada, holders of tax-favored savings plans must at age 69 either buy an annuity or set up what is known as a "discretionary managed" withdrawal plan to avoid paying tax on distributions. The tax treatment of annuity income depends on the source of its funding, as Chapter 7 will discuss, and in particular whether the funds are deductible (come from before-tax income) or not deductible (come from after-tax income) from taxable income. When the tax treatment of the source of funding for annuities is taken account of, it is usually the case that OECD country tax systems treat individual annuities less favorably than they treat employer-provided pensions. The tax incentives that the Netherlands gives to annuities (described earlier) are not typical of OECD countries.

---

[9] Favorable tax treatment is not the only good reason to prefer owning to renting. Apart from pride of ownership, a house is to some extent a hedge against inflation (and rent increases).

Reverse Mortgages

Markets for reverse mortgages are found in Australia, the United Kingdom (where the arrangement is known as a lifetime mortgage with a roll up feature), and the United States. These markets are very little developed in other countries if they exist at all, although other countries are considering the potential role they might play in increasing the cash income of the elderly. In the United States, a reverse mortgage allows an older homeowner to draw on that part of her wealth embodied in her principal residence to finance consumption without requiring her either to give up title to the home or to service a mortgage. Specifically, with a reverse mortgage, a financial institution lends money to an older homeowner, but no payment of either interest or principal normally takes place until the homeowner or owners die, move out or sell the home (Eschtruth and Tran, 2001). Instead, the balance of the loan is capitalized at the rate of interest stipulated in the contract. The proceeds of the loan take the form of a certain annuity, a life annuity, or a line of credit (where the available balance under the line of credit increases at the rate of interest). The most popular forms of the loan are the line of credit and a certain annuity, or a combination of the two. Reverse mortgages are not a tax-favored form of borrowing, but demand for them may be indirectly stimulated by the favorable tax treatment of owner-occupied housing.

The comparative lack of popularity of reverse mortgages taking the form of life annuities could also result from the protection from eviction that the reverse mortgage contract provides even if it does not take this particular form. It is useful to think of a reverse mortgage loan as a combination of a conventional loan, albeit one that is rolled over, and a deferred life annuity that starts when the equity in the home has been reduced to zero, with payments equal to the accruing interest on the loan. This feature of a reverse mortgage provides some longevity insurance even if the loan is taken in a line of credit or certain annuity.

In the United Kingdom, the lifetime mortgage is one of two means of unlocking the equity in a home. The other is an equity reversion, where the provider of the funds becomes part or whole owner of the property. The lifetime mortgage takes a number of forms: under the home income plan, the lender makes a lump-sum payment that is used to buy a fixed nominal annuity, part of which pays the interest on the mortgage. Title to the home remains with the original owner, who receives income from the annuity for the rest of her life. The extra income this arrangement provides increases with the age of the homeowner. A failure to make the interest payments could result in the owner's losing her title to the home. Under a roll-up mortgage, which is similar to the U.S. reverse mortgage, interest is not paid, but accrues (FSA, 2005).

The U.S. market for reverse mortgages appears to be growing rapidly, albeit from a very small base. As of 2000, there were only 60,000 reverse mortgages outstanding, or less than 1 percent of the estimated market (Eschtruth and Tran, 2001). More recently, a trade association report shows that new federally insured reverse mortgages amounted to 18,000 in the twelve months ending in September 2003, which suggests that market penetration has increased somewhat, even if it remains very low in comparison with that for conventional mortgages. The lack of popularity to date of reverse mortgages in the United States has been attributed to a stigma associated with the reverse mortgage that deters many potential applicants, to the inhibiting impact on the lender of the protections given the borrower, and to high settlement and closing costs, among other factors.[10]

Data on the size of the UK market are not comprehensive, although the fact that 24,440 new loans were taken out in the year ending in June 2004 suggest that the outstanding number of such loans must be larger in absolute terms, and substantially larger in relative terms, than their number in the United States (Ernst and Young, 2004). The Financial Service Authority of the United Kingdom, the regulatory authority for the country's financial sector, publishes fact sheets for potential borrowers explaining the advantages and pitfalls of equity release and lifetime mortgage schemes.

The demand for reverse mortgages may be inhibited by the bequest motive, as Mitchell and Piggott (2003) suggest. Whatever form the loan on the property takes, taking out a reverse mortgage means that the consumption of the homeowner can be higher than it otherwise would be, and the size of the potential bequest she could make would be lower.

Nonetheless, taking out a reverse mortgage is compatible with having a bequest motive. Its impact on the size of a bequest depends on the size of the loan, and on the form it takes. If all of the homeowner's wealth took the form of the equity in the home, then a reverse mortgage in the form of a life annuity for the maximum value the lender allowed could greatly reduce

---

[10] The homeowner is not obliged to sell his home to pay off the mortgage, and his liability is limited to the value of the house. The lender is effectively assuming mortality risk, since the outstanding balance can accumulate as long as the homeowner is alive. For further discussion, see Eschtruth and Tran (2001) and Mitchell and Piggott (2003).

the size of the potential bequest the homeowner could make. But the homeowner could choose a smaller annuity, or a combined life annuity and line of credit. As the chapter has discussed, someone wishing to make a bequest of a specified amount or range maximizes welfare by investing at least part of her retirement nest egg in a life annuity. Similar arguments apply to some of the lifetime mortgages available in the United Kingdom, specifically those that offer a "no-negative-equity" guarantee (FSA, 2005).

The impact of reverse mortgages on the annuity market is uncertain. A flourishing market for reverse mortgages might stimulate an increase in demand for annuities by older people, because they may opt for either a life or certain annuity. The popularity of the line of credit in the United States implies that the bequest or precautionary asset holding motives are more important than longevity insurance. Nonetheless, the further growth of the market could stimulate demand for annuities, particularly among childless homeowners, for whom the bequest motive would presumably be less strong.

The Public Pension System

The public pension system provides potent competition to the private annuity market. Introducing a public pension system into an intertemporal choice model has the predictable effect of reducing demand for private annuities — the public pension, which takes the form of an indexed life annuity is a substitute for the private pension — although the exact effect depends on the characteristics of the public benefit (see Sub-section, Competition from the Public Pension System in Appendix 1). Assuming for simplicity that the implicit rate of return of the public system equals the expected rate of return of a private annuity, the introduction of the public pension should have no impact on consumption in working life or in retirement if the public pension remains below the value of the regular payment made by the annuity that would be demanded in its absence. What happens is that private saving during working life to purchase an annuity is reduced by exactly the amount of the taxes levied to pay for the public system. In effect, the payroll tax that finances the public pension is treated as forced saving.

If the benefit that the public system provides is large enough, the model predicts that its introduction could eliminate the private annuity market altogether. If the average public pension is so large that the value of the taxes that finance it exceeds the value of the regular payment of the annuity that would have been purchased were there no public pension, the demand for private annuities is eliminated and consumption during working life will fall. The model also predicts that a reduction in the size of the public pension system can increase the demand for private annuities. In the case just described, this increase might not occur in response to a modest reduction in the size of the public system, if people were initially over-annuitized. Parenthetically, we should recognize that the family itself — the state writ small — can offer competition to a life annuity because, like a formal insurance arrangement, it facilitates risk pooling (Kotlikoff and Spivak, 1981). However, single-earner or single adult families are more prone to longevity risk than two-earner households are, because there is less scope for risk-pooling.

Some public pension systems are designed to replace a large share of the typical worker's income upon retirement. The systems of many euro area countries, including France, Germany, and Italy fall in this category. In Italy, for example, the replacement rate (after tax) for a worker earning 1.5 times the average pensionable wage in 2002 was close to 100 percent. In Germany and France, it was about 80 percent (OECD, 2004). These rates fall off as income increases. Nonetheless, the comparative generosity of the pension system must inhibit demand for private annuities for even relatively well-off retirees. In the United States, social security aims to replace quite a high share of the income of the low-paid, but the replacement rate falls to 15 percent once average indexed monthly earnings (the concept used to calculate the pensionable base) rises above about $3700. Consequently, its inhibiting effect on annuity demand might be muffled for the better paid.

Employer (occupational) pension plans should crowd out demand for annuities in the same way that public plans do, particularly if they take the form of defined benefit plans. The move away from defined benefit plans in the United States, the United Kingdom, Australia, and Canada that the introduction noted may attenuate this effect. With defined contributions plans, the employee may normally elect to buy an annuity, and this may lead to an increase in demand for individual annuities. There are no signs that this is occurring as yet.

One way to analyze the impact of changes in the generosity of the benefit of the public pension system on the size of the private annuity market is to calculate the share of a person's wealth that takes the form of an annuity. Annuitized wealth is a measure of the current or present discounted value of a stream of annuity and other regular payments, like the benefits of a public pension system. It can be calculated and compared with the value of conventional assets, like a house, savings accounts, and mutual funds. If the ratio of annuitized wealth to total wealth — the sum of annuitized and non-annuitized wealth — of a retired person is high, he may well be over-annuitized, in the sense that the share of his wealth that is annuitized is greater than he would choose if free to do so. One sign that a retired person is over-annuitized could be holdings of life insurance — unless he has also purchased an annuity voluntarily — since life insurance is one way of undoing the impact of involuntary annuitization and allowing the policy holder to make a larger bequest than he otherwise could (Brown, 1999). Under-annuitization is also possible.

Although the optimal degree of annuitization can be modeled under certain assumptions, its practical determination for a particular individual is very difficult. If a person has no pension or annuity, but is free to buy an annuity, we could conclude that he is not under-annuitized, because he can choose to annuitize more of his wealth but has not done so. But we might also conclude that problems with annuities markets discourage him from buying one, or that he fails to appreciate the longevity insurance that a life annuity provides.

Lack of Understanding

The lack of understanding by potential annuitants of an annuity's properties deserves a place, and probably a prominent one, among the influences that have inhibited the growth of the annuity market. People may not be aware that the conditional rate of return to an annuity is significantly higher than the rate of return to more conventional fixed interest instruments. One large U.S. annuity provider argues that people do not understand the concept of a "shared risk pool," and how it allows an insurance company to make the same promise of income for life to all holders of a life annuity (TIAA-CREF, 2004). In a similar vein, but in more academic language, Diamond (2004, p. 6) refers to: "the failure of much of the population to understand the properties of stochastic variables, as has been documented by cognitive psychologists." Simple short-sightedness may also be playing a role in inhibiting demand for annuities. If a person heavily discounts the future, not because he believes he is going to die soon but because he simply pays no regard to the future, he will place little value on the more distant payments of the stream he expects to receive.

Adverse Selection and Moral Hazard

A final inhibiting influence on demand for annuities is adverse selection. Annuity annuitants tend to live longer — as Mrs. Dashwood observes in Austin's (1811) *Sense and Sensibility* — than the population at large. This greater longevity is reflected in the premiums that annuity providers charge their customers. Women live longer than men, and that is also reflected in differentiated premiums. The problem of adverse selection arises because, although men and women can be distinguished, it is not possible to easily distinguish within the sexes between groups with different life expectancies. Annuity providers cannot offer everyone the premium they would offer the group with the shortest life expectancy, even if they could identify that group in the first place. As a result, the cost of annuities for groups with short life expectancies may be prohibitively high. Income and life expectancy are correlated, so that this feature of the annuity market disadvantages the poor.

Adverse selection is often fingered as the chief culprit behind small annuity markets. In fact, it is very difficult to know what effect the mitigation or elimination of adverse selection would have on the size of annuity markets. The premiums paid by the longer lived would rise, since they would no longer be partly subsidized by the premiums paid by the shorter lived. This would tend to reduce the former group's demand. The premiums paid by other groups would decline. If they had participated little in the annuity market before, and the difference in life expectancy between them and the longer lived were sufficiently great, then their premiums might decline substantially.

Universal mandatory annuitization of part or all of the balances in individual accounts would lower the average life expectancy of the annuitant population, and should lower the average premium for each sex. In this respect, it differs from the reduction or elimination of adverse selection that results from better information on the longevity of different sub-groups in the population. The findings of Palmon and Spivak (2002) suggest that mandatory annuitization may not have a sizeable impact on premiums. They note that as long as the conditional return to the annuity exceeds the rate of interest, and the bequest motive and other inhibiting influences on demand are weak enough to be ignored, a group with a below normal life expectancy will be participating in the market even before annuitization becomes mandatory. It follows that annuity premiums will already be reflecting the participation of this group to some extent. Mandatory annuitization should increase the (involuntary) demand for annuities by this group, but the size of the increase and the impact on the average premium will depend on the terms of the mandatory annuity, and the size of the short-lived group compared to the population as a whole. This topic is pursued further in Chapter 7 and in the Section, Adverse Selection in Appendix 1, where a model is presented that can be used, given some simplifying assumptions, to make a rough estimate of the impact of mandatory annuitization. Walliser (2000) estimates that mandatory annuitization in the United States would reduce premiums by 2–3 percent, which seems modest.

In property and casualty insurance, the constricting impact of adverse selection on market size can be mitigated not only by information on the actual experience of the insured, but also by the way the insurance contract is designed. Ideally, a contract may be so structured that members of different risk groups reveal themselves by the amount and form of the coverage they choose. In the specific case of automobile insurance, providers can distinguish between good and bad drivers based on their driving experience, if reliable information on that experience is available. However, the design of the contract – in the case of auto insurance, the deductible, or the value that insurance will not cover in a single loss – can serve a similar purpose. For example, policy holders who elect a deductible of $1000 – which means that the first $1000 of loss from an incident is not covered – pay less for their insurance than policy holders who elect coverage with a deductible of $500. The first option is likely to appeal to good drivers, if they are not too risk averse and the second to bad. By their choice of policy, good and bad drivers identify the characteristics that are relevant to their insurability but cannot be otherwise verified.

In a study of the UK annuity market, Finkelstein and Poterba (2000) find that in the voluntary segment of the market a relationship exists between the form of the annuity chosen and the longevity of the annuitants. In both the voluntary market and the compulsory market (i.e. the market for those who, having opted out of the state system, are obliged to annuitize at some point), they find strong evidence that annuitants who select more backloaded annuities (with tilt) are longer-lived than those who do not. Similarly, among voluntary annuitants, those who pick an annuity which guarantees a repayment of principal to the estate are shorter-lived than those who do not select this option. They also find that there is a relationship among compulsory annuitants between the size of the premium and longevity, but not among voluntary annuitants. These findings suggest that the design of an annuity contract may promote the kind of self-selection that takes place with other kinds of insurance.

In the United States, anti-discrimination law may cause some degree of adverse selection. It is not lawful to discriminate racially in pricing annuities, despite the significant differences in longevity across the races. Even so, it would be technically possible for annuity providers to use the kind of rating system that insurance companies use when underwriting life insurance. At present, most annuity providers use only age and sex/gender to classify potential annuitants, although at least one insurer has recently offered an annuity for the seriously ill. Diamond (2004) suggests that U.S. annuity providers do not use a risk classification system because the market for individual annuities, unlike the market for life insurance, is too small to make the start-up costs for the system worth while. In contrast, there is a thriving market in the United Kingdom for enhanced annuities, which are intended for people whose unhealthy life-styles reduce their life expectancy below normal, and for people with life-threatening illnesses.

Moral hazard is the other inherent characteristic of insurance markets that is thought to impair their efficient functioning. It is a basic fact of life that when people insure against a risk, they are more likely to engage in the risky behavior, or exercise less care in avoiding it. (As an example of the latter, the insured auto is more likely to be left out on the street, and not put safely in the garage than is the uninsured auto.) In the life annuity market, moral hazard would manifest itself in healthier behavior: upon signing the contract, annuitants would quit smoking, exercise more, live a more sober if not a more godly life, and so on. Evidence on the importance of moral hazard with life annuities is slim. One (not entirely facetious) reason for thinking it is probably unimportant is that it entails giving up vices, and exercising more self-control. The opposite is the case with life insurance, which creates an incentive for (or reduces the disincentive against) dangerous or rash behavior and unhealthy lifestyles.

ANNUITY PRICING

A Simple Model

Aside from noting that the premium for a life annuity will be less than that of a long-term bond, we have not addressed what determines annuity premiums. Anticipating the discussion of Chapter 2, and making some simplifying assumptions, it is possible to show how annuity premiums and bond prices are related.

To price annuities, the provider must project both interest rates and mortality rates. Taking the case of a female annuitant aged 65, we assume that that rate of interest is a constant, and that the probabilities that the annuitant will survive one, two, three, four ... thirty-five years after annuitization are known and constant. We assume that no one survives past age 100.[11] This implies, as Chapter 2 will discuss more fully, that there is select mortality risk but not aggregate mortality risk. To simplify the exposition further, we will also assume that the annuity payment is made annually (not monthly, as is customary), starting one year following annuitization.

Denoting the interest rate by r, and the probability of survival of female annuitants to year i after annuitization by SP_i, the present value of the expected stream of one dollar annuity payments (PVAP) to a woman aged 65 at annuitization will be:

$$PVAP = \sum_{i=1}^{35} \frac{SP_i}{(1+r)^i} \tag{1.1}$$

As Chapter 2 will explain, Eq. (1.1) assumes that the annuity provider funds annuities with bonds whose maturities match those of the expected payments to annuitants. If the annuity provider incurred no costs, and if it had a sufficiently large number of policy holders, this expression would be a good approximation of what it could charge per dollar of regular annuity payment, and not make losses.

If we assume that the probability that a member of the group of annuitants aged 65 upon annuitization and alive in year $i-1$ will survive to year i is ps_i and define ϕ_i equal to $(1-ps_i)/ps_i$ for all i then the formula can be re-expressed as:

$$PVAP = \sum_{i=1}^{35} \frac{1}{(1+r)^i \cdot \prod_{i=1}^{35}(1+\phi_i)} \tag{1.2}$$

where $(1+\phi_i) = 1/ps_i$ and

$$\frac{1}{\prod_{i=1}^{t}(1+\phi_i)} = SP_t$$

[11] As a practical matter, the combination of the low probability of attaining that age and the discount factor means that this simplification would have little effect on the calculation.

For the sake of illustration, it is useful to assume that the *ps* and ϕ terms are constant, in which case Eq. (1.2) becomes:

$$\text{PVAP} = \sum_{i=1}^{35} \frac{1}{(1+r)^i \cdot (1+\phi)^i} \tag{1.3}$$

This expression effectively discounts a certain stream of payments by a factor that is (roughly) equal to the sum of the regular discount rate and the year by year mortality rate. As an example, if the annual rate of interest *r* equals 5 percent and ϕ equals 3 percent (which implies that the annual mortality rate is about 3 percent), then the effective discount rate used to price the annuity is about 8 percent, which is the conditional rate of return referred to earlier. (When *ps* is close to one, ϕ is approximately equal to (1−ps).) A price of a bond that paid one dollar for thirty five years (with no final payment of principal) is given by Eq. (1.3), but with ϕ set equal to zero. The greater the mortality rate, the cheaper the annuity is relative to the bond.

Empirical Studies of Annuity Premiums

The mechanical application of Eq. (1.1) to actual data on annuity payments and interest rates should produce a result that understates the actual premium that a life insurance company would charge. There should be a discrepancy, simply because financial intermediation is not costless. A growing body of research has investigated the size of the discrepancy – the gap between the premium annuitants pay per dollar of regular payment and the present discounted value calculation of Eq. (1.1).[12] These studies calculate the ratio of the present discounted value calculated using Eq. (1.1) to actual premiums per dollar of regular payment, which is known as the money's worth ratio (MWR or MW ratio).

Studies of annuity markets in the small group of countries where they flourish have found that the MW ratio is usually less than one for the general population (i.e. when the survival probabilities used in Eq. (1.1) are those of the general population). This is especially true of the United States and the United Kingdom (see Table 1.2).

[12] Recent studies of the U.S. market include: Brown (2001) and Mitchell et al. (2001). On the UK, see Finkelstein and Poterba (1999 and 2000); for the UK, Chile, and other countries, see James and Vittas (2000) and James and Song (2002). For a study of Chile, see Rocha and Thorburn (2006).

Table 1.2. *Money's worth ratio values for a group of countries: nominal annuities*

	Australia population		Canada population		Singapore population		Switzerland population		United Kingdom population		United States population	
	General	Annuitant	General	Annuitant	General	Annuitant	General	Annuitant	General	Annuitant	General	Annuitant
Using government bond rate or yield curve												
Male, aged 55	–		0.949	1.000	–	0.990	1.043	1.195	–	0.985	0.838	0.904
Male, aged 65	0.914	0.986	0.925	1.014	–	1.256	0.965	1.169	0.897	0.966	0.816	0.916
Male, aged 75	–		0.889	1.036	–	–	0.854	1.111	0.850	0.940	0.797	0.922
Female, aged 55	–		0.950	0.999	–	0.985	1.084	1.169	–	–	0.845	0.891
Female, aged 65	0.914	0.970	0.937	1.015	–	–	1.029	1.152	0.910	0.957	0.829	0.893
Female, aged 75	–		0.933	1.035	–	–	0.947	1.095	0.871	0.942	0.833	0.902
Using the corporate bond rate or yield curve												
Male, aged 55	–		0.877	0.919	–	–	0.976	1.103	–	–	0.745	0.796
Male, aged 65	0.846	0.906	0.869	0.947	–	1.073	0.922	1.104	0.854	0.916	0.742	0.825
Male, aged 75	–		0.851	0.984	–	–	0.833	1.072	0.823	0.907	0.744	0.852
Female, aged 55	–		0.872	0.911	–	–	1.000	1.074	–	–	0.743	0.778
Female, aged 65	0.839	0.885	0.874	0.941	–	–	0.974	1.083	0.860	0.901	0.745	0.797
Female, aged 75	–		0.885	0.977	–	–	0.917	1.054	0.838	0.903	0.768	0.827

Source: For the United States: Mitchell et al. (2001). For countries other than the United States: James and Vittas (2000)
Note: All annuities are immediate single-payment life annuities. U.S. data are for 1995

In a study of the United States, Mitchell et al. (2001) find that the MW ratio for the general population, calculated using the government bond rate as the discount rate, can be as low as 80 percent, and lower still when a corporate bond yield is used instead of the government bond yield. Finkelstein and Poterba (1999) derive somewhat higher estimates for nominal life annuities in the United Kingdom. However, James and Song (2002) estimated ratios for both countries that were close to 100 percent. This study also estimated MW ratios for Australia, Canada, Singapore, and Switzerland, and found that they were either close to or exceeded 100 percent. James and Vittas (2000) came to a similar conclusion regarding the same group of countries. James and Vittas conjecture that in Switzerland and Singapore's case the relatively high estimate of the ratio may reflect the impact of a steep yield curve (where interest rates rise markedly as the maturity of the bond increases) on life insurers' funding decisions, and specifically on the average maturity of the portfolio of assets backing the annuities. When the yield curve slopes upwards, as it usually does, the insurer can increase the average interest rate that its portfolio earns by tolerating a shortfall of assets from expected liabilities at the short end and increasing holdings at the long end. Insurance companies may feel able to offer highly competitive premiums in consequence. However, a maturity mismatch could entail capital losses as bonds are sold to finance annuity payments when interest rates are rising, whether or not the increase had been expected. In fact, it will entail losses even if interest rates change over time in the way in which the term structure implies.

All the studies cited find that the MW ratios for the annuitant population (which are calculated by inserting the survival probabilities of annuitants in Eq. (1.1)) are consistently higher than the MW ratios for the general population. This finding points to the ubiquity of adverse selection. Finklestein and Poterba (1999) find that the MW ratio for the population of voluntary annuitants in the United Kingdom is higher than that of compulsory annuitants, which in turn is higher than that of the general population. Since even the compulsory annuitant has a choice whether to opt out of the state earnings-related scheme, this last result might reflect a degree of adverse selection. The study by Mitchell et al. (2001) finds that the gap between the MW ratios for the general and annuitant population in the United States varies from about four cents on the dollar to more than ten cents (see Table 1.2). James and Song (2002) report similar differences.

The findings of MW ratios that exceed 100 percent are on the face of them inconsistent with the chapter's pricing model (discussed at greater length in Chapter 2). Annuity providers incur expenses in marketing and administration and in funding their products, and it would seem that the MW ratio would have to fall short of 100 percent simply to allow insurers to break even. The finding could be explained by the fact that the studies used as their discount rate the (risk free) government bond rate, while life insurers do invest in higher yielding assets, like corporate debt, equities and real estate, which normally have a higher yield than the government bond rate. In addition, the life insurer may be able to diversify some risk in ways not effectively open to individual investors (the use of options may not be feasible for the small investor, for example). If, however, the higher return on the insurer's portfolio comes at a cost of an increased risk of default on its policies to annuitants and others, the government bond rate — normally considered the risk-free rate — is not the appropriate discount rate to use in the calculation of the MW ratio. A higher rate, possibly a corporate bond rate, should be used, which would reduce the calculated ratio.

A further qualification needs to be made about the MW ratio calculation, which is that it takes no account of the costs that potential annuitants incur if they choose to self-insure. The calculation typically assumes that the prospective annuitant incurs no trading or other transaction costs when he or she acquires bonds or other financial instruments. This means that the relevant discount rate is a bond rate unadjusted for the costs of financial intermediation. This assumption may cause the MW ratio to be substantially underestimated in countries where brokerage fees or commissions are substantial. It may be less of an issue in countries like the United States, where the costs of administration of the large broad market index funds are quite low. However, taking advantage of these low costs requires that the investor allocates most of his portfolio to these passively managed funds and avoid actively managed funds. In principle, the rate of return of an annuity (which is a net rate of return) should be compared to the net rate of return to direct investing by the annuitant. Arguably, the calculation should also reflect the fact that a retiree who does not annuitize incurs other costs in managing regular draw downs of his retirement nest egg.

THE INSURANCE VALUE OF ANNUITIES

Studies of MW ratios are extremely valuable. Among other things, they may shed some light on the size of the costs incurred — or the margins charged — by annuity providers. They also make clear the importance of adverse selection. Nonetheless, the fact that a MW ratio is below some set level like 0.90 or 0.85, says nothing about the value of annuities as insurance. In particular, a low MW ratio does not necessarily imply that the conditional rate of return to an annuity is less than the return to a bond. The point is not simply of theoretical or academic interest. Calculations of the MW ratio for African Americans yield estimates that are lower than those calculated for the general population because African Americans have a shorter life expectancy — even at age 65 — than the general population of the same sex (Brown, 2001; Cohen, Steuerle and Carasso, 2001). Nothing follows from this finding, however, about whether annuities are a good buy for African Americans, although this is one case when anti-discrimination laws may disadvantage a group they were intended to protect.

The longevity insurance a life annuity provides to a retired person depends on the difference between the annuity's (conditional) rate of return and the bond rate, on the degree of aversion the person has for a decline in consumption and on the subjective discount rate. It is always possible to self-insure against longevity risk. As the chapter has discussed, however, if a retired person has the choice of investing in an annuity, instead of simply self-insuring, she can have a higher standard of living throughout retirement with the annuity.

The lower the subjective discount rate, the greater the value of the extra future consumption that an annuity makes possible. For a given discount rate, the extra future consumption an annuity makes possible is valued more, the more shifting consumption back from the future to the present causes a loss in welfare, or the more consumption is back loaded. The lower the discount rate, and the greater the loss in welfare from spending it all now, the greater is the gain from annuitization. By making appropriate assumptions about the form of the utility function, it is possible to calculate the extra wealth the retired person would need to feel indifferent about foregoing the chance to annuitize.

Mitchell et al. (2001) estimate the insurance value of annuities in this manner. Specifically, Mitchell et al. calculate the utility level reached with and without the possibility of annuitization, and then calculate the wealth that would be necessary to restore an individual without the possibility of annuitization to the same level of utility that annuitization makes possible. The increase in wealth is an estimate of the insurance value of annuitization. This study found that under what the authors considered fairly conservative assumptions about risk aversion, it would take an increase in wealth at retirement of 30 percent or more to make up for the

lack of opportunity to annuitize (Mitchell et al. 2001, p. 95). Brown
(2001) came to similar conclusions. Appendix 1 presents the results of
an exercise that computes the increased wealth that would be necessary to
achieve the same level of welfare as is possible with annuitization, using
simpler assumptions than Mitchell et al. (see the Section, The Insurance
Value of Annuities). As Mitchell et al. point out, the results of the study
should be considered provisional, since it does not take into account the
inhibiting influences on the demand for annuities that this chapter has
discussed. In particular, the study takes no account of the bequest motive
and the need for precautionary balances.

ANNUITIES AND ALTERNATIVE INVESTMENT STRATEGIES

Annuities can only dominate other fixed income investments, as they do in
Yaari's model, if the conditional rate of return to an annuity exceeds that of
a bond of equal maturity. It is easy to verify that this is so. For example,
as of August 2004, some 40 U.S. life insurance companies surveyed by
Comparative Annuity Reports were advertising a life and 10 year certain
annuity for a 70-year-old female that paid from $638 to $706 per month
per $100,000 premium. Assuming a maximum life-span of 30 years, this
would imply a conditional return of 6.6–7.7 percent. By way of
comparison, the contemporary long-term bond yield – i.e. the discount
rate at which the present discounted value of the interest payments and
repayments of principal equals the current market value of the bond – was
less than 5 percent.

   The introduction of risky assets like equities into the analysis means that
the assumption that the conditional return to an annuity exceeds the rate
of return to the competing asset may no longer hold. The standard
assumption is that the expected return to risky assets will exceed the rate of
return to safer assets. The evidence for this proposition is certainly
not clear-cut. Malkiel (1999) puts the standard assumption to the test by
examining the performance of U.S. stock markets in good times and bad.
He divides the post-war period in three sub-periods (1946–68, 1969–81,
and 1982–98). During the first and third, stock markets did well; during
the second, they performed poorly. He finds that over each of the three
sub-periods, stocks outperformed long-term high-quality corporate bonds.
Shiller (2000, p. 195), taking the contrary view states that: "The evidence
that stocks will always outperform bonds over long time intervals simply

does not exist." A basic issue, of course, is the difficulty of inferring future from past performance, which Malkiel acknowledges.[13]

With equities and other high-yielding but risky investments as alternatives, the possibility arises that for some retired people a portfolio that includes equities and other financial assets might dominate a portfolio that includes an annuity. The standard approach to tackling this question is to treat it as a multi-period expected utility maximization problem. Appendix 1 provides a simplified version of such a problem, using a two-period framework in which a person chooses between an annuity and a risky asset with an expected return that exceeds the conditional return of the annuity (see the Sub-section, Competing Assets − Risky Financial Assets). The main result is that the share of the portfolio invested in the annuity will vary inversely with the expected rate of return to the risky asset. Although the model of Appendix 1 does not introduce risk aversion explicitly, it is relatively straightforward to show that the share of the portfolio devoted to the annuity will also vary inversely with the degree of risk aversion the annuitant exhibits. These findings are not surprising − the greater the expected return to an alternative investment, other things being equal, the more attractive the investment will be. Similarly, the less risk averse investors are, the more attractive will be the superior expected return to equities. Liquid financial investments have the added advantage that − provided the variance of their return is not too large − they can serve to defray unexpected lump-sum expenditures.

The availability of alternative investments with a higher expected return need not reduce the demand for annuities to zero, unless the investor is risk neutral, provided the conditional rate of return to an annuity continues to exceed the rate of return to a fixed interest investment. The latter condition may not hold if there is a sizeable lump-sum cost element in providing an annuity. In this case, the conditional rate of return to an annuity with a premium below some threshold value may drop below the rate of return on a safe asset.

In addition to reducing the share of wealth devoted to an annuity in favor of a portfolio of more risky assets, a person on the verge of retirement might choose to defer purchase of an annuity until later in the retirement period, and invest her entire portfolio in conventional financial assets.

---

[13] Bodie (2001) and Shiller (2000) have emphasized that the standard practice of assessing the comparative long-run performance of stocks and bonds by using overlapping 20-year periods is misleading, since the results of one or two years can affect the average rate calculated over a number of periods.

There is a superficial rationale for this approach, since the conditional rate of return to an annuity increases with the age of the annuitant.[14] However, if the alternative to a life annuity is a government bond, and annuities have an actuarially fair rate of return, deferral actually reduces consumption possibilities (See the Section, An Aside on the Timing of Annuitization in Appendix 1).

Deferral can be advantageous, however if risky assets with an expected return greater than the conditional return to the annuity are available, and if risk aversion increases with age (Milevsky and Young, 2002). In this case, it might benefit the prospective annuitant in the early stages of retirement to defer annuitization. Instead, he would invest in stocks and bonds on the expectation that the higher expected rate of return justifies the greater risk. However, as Mike Orszag (2000, p. 10) notes, beyond some age, the return to holding an annuity will exceed the mean return on equity. Deferred annuitization is better than no annuitization at all as far as reducing the risk and the size of a shortfall of assets from a benchmark consumption level (Dus, Maurer, and Mitchell, 2004).

In practice, this strategy is much more risky than it appears. First, while someone aged 60–65 might conceivably be more willing to take investment risks than someone ten years older, older persons would have less opportunity to make up a serious investment loss by working longer hours or saving more. The number of years of productive working life that remain to them will fall as they age, and their skills will deteriorate or become obsolete. Forsaking annuities also means that more time has to be devoted to managing the stream of withdrawals, a task for which people may not have the requisite skills and self-control (or the means to afford the services of a competent financial planner). The variability of the premium per dollar of regular payment is another important consideration. This figure has varied substantially over time in the past (Warshawsky, 2001). Data on a representative premium for the U.S. market for the period since 1995 are not readily available. However, Mackenzie and Schrager (2004) show, using an indirect approach that derives estimates of the variability of premiums from the behavior of the term structure of interest rates, that the premium per dollar varied substantially in 1990–2002.

---

[14] According to the August 2004 number of *Comparative Annuity Reports*, the average monthly payment available from a group of 40 "top" providers for a $100,000 single premium life and 10-year certain annuity was $663 for a 70-year-old female. The payment increases to $744 for a 75-year-old female.

An alternative approach to expected utility maximization, which retirement planners use to develop concrete investment strategies for their clients, is based on Monte Carlo simulations of the range of returns to alternative investment portfolios, assuming a rate of drawdown of the assets to finance consumption that is greater to or equal to the regular payment that an annuity finances. The simulations, which are based on actual past rates of return, are used to calculate the probability that the portfolio's assets will be exhausted by various dates. This second approach gives an idea of the risk a retired person is taking of prematurely exhausting his resources under different investment strategies.

Ameriks, Veres, and Warshawsky (2001) use the second approach to address the question of the role of an annuity in reducing the risk of outliving retirement resources. This study sheds light on the complexities of investing for retirement, and on the role of annuities in generating a more secure income source, and for that reason is worth discussing at some length. The study first compares the relative performance of four different investment strategies in which annuities play no role. These strategies range from a conservative portfolio invested 50 percent in bonds, 30 percent in cash, and only 20 percent in stocks to an aggressive portfolio with 85 percent in stocks. It uses a Monte Carlo technique to simulate rates of return based on actual rates of return derived from the historical performance of stock and bond markets post-WWII.[15] The simulations also assume an asset management fee of 1 percent of the value of the portfolio.

The basic test to which these different portfolios are put is how long they can generate returns that will allow a withdrawal that is initially set at the equivalent of 4.5 percent of the original portfolio value and is then indexed to inflation. The conservative portfolio, with only 20 percent invested in stocks proved to be the most likely to be exhausted. The study estimated that the probability of exhaustion exceeded 90 percent over a horizon of 30 years. Playing it safe, the study implies, is living dangerously.

The result is less surprising when we remember that the annual real return to safe fixed interest investments in the United States has typically been well below 4.5 percent. At end-2004, for example, the real rate of

---

[15] The samples were generated by drawing randomly, with replacement, from monthly return and inflation data, from the period 1946–99. Ameriks, Veres, and Warshawsky note that this method overcomes the problems associated with using overlapping multi-period returns. The approach requires that the returns in different periods are independent of one another.

54   *The Demand Side of the Annuity Market*

return on long-term Treasury bonds was about 2 percent, and short-term real rates were even less. Thus, exhaustion at some point would be certain. With the conservative portfolio, the risk of a big loss in any given year is small, but the average return is significantly less than the return of the aggressive portfolio. This explains why the probability of a shortfall of any size for a horizon of 20 years or less is substantially less for the conservative portfolio than for the aggressive portfolio.

The best way to minimize the probability of a shortfall *of any size* with a long horizon is found to be adopting the aggressive strategy. However, this approach would also have the greatest chance of generating a *large* shortfall. In contrast to the conservative strategy, the aggressive strategy can entail big gains or big losses.

These simulation experiments were then repeated assuming that either 25 percent or 50 percent of the portfolio was used to buy a life annuity, with an annual nominal payment of 9.05 percent of the premium. Since the 4.5 percent withdrawal rate is indexed, and the life annuity is fixed in nominal terms, the share of the income generated by the annuity has to fall over time. Nonetheless, for all portfolios, the annuitization of even 25 percent of the portfolio reduced significantly the chances of a shortfall. The annuitization of 50 percent of the portfolio had, as could be expected, an even greater effect.

Another approach to evaluating the adequacy of alternative investment strategies in securing an adequate income in retirement is to compare the effects of different rules governing the withdrawal of funds from the portfolio. Dus, Maurer, and Mitchell (2004), who take this approach, rely on a broader concept of exhaustion of resources that takes into account the expected value of the shortfall in the income a particular strategy generates compared with the benefit obtainable from a real life annuity.

Among the withdrawal rules they consider, two are of particular interest, since they illustrate the problems inherent in a strategy that avoids annuitization in favor of more flexible strategies that increase the expected value of bequests, and even income or benefit levels, but also increase the risk of shortfalls. The first is deliberately conservative, and can be expressed as withdrawing a fraction of wealth equal to $1/T_M$, where T_M is the maximum lifespan left to the person. For example, if we assume that no one can live past the age of 100, the maximum span for someone aged 65 would be 35 years, and for someone aged 75 would be 25 years, and so on. The second rule would set the withdrawal fraction as $1/T_E$, where T_E equals remaining expected life span. Thus, the remaining expected life span of someone aged 70 might be 15 years, someone aged 75 might be 12 years, and so on.

With an annuity with a return of over five percent, the $1/T_M$ rule automatically entails shortfalls in the initial years of retirement, since it entails withdrawals of about 3 percent of capital. However, assuming that the portfolio is invested in a mix of stocks and bonds with an average return well above the rate of withdrawal, the portfolio grows in size. This approach is good for the retiree's heirs unless he lives a very long life, since the value of his withdrawals can increase substantially as he ages. However, the approach can also effectively entail privation in the early post-retirement years. The second approach does not entail the same initial build-up, which means that as the encroachments increase ($1/T_E$ increases as the retiree ages), the value of the residual capital dwindles.

It is difficult to draw categorical conclusions from these types of studies as to the superiority of life annuities, or the share of a retiring person's portfolio that should be invested in them. The results are inevitably sensitive to the periods from which the estimates of the variances, covariances, and average rate of return of the competing assets are derived. Three general observations should be made, however. First, there is always some risk of a shortfall – i.e. of running out of money – when a portfolio of a retired person includes risky assets, and even when it does not, unless the person is self-disciplined enough to stick to a conservative rate of withdrawal. Second, to echo the mantra that U.S. investment dealers are obliged to repeat to their clients, past performance is not necessarily a good guide to the future. Finally, it would be unwise to underestimate the ease with which even smart people, or their financial advisors, can make foolish financial decisions.

CONCLUSIONS

The small size of the annuity market in any country where purchase is not compulsory or strongly encouraged has puzzled economists. At the same time, they have recognized that demand for life annuities – annuities that provide longevity insurance – can be inhibited by many influences, and not least by competition from the indexed life annuity that most public pension systems provide. In addition, the favorable treatment most tax systems accord residential investment, which is probably reinforced by a basic preference to be one's own landlord make a house more attractive than an annuity. Adverse selection probably reduces demand among people with relatively short life expectancies. A simple lack of understanding of

this unusual financial instrument may also reduce its popularity. Its value
as longevity insurance appears to be poorly appreciated.

Even when the effects of a bequest motive and the other inhibiting
influences on the demand for annuities are recognized, however, most
people will benefit from some degree of annuitization of their wealth.
Annuitization does reduce a person's flexibility to defray unexpected
expenditure, and means that early death will reduce the size of the person's
estate. Nonetheless, neither the precautionary motive for holding liquid
assets nor the bequest motive need imply that the optimal degree of
annuitization is zero. In fact, if people wish to leave an estate whose size
is less than their total wealth at retirement, they are clearly better off
annuitizing some part of the wealth they do not intend to bequeath than
holding it in fixed interest investments. One indirect sign that annuitization
is appreciated is the general acceptance of the form that public pension
benefits take.

Annuities ought to play an important role in retirement security, and the
demand for them could grow strongly as the competitive role of the public
pension diminishes, employer-provided pensions shift from defined benefit
to defined contributions, as they are in a number of countries, and
populations age. The growth in the market should encourage insurance
companies to make investments in the information that would allow them
to make finer distinctions among different groups with differing life
expectancies. Greater discrimination in premium setting would reduce
adverse selection, and probably increase demand for annuities by the less
well off. In addition, the increase in the size of the market, not just in the
United States but elsewhere, would reduce the risk premium entailed by
type one or select mortality. This could be particularly important for older
annuitants (e.g. age 75 and above), given the way their numbers decline as
they age.

Self-insurance against longevity risk may work for some older people.
To be successful, the self-insurer should be able to choose an efficient and
not excessively risky investment portfolio and to stick to a conservative
withdrawal strategy. Nonetheless, the risks entailed by a strategy of self-
insurance should not be downplayed. Many people, including well-
educated and intelligent people, have a lot of difficulty turning a stock of
wealth into a sustainable flow of income. The standard test of this difficulty
is to ask people how much money they will need at age 65 to sustain their
current standard of living. Few people realize how small the rate of
withdrawal has to be to prevent premature exhaustion of what may seem, at
the start of retirement, to be a handsome sum of money. Given the

divergent views of financial professionals on the matter, this failure is understandable. Nonetheless, its consequences can be anxiety, privation, and misery.

If annuities can be reasonably well priced, and administrative and sales fees (a topic Chapter 2 takes up) are not prohibitive for small annuities, most retired people without a relatively comfortable pension income from public and private sources would surely benefit by acquiring one.

The Supply Side of the Annuity Market

INTRODUCTION

The insurance industry is an institution that reduces the risks of economic and financial loss that individuals and businesses confront in the daily business of life by pooling them. Property and casualty insurance pools the risk of catastrophic loss faced by business and property owners, and by doing so reduces a prohibitive risk to a manageable one. Life insurance pools the risks associated with death, and in particular the risk of loss of income that the death of a breadwinner entails to reduce the economic insecurity that families confront.

The life annuity branch of the life insurance business pools the risk of excessive longevity. If a market for life annuities is to develop and function effectively, two conditions must be met. First, annuity providers must have a reasonably large number of annuity policy holders, and the group's life expectancy must be predictable with some accuracy. Second, annuity providers need investment vehicles that will generate a cash flow that matches the expected future stream of payments to annuitants.

Life insurance companies have traditionally monopolized the sales of annuities to the private market, because the actuarial skills and financial acumen required to price and fund life insurance contracts are the same as those required to price and fund annuities. A lesser reason is that the sale of annuity contracts can be a partial hedge against the mortality risks that life insurers face. The early death of the holder of a life insurance policy causes the insurer to lose money, but the same event in the case of a life annuity has the opposite effect.

As Chapter 3 will discuss at greater length, the life insurance business in the larger OECD countries has moved in the past 30 years well beyond its more traditional confines of life insurance, annuities and related products.

It now funds and markets many products that are essentially investment vehicles. In some of these, the investor bears all of the risk; in others, the insurance company incurs risk by extending interest rate or minimum return guarantees. Chapter 1 has already noted the importance in the U.S. market of the variable annuity, which is essentially an investment vehicle, despite its name. Chapter 2 concentrates on the life annuity business, and does not discuss the rest of the life insurance business. Chapter 3 will briefly discuss the regulatory implications of this diversification of the life insurance business, because the soundness of life insurers as annuity providers cannot be judged in isolation from the soundness of the business as a whole.

MAJOR RISKS OF THE ANNUITY BUSINESS

A life insurer selling annuities faces a variety of risks. These can be variously categorized, and the categories this chapter proposes are by no means exhaustive. For the book's purposes, the main risks are: mortality risk, investment risk, credit risk, liquidity risk, and business risk. A well-designed regulatory framework is intended to create strong incentives for life insurers to adopt procedures and practices that will reduce these risks to an acceptable level. Nonetheless, as the discussion of regulatory issues in Chapter 3 will explain, the nature of the annuity business itself and a changing commercial, regulatory and economic environment may have weakened the incentives for prudence in a number of annuity markets in recent years.

In funding annuities, the life insurer faces two kinds of mortality risk. The first, *select mortality risk* was introduced in Chapter 1, and is the risk that the insurer's particular group of annuitants lives longer than the annuitant population. Provided the probability of the survival of individual annuitants is independent of that of others, this particular risk is reduced by issuing more policies, since that will pool risks. It should be a problem only for small companies, or companies that are just entering the annuity business.

The second, *aggregate mortality risk* is the risk that the life expectancy of the population as a whole is uncertain, and might be underestimated. This risk is not so easily addressed, because despite a clear trend over time to increasing life expectancies, not simply life expectancies at birth, but life expectancies of people aged 65 and older, no model has yet been developed that gives accurate predictions of the rate at which longevity is increasing. The availability of accurate demographic data and advances in modeling techniques notwithstanding, life insurance companies have tended to underestimate the recent increase in longevity. In the late 1990s, some UK life insurance companies reportedly underestimated the average life expectancies of their pool of annuitants by up to two years (Blake, 1999). In the case of a 65-year-old male, an underestimate of average longevity of even $1\frac{1}{4}$ years could cost a U.S. insurance company about $8000 for every $100,000 in premiums.[1] Consequently, insurers confront some irreducible aggregate mortality risk.

Investment risk takes a number of forms. *Interest risk* is the risk that when the fixed interest instruments that the life insurer holds are redeemed at maturity, the principal must be reinvested at rates of interest lower than the insurer had assumed when it issued the policies that the investments are funding. Some interest risk is inevitable if the maximum maturity of a bond is less than the period over which the life insurer might have to make payments. As an example, if neither government nor corporate bonds have a maturity exceeding 20 years, and are used to fund life annuities sold to 65-year-olds, some bonds will mature before all the annuitants have died, and will have to be reinvested. Interest rates at that time may be significantly lower than the life insurer had assumed when it priced the annuities. *Capital risk* is the risk that long term bonds may have to be sold before they mature at a time when interest rates are unexpectedly high and their prices are depressed, or that equities may have to be sold in a depressed market.

Liquidity risk is the risk that assets have to be sold at a time when a preference for liquidity has caused bond markets to freeze up. This is more of a risk for high-yield (junk) bonds than high-grade securities, but can affect even highly rated bonds at times. The financially turbulent period of August–September 1998, when Russia defaulted on its debt, the hedge fund Long Term Capital Management was pushed to the wall, and Brazil was caught in a financial crisis was such a time. Lowenstein (2000, p. 151), in his account of the crisis at Long Term Capital Management, puts it this way: "Despite the ballyhooed growth in derivatives, there was no liquidity in credit markets. There never is when everyone wants out at the same time."

Credit risk is the risk that the issuer of the obligation or loan that the insurer holds is unable to service or redeem it. It should be very small with

---

[1] In other words, the expected present discounted value of annuity payments would increase by about eight cents for each dollar of premium, which would wipe out any profit on annuities. The figure of $8000 is based on the author's simulation of the impact of increasing life expectancy using a table from United States Life Tables 1988 for 65-year-old American males and simulating the impact of an increase in life expectancy of $1\frac{1}{4}$ years.

holdings of government bonds in most OECD countries, but will be greater with corporate debt, particularly high-risk debt, and other forms of credit. Counterparty risk is related to both credit and liquidity risk, and is the risk that the counterparty to a trade will not have sufficient funds to honor its obligation.

Finally, *business risk* includes all the risks that result from problems of corporate governance, faulty control systems, and the like. The risks subsumed under this heading would thus include the risks of defalcation, fraud and embezzlement, and the incompetence of employees or company officers, as well as acts of God. Cyber risk has become an important component of business risk.

A SIMPLE MODEL OF FUNDING

A useful way of tackling the pricing and funding problems of an insurance company selling life annuities is to start with a very simplified version of the environment in which they operate. Specifically, the exposition here, which Chapter 1 anticipated, assumes that life insurers confront select but not aggregate mortality risk, and leaves a fuller discussion of the consequences of aggregate mortality risk until later. It is also assumed that insurance companies can invest in risk-free fixed-interest instruments, like government bonds, and that the maturity range of these instruments spans the remaining life time of even the longest-lived annuitant. For example, if annuitants are 65 years old at annuitization, and the longest available maturity is 35 years, then no annuitant survives past the age of 100.

Given these assumptions, the life insurer can exactly match its expected annuity payments with holdings of government bonds of the same maturity. If the government bonds are zero coupon bonds — where the interest is not paid out but accrues until the bond is redeemed, the insurer simply matches the payments it expects to make 10, 15, 20 years from now with zero coupon bonds of the same maturity, and the same present discounted value. A similar and only slightly more complicated procedure applies if the bonds bear coupons and pay interest regularly (see the Section, The Cost and Funding of Annuities in Appendix 1).

With this strategy, the life insurer avoids both interest risk and capital risk. It redeems bonds when they mature at their face value to make the regular payments on its annuity contracts. There is no capital loss, because the bonds are risk-free, and there is no credit risk. Similarly, there is no interest risk, because the proceeds of the bonds do not have to be reinvested. Equation (2.1) shows the relationship between the value of expected payments n years from now, AP_n, and the current value of the zero-coupon bonds, DB_n that the insurer buys to fund these payments. The interest rate on n year bonds is denoted by r_n, and interest is assumed to be compounded annually:

$$DB_n = AP_n/(1 + r_n)^n \qquad (2.1)$$

This strategy is an example of a perfect matching between the timing of future payments and future receipts. Defining the surplus as the difference between the present discounted value of the assets funding the annuities and the present discounted value of expected annuity payments, we see that the surplus is completely unaffected by interest rate fluctuations. In every period, the undiscounted value of assets equals the undiscounted value of expected liabilities, so the present discounted value of the surplus is always zero regardless of the rate of interest used to discount expected future payments and assets. The sum of the assets that an insurer holds to fund its potential liabilities are known as technical or mathematical reserves.

The life annuity the state provides is typically indexed. If annuity providers are to be able to offer an indexed life annuity, and to match their liabilities with their assets in exactly the same way as they would with nominally fixed annuities, a complete maturity spectrum for indexed bonds must exist. The governments of Australia, Canada, France, the United Kingdom, and the United States all issue indexed bonds – Japan issued indexed bonds for the first time in 2004, and Germany for the first time in 2006 – although the share of indexed debt in total public debt varies considerably across these countries (IMF, 2005, p. 39). In practice, only governments are able to assume the risks entailed by issuing indexed debt. A private corporation is able to influence its own credit rating by its business decisions, but it has absolutely no control over inflation, and has no natural hedge against it. Governments, on the other hand, have the means if not always the political will to control inflation, and the issue of indexed debt could increase their incentive to avoid inflationary finance.

RELAXING THE ASSUMPTIONS OF THE SIMPLE MODEL

Incomplete or Short Maturity Spectrums

The simple model assumes that there is a bond with a maturity to match each annuity payment. In some bond markets, however, the supply of bonds at particular maturities may be a little thin. Gaps in the maturity spectrum expose insurance companies to losses. The strategy that minimizes losses is normally a portfolio of bonds with maturities both shorter and longer than the maturities of the expected payments in the interval or intervals when there are no matching maturities available. This strategy ensures that unexpected interest rate fluctuations are at least partially hedged. When interest rates fall unexpectedly, the capital gain on longer term bonds offsets the interest loss on maturing short-term bonds, and vice versa. It can be shown that if interest rates move by the same amount at all maturities – i.e. the yield curve shifts uniformly up or down – the impact of small fluctuations in interest rates on net worth can be immunized by ensuring that the *duration* of liabilities (roughly, the terms or maturities of the expected payments weighted by the share of the present discounted value of future payments in the value of the bond) is equal to the duration of assets. (See the Sub-section in Appendix 1, "Relaxing the Assumptions: Nonmatching and immunization" for further discussion.)

Gaps in the maturity spectrum may be of no great moment for life insurers if the gaps are relatively small. As a simple example, suppose that expected payments seven years from now are funded by bonds with maturities of five and nine years. It would take a major fluctuation in interest rates to cause significant losses.

The problems posed by a shortage or absence of longer term bonds are less tractable. Taking the UK market as a case in point, the humped yield curve that characterizes the market for gilts (government bonds), so described because 30-year-gilt yields are lower than those of shorter maturities, is thought to result in part from the strong demand of life insurers for long-term bonds to match their long-term liabilities (Association of British Insurers, 2005). Of course, the lower the yield of the insurers' assets, the higher the premium per pound of annuity income they will charge. Any shortage at the long end of the market for gilts will be aggravated by a shift in the portfolios of pension plans away from equities and in favor of bonds (see below). High quality corporate paper might substitute for gilts to some extent, but British companies do not tend to issue such debt, and the debt they do issue at long maturities is typically at variable rates, which means that it does not exactly match the liabilities entailed by either fixed nominal or indexed annuities. The possibilities for reinsurance (when insurance companies lay off their risk on a reinsurer) for the risk of maturity mismatches are limited. The conclusion to draw from these arguments is that a solution to any shortage of long-term bonds will require that the government increase its reliance on long-term debt (ABI, 2005).

This "capacity" problem is evident in some degree in other countries as well. However, until quite recently, governments were not disposed to increase their reliance on long-term debt. In fact, in 2001, the U.S. Treasury announced that it was discontinuing the issue of 30 year bonds. However, in February 2006, the Treasury resumed auctions of these instruments. Among the Group of Ten industrial countries (G-10), the shortest maximum maturity is 15 years, in Sweden. Until recently, the longest maturity among the G-10, apart from perpetuities issued occasionally by Belgium and the Netherlands, was 44 years, in Switzerland. In many financial markets elsewhere, the longest-dated government bond maturities will be substantially shorter than 30 years.

Most recently, and partly in response to the very concerns this chapter has discussed, France has begun issuing a 50 year bond. The United Kingdom's Debt Management Office announced in March 2005 that it would begin issuing conventional (nonindexed) 50 year bonds in May 2005 and in September 2005 it began issuing 50 year indexed bonds.

The outright lack of sufficiently long maturities can entail a serious maturity mismatch between the expected annuity payments and the bonds that fund them. As an example, consider an insurer operating in a financial market where the longest actively traded government bond is 15 years, and assume that it needs to fund the annuities of a group of people aged 65. Female annuitants aged 65 in the typical OECD country will have a life expectancy of about 20 years, and some may live as long as 35–40 years from the date they buy their annuity. Given the lack of long maturities, the immunization strategy described earlier requires a portfolio of bonds that clusters near or at the end of the available maturity spectrum of 15 years. In fact, it might not be possible to equalize the duration of the portfolio of bonds and expected future annuity payments. In such a case, the insurer could be substantially exposed to interest risk.

In general, unless it is possible to match exactly future payment obligations with future income and the proceeds of bond redemptions, it will not be possible for the insurer to immunize its portfolio completely.[2] It is, however, often possible to construct bond portfolios that are relatively immune to moderate interest rate fluctuations.

[2] De la Granville (2001) advances a proof that complete immunization is possible given certain assumptions about the behavior of the term structure of interest rates.

More Risky Investments

A life insurer might back its annuities fully with bonds, but choose to forego a matching strategy, even if one were feasible. The risk this alternative strategy entails could seem attractive in some circumstances. In early 2004, the yield curves of major financial markets — particularly the U.S. market — were sloping steeply upward and short-term rates were near historical lows. In these circumstances, a life insurer might wish to fund near-term payment obligations with longer-term maturities. The yield curve is normally assumed to reflect (at least in part) expectations of the future course of interest rates. A life insurer, relying on its own forecasts, might decide that the slope of the yield curve overstated the increase that will actually occur. This strategy would have the advantage of increasing cash flow now. Chapter 1 noted that it might explain relatively high money's worth (MW) ratios in certain countries. However, it runs the risk that the insurer will incur a sizeable capital loss later. As the Section "The Cost and Funding of Annuities" in Appendix 1 explains, if the yield curve perfectly predicted the future course of interest rates, the extra income the insurer would obtain from this strategy would be exactly offset by the capital losses it would incur when the longer maturities were sold to fund the near-term payments they were backing. An *unexpected* increase in interest rates, however, would cause a greater than planned capital loss when the bonds were sold.

The insurer would also have to take into account the impact of a duration mismatch on its reserve or provisioning requirements. In somewhat different ways, both the UK system of reserve requirements (discussed in Chapter 3) and the Chilean system (discussed in Chapter 4) would stipulate an increase in reserves if such a strategy were adopted. In Chile, a shortfall of assets from liabilities at any maturity increases the provisioning requirement. In the United Kingdom, the impact of a shortfall of assets from liabilities at some maturities depends on the sensitivity of net worth to fluctuations in the yield curve.

The simple model with perfect matching is virtually risk free, if there is no aggregate mortality risk and select risk can be reduced to manageable proportions by increasing the number of annuitants. (We neglect business risk.) The cost of such conservative investing is a low rate of return. When the maturity spectrum is insufficient to allow perfect matching, there will be some investment and some interest risk. One way of hedging this risk and raising the overall expected rate of return of the portfolio may be including equities in the portfolio. Similarly, the expected rate of return may be raised by including corporate debt, which pays a higher interest rate than government bonds.

The appropriate balance between equity and bonds in insurance companies' portfolios has been a controversial issue. Recently, the same issue has been actively debated in the case of private (employer-provided) pension funds, particularly European funds. The decade of the 1990s witnessed an increase in the share of equities in the portfolios of pension funds, reflecting the very high rates of return — mainly in the form of capital gains — that stocks were earning during this period. The substantial losses of the early 2000s inspired some rethinking on the appropriate weight equities should have in a pension fund's portfolio.

The pension plan funding debate has some bearing on insurance company practices, and the funding of annuities. European life insurers have reduced their equity exposure substantially since 2000 following the bursting of the equity bubble (IMF, 2004a, 93–94). Despite big differences in the way they are funded and the way their obligations or liabilities are affected by wage and price inflation, the life annuities business and a defined benefit pension fund are similar in that both the insurer and the plan sponsor are expected to bear actuarial and investment risks.[3] The pension fund is expected to be able to fund an employee's pension whose value is determined not by the performance of stock and bond markets but by the employee's length of service and salary history. If the pension fund becomes under funded because of a bad investment experience, the sponsor is expected to make up the difference. The same is true of the annuity provider.

Advocates of substantial holdings of equities in pension fund portfolios have argued that stocks can be used to fund longer-term liabilities like the payments that a pension fund expects to make to its future pensioners. The basic argument is that stocks vary more closely with salaries — which determine the value of defined benefit pensions — than bonds do. In more technical language, stocks and salaries are cointegrated (Cardinale, 2004). It is also argued that their inclusion in a portfolio reduces portfolio risk overall, because their returns tend to be negatively correlated with those of bonds.

---

[3] The future obligations of a defined benefits pension plan will depend, among other influences, on wage inflation, which will depend, because of indexing arrangements, on consumer price inflation. Changes in the rate of wage inflation have no direct bearing on funding of a life annuity with nominally fixed payments.

Bodie (2001) maintains that this view, at least in its application to retirement planning, is fundamentally flawed. Long-run investments in equities have a low probability of losing money, because the probability of a loss of any size declines with time. However, even if there is some limit on the size of the loss that can be incurred in a single year, the probability of a large loss will grow as time passes. Put another way, the probability of the maximum possible loss will decline as time passes, but the size of that loss will increase.[4] If a fund sponsor is sufficiently risk averse, it would not want to maintain significant equity holdings. A pension fund that is funding some of its future expected annuity payments with equities is vulnerable not only to loss, but to insolvency, because its liabilities are bond-like. Hence, the pension fund should be investing in bonds and following a strategy of immunization, as the chapter has discussed. The argument for bonds over equities is stronger if, as Munnell, Sass, and Soto (2005, p. 7) note, there is a moral hazard problem that creates an incentive for the plan sponsor to make excessively risky investments.

One basic difference between a pension fund sponsor and an annuity provider is related to the predictability of their future liabilities. A pension fund may not be able to predict even the initial cost of the pensions it is obliged to pay successive cohorts of retiring plan participants until shortly before the date of retirement. A provider of immediate life annuities agrees on the premium per dollar when the contract is ratified. Nonetheless, annuity providers do incur risks in investing in equities. Even if these can be mitigated to some extent by the use of derivatives and by portfolio insurance techniques, they should not be understated. If a lack of longer maturities entails a mismatch for annuity providers, however, then they are going to incur interest rate risk when the bonds that fund their long-dated annuity payment obligations mature and have to be reinvested. The risk entailed by this strategy needs to be compared with the risk entailed by including equities in the assets backing the claims of policy holders. The decline in international interest rates that took place in the late 1990s caused substantial losses to some European insurers, and to the British insurer Equitable Life, which sold guaranteed income products on the assumption that the higher interest rate environment of the early 1990s would continue.

---

[4] The point can be illustrated with a simple example. Suppose that a stock will either earn 15 percent per annum or lose 10 percent per annum, each result being equally likely. A loss of 50 percent may not be very likely, and cannot occur if the investment horizon is less than seven years. At longer horizons, however, larger losses are possible, although the probability of a loss of a given size declines as the horizon increases.

The Discount Rate

The choice of the rate at which future obligations of annuity providers are discounted is of critical importance to the funding decision, because it determines the value of the assets that the insurance company has to hold to maintain solvency. The choice of discount rate also has a bearing on the composition of the asset portfolio, and on the bonds versus equity debate the previous section has reviewed.

The simple model of funding set out earlier assumes that annuity payments should be funded by government bonds, and that the discount rate that should be used in determining the funding for these obligations is the government bond rate, or the risk-free rate. Although, as discussed below, this choice can be criticized for being too cautious, it poses no practical problem if there is a complete maturity structure. In this case, a discount rate can be derived from bond yields for the whole range of maturities right up to the maturity of the most distant obligations. If the maturity spectrum does not extend to cover the most distant obligations, however, then some procedure for estimating a discount rate for distant maturities needs to be worked out. One procedure, assuming that the yield curve is flat at the longer maturities, is to extrapolate a rate for the most distant maturities from the discount rate of the longest available bond and the slope of the yield curve at that maturity. If the maturity structure is reasonably long – say 25 years – the impact of a wrong guess about this rate on the pricing of annuities may not be significant, because the combination of discounting payments over a long period and taking account of the impact of mortality will reduce the present discounted value of such distant liabilities to a small number.

A thornier issue arises when insurance companies do not rely exclusively on government securities to fund their obligations, but rely instead on a mix of bonds, equities, and other financial assets. Equity financing, as Chapter 3 will discuss, has traditionally been more important in Europe and Japan than in the United States. These mixed portfolios are expected to have a higher return and a greater variance than a portfolio composed exclusively of government bonds. Since on average a mixed portfolio will outperform a portfolio with no risky assets, it can be argued that the rate used to discount future obligations should be an estimate of the expected rate of return on the mixed portfolio, rather than the risk-free rate. Another possibility is a blend of the two rates.

The appropriateness of the choice of discount rate, like the appropriateness of indicators of a government's fiscal position, depends crucially on the purpose it is to serve. Consider a choice between the (risky) portfolio rate and the risk-free rate. Using the risky rate to discount a future obligation has an obvious advantage that it reduces the cost of funding. However, reliance on the rule will also ensure that there is a substantial risk of shortfall.

In practice, to make a reasonable estimate of the probability of a shortfall in the annuity business would require an elaborate procedure using a multi-period model to run Monte Carlo experiments. However, the basic point is easily illustrated if we consider the investment needed in one period to meet an obligation in the second assumed to take the value of $104 million. With a risk-free return of 4 percent used as the discount rate, the required assets in the first period are $100 million. A risky portfolio that returns a gain of 6 percent with a probability of 50 percent, a loss of 1 percent with a probability of 25 percent and a gain of 10 percent with a probability of 25 percent has an average return of $5\frac{1}{4}$ percent. Using $5\frac{1}{4}$ percent as the discount rate, the necessary funding is reduced to $98.8 million. However, adopting this strategy means that there is a 25 percent probability of a shortfall of $6.2 million. The choice of a blended rate increases the amount of funds required, and reduces but does not eliminate the chance of a shortfall. As the previous section and Chapter 1 have discussed, proponents of stocks as a long-run investment argue that the chances of a loss over a period of many years is not large. However, it is easy to extend the one-period example to many periods, to show that the probability of sub-par, if not catastrophic performance is by no means trivial.

Given the book's concern with security of income in retirement, the vital consideration in the choice of a discount rate is the risk of default on a life annuity that the policy holder expects (or can be expected) to bear. Presumably, that risk should be very low. Using a discount rate derived from a portfolio with risky assets rather than the risk-free rate creates an incentive to rely excessively on the risky asset for funding, which the choice of a discount rate based on the risk free rate avoids.

Even with a risk-free discount rate, the funding of annuities by a portfolio of risky assets will entail some risk of default. With the assumptions of the previous example, a balanced portfolio entails a 25 percent probability of a shortfall of $2\frac{1}{2}$ percent. The mean expected return to the portfolio will exceed the risk-free rate, but the realized return can also fall below it. There is nothing, in principle, wrong with an annuity provider funding its annuities with a portfolio with an uncertain return. The key issue is whether the annuity provider has made adequate provision for losses, a subject that is taken up in Chapter 3.

Aggregate Mortality Risk

By its nature, aggregate mortality risk cannot be reduced by increasing the number of policy holders, because it derives from the uncertain life expectancy for whole populations or age cohorts. The ideal hedge against aggregate mortality would be a security that life insurers could buy with a stream of payments that was contingent on the life expectancy of the general population, or, were it possible, the life expectancy of their policy holders. A life insurance contract is not a good hedge. In particular, the average holder of a life insurance policy is younger than the average annuitant, and aggregate mortality risk does not affect each age group in the same way. Many life insurance policies, particularly term life insurance, which is pure life insurance, are taken out to provide insurance to family members in the event of the loss of the family's principal income earner, and are allowed to lapse as the policy holder ages. Term insurance (where the premium increases as the policy holder ages to reflect the increased probability of his dying) has no cash value to the policy holder once it lapses.

Both select and aggregate mortality risk increase, for a given number of insured, with the age of the annuitant. For example, the conditional life expectancy of the very old (80 plus) is less than the conditional life expectancy of 65-year-olds, but even without aggregate mortality risk, the standard deviation of the number of additional years lived is much higher at the older age. If the average age of annuitants increases, select mortality risk might become more of a problem, in that it will take a larger pool of annuitants to reduce it to an acceptable level. That said, the sheer number of older annuitants should also increase. However, it is also likely that aggregate mortality risk will increase.

The intractability of aggregate mortality risk has led to the development of financial instruments that allow the annuity provider to lay off part of the risk on a reinsurance company. The European Investment Bank (EIB), which is a public financial institution, recently issued a bond with a 25 year maturity that makes payments that are related to an index based on the number of men in England and Wales aged 65 at the time of the bond's issue, who are still alive at the time each successive payment is made. The payments, which are annual, are expected to start at about 9 percent of the bond's initial market value, and to decline over 25 years to zero. The payment stream of the bond will consist of these 25 annual payments; there is no repayment of principal (see IMF, 2005 p. 80 for further details).

This instrument allows annuity providers to hedge against the risk that general longevity exceeds their actuarial projections. The more similar the demographic characteristics of the insured population are to the population of English and Welsh males, the better the hedge will be. The bond does not provide insurance against extreme longevity (i.e. the risk that the number of annuitants living past the age of 90 exceeds the projected figure). Blake and Burrows (2001) propose that the government issue what they term survivor bonds, which would, depending on their conditions, provide annuitant providers with an even better hedge against aggregate mortality risk. The instrument they propose would have a payment pattern similar to that of the bond that the EIB has issued, but the government, rather than a financial institution would assume not just most but all the longevity risk. The UK government has said that, although it was not planning to issue longevity bonds in 2005–6, it might revisit the issue subsequently (IMF, 2005, p. 80).

By issuing survivor bonds, the government would be assuming the same kind of risks it assumes with a public pension system, except that altering the terms of the bonds would entail a default. Effectively, the taxpayer would assume the risk. Blake and Burrows note that to the extent older taxpayers bore more than their share of the tax burden, they would end up sharing the risk of unexpectedly large improvements in longevity with the government. Otherwise, the risk would be spread over the population as a whole. The survivor bonds proposal, ingenious as it is, does raise the question as to whether the government should not supply annuities directly to potential annuitants. This issue is revisited in Chapter 8.

Another way of dealing with aggregate mortality risk is to share it. In the United States, the teachers' insurance company TIAA-CREF offers a participating annuity that shares the risk of unexpected longevity gains between it and its policyholders (Reno et al., 2005, p. 77). It is possible to conceive of an annuity where the policyholder bears all the risk, where the regular payment would be reduced in proportion to unexpected increases in longevity. Both risk-sharing and a 100 percent transfer of risk to the annuitant would require a means of calculating the extent to which observed survival rates exceeded a norm. An instrument like this would still provide some longevity insurance to long-lived individuals; the reduction in payments would be related to increases in *average* lifespans, not the lifespan of a particular annuitant. For example, if an annuitant reached the age of 90, and the longevity of his age cohort was 10 percent higher than projected, his annuity payment would be reduced by about 10 percent.

Impavido, Thorburn, and Wadsworth (2004) propose another means of mortality risk sharing. This entails annuity providers issuing a series of temporary annuities — i.e. annuities with a payment that ceases at the end of the contractual period or upon the annuitant's death, whichever comes first — for relatively short periods. The terms of the annuities would change over time as they were recontracted, and unexpected increases in longevity would be reflected in higher premiums.

The strategy of a series of temporary annuity contracts may reduce insurance company risk; it is less clear that it is an attractive alternative for an annuitant. If all the funds that would otherwise have been invested in a life annuity are invested in a temporary annuity, the annual income would be much higher than the income of a life annuity, and much of it will have to be reinvested at a lower rate than the annuity would earn. Alternatively, if the investment in the temporary annuity is calibrated to generate the same income that a life annuity would have generated, then the share of the annuitant's portfolio devoted to annuities would be much lower than it would be with a life annuity, and the share devoted to conventional instruments, again with a lower rate of return, would be much higher. The discussion in Appendix 1 of deferring annuitization is applicable to this strategy, and it can be shown that a series of temporary annuities — even without uncertainty about the terms of future annuities and additional costs because of the short terms — can reduce an annuitant's consumption possibilities. The reason for this is that part of the annuitant's stock of savings has to be invested in conventional assets, with a rate of return below that of an annuity of a comparable term.

OTHER ASPECTS OF ANNUITY PRICING

Statistics and Statistical Issues

Life insurance companies need reliable data on the mortality rates of their policyholders, and some means of projecting improvements in their mortality rates. Information on the mortality rates of the population as a whole may not be of much use to insurers in pricing their products, because annuitants live longer than the general population. However, statistics for the general population are essential to have an idea of the effect of adverse selection on annuity premiums. Moreover, in some countries, as Atkinson and Dallas (2000, p. 132) point out, the insurance industry has no good database of its own. In certain circumstances, the statistics for the general population may be a necessary if not an ideal starting point for the industry. Consequently, before discussing the life insurance industry's own data, the section briefly discusses the mortality statistics that governments prepare for national populations.

Governments prepare life tables that set out the mortality rates of the population at different ages. Life tables take two basic forms. A period life table presents the experience with mortality over the whole age range of a population during a period that might range from one to five years. (See Table 2.1 for an excerpt from a life table prepared by Statistics New Zealand, the New Zealand government agency responsible for demographic studies). When demographic statistics are reliable and comprehensive, a period life table may be constructed from census data by counting the members of the population at each age that are alive at the beginning and end of the year (or, depending on the interval between censuses, a longer period), after taking account of net immigration. The year to year mortality rates derived from this data are often presented in a table with the starting population (at age zero) set at 100,000 to show how the numbers of persons alive at each age will decline over time. However, because the calculation is based on the mortality rates of different birth cohorts over the same period, it is not a reliable indicator of the experience of a given birth cohort.

In contrast to a period table, a cohort life table portrays the experience of a given birth cohort over time. For example, a table might illustrate the mortality rates of the cohort of women aged 40 in 1970. In principle, actual data would be available, as of 2005, to construct the entries for such a table up to age 75, since there would be 35 years of data following the base year. Mortality rates for ages greater than 75 would have to be extrapolated.

If period life tables have been prepared regularly over a sufficiently long interval, it becomes possible to derive projections of mortality rates by extrapolating from changes in mortality rates for particular age groups over the period covered by the life tables. Statistical techniques can be used to estimate a relationship between time and increased longevity.

A surprisingly large number of countries lack the demographic data that are necessary to construct such projections, and their insurance companies may lack good industry data. In Australia, because of a lack of sufficient industry data on mortality experience, actuaries often use data from UK insurance companies (Cardinale, et al., 2002, p. 20). The life insurance industries of Peru and other South American countries that have adopted a variant of the Chilean individual accounts system also rely on data from other countries. Ideally, the country used as a model should have a similar demographic and economic profile.

The Supply Side of the Annuity Market

Table 2.1. *Period life table, New Zealand, male population 2000–2002*

Age (in years)	Number of lives	Probability of death	Life expectancy (in years)	Age (in years)	Number of lives	Probability of death	Life expectancy (in years)
0	100,000	0.0061	76.3	69	77,761	0.0240	13.8
1	99,392	0.0007	75.8	70	75,892	0.0266	13.1
2	99,321	0.0003	74.8	71	73,873	0.0294	12.5
3	99,289	0.0003	73.9	72	71,700	0.0325	11.8
4	99,260	0.0003	72.9	73	69,369	0.0359	11.2
5	99,235	0.0002	71.9	74	66,879	0.0396	10.6
10	99,156	0.0001	67.0	75	64,231	0.0436	10.0
15	99,028	0.0006	62.1	76	61,430	0.0480	9.5
20	98,596	0.0011	57.3	77	58,483	0.0527	8.9
25	98,031	0.0012	52.6	78	55,399	0.0580	8.4
30	97,444	0.0012	47.9	79	52,186	0.0639	7.9
35	96,849	0.0013	43.2	80	48,850	0.0707	7.4
40	96,186	0.0016	38.5	81	45,399	0.0783	6.9
45	95,322	0.0022	33.8	82	41,844	0.0869	6.4
50	94,061	0.0034	29.2	83	38,208	0.0964	6.0
51	93,738	0.0038	28.3	84	34,525	0.1068	5.6
52	93,385	0.0042	27.4	85	30,838	0.1181	5.2
53	92,997	0.0046	26.5	86	27,195	0.1307	4.8
54	92,571	0.0051	25.7	87	23,642	0.1446	4.5
55	92,103	0.0056	24.8	88	20,224	0.1602	4.2
56	91,587	0.0062	23.9	89	16,985	0.1775	3.9
57	91,019	0.0069	23.1	90	13,971	0.1960	3.6
58	90,395	0.0076	22.2	91	11,233	0.2152	3.3
59	89,707	0.0084	21.4	92	8,816	0.2345	3.1
60	88,950	0.0094	20.6	93	6,749	0.2534	2.9
61	88,117	0.0104	19.8	94	5,039	0.2720	2.7
62	87,199	0.0116	19.0	95	3,668	0.2911	2.6
63	86,189	0.0129	18.2	96	2,600	0.3107	2.4
64	85,080	0.0143	17.4	97	1,792	0.3306	2.3
65	83,863	0.0159	16.7	98	1,200	0.3508	2.1
66	82,530	0.0177	15.9	99	779	0.3713	2.0
67	81,073	0.0196	15.2	100	490	0.3917	1.9
68	79,486	0.0217	14.5				

Source: Statistics New Zealand. Some years omitted

Life insurance companies in the major markets develop their estimates of mortality rates from industry data. Atkinson and Dallas (2000, p. 131) note that the largest American companies do not assume that the mortality rates of their policyholders will equal the industry average, and usually analyze their experience as a percentage of the industry rates. Smaller companies tend to rely on the industry average.

As Chapter 1 noted, apart from the United Kingdom and, to a very limited extent, the United States, no rating system like the one insurance companies use for life insurance applies to annuities. This lack, which limits the extent to which insurers can discriminate among groups of annuitants with differing life expectancies, may simply reflect the fact that members of such groups cannot be readily identified. However, the small size of annuity markets might make the effort of putting together such statistics not worth the cost to an individual insurer.

Cardinale et al. (2002) suggest that there is a case for the government to collect data to build a rating system like that used for life insurance. This kind of information is a public good, in that while the benefits to the industry and society from its collection exceed the cost of collection, the benefits to the individual insurance company are insufficient to warrant the effort. A cooperative arrangement among insurers that spreads the cost among them, as now happens with the data used for life insurance, could make government intervention unnecessary, however.

Administrative and Marketing Expenses

The information on the cost of provision of annuities – the marketing and administrative expenses they entail – is partial and fragmentary.[5] The indirect evidence from studies of the MW ratio is hard to interpret, since, depending on the investment strategy of the insurer (and the assumptions of the particular study), the estimated MW ratios suggest that such costs can be high or low. To judge from the available evidence, marketing costs vary a good deal from country to country. James and Song (2002), reporting on data they have culled from a variety of sources, state that sales commissions on immediate annuities in the United States are

---

[5] Given the subject of the book, this chapter addresses the administrative and sales costs associated with annuities; that is, with the distribution end of individual accounts. A number of observers have drawn attention to the high costs associated with the establishment and maintenance of individual accounts, including Murthi, Orszag, and Orszag (2001) (regarding the United Kingdom) and James, Smalhout, and Vittas (2001). The Chilean regulatory authorities have acknowledged that the commissions are high.

4 percent of the premium, with total distributional costs amounting to 5–6 percent. They estimate that the present discounted value of all other expenses, both up-front and ongoing – apart from the cost of maintaining prudential reserves in relatively low-yielding assets – amounts to 7–8 percent of the premium, bringing total costs to 12–14 percent of the premium. James and Song maintain that administrative costs (which do not include the costs associated with portfolio management or actuarial services) should, in principle, be low for immediate life annuities, since the premium is collected in a single payment, and the costs entailed by the regular monthly payment, which never changes, should be modest. (Life insurance is normally paid out in a single payment, but collection costs, which would include dealing with late payments, bounced checks, etc., would be greater). A number of these functions would, however, be subject to economies of scale.

Elsewhere, sales commissions range from 1 percent of the premium in Singapore – where total costs are also very low, being estimated at only 4 percent of the premium – to 5–6 percent of premiums in Chile. More recently, as Chapter 4 discusses, commissions in Chile have substantially declined. The United Kingdom, with commissions of $1\frac{1}{2}$ percent of premium (Cardinale et al., 2002, p. 14) rivals Singapore. James and Song note that in Singapore the Central Provident Fund standardizes the product – the only annuity product is a simple nominal life annuity – and prepares a list of approved insurance companies among which annuitants may choose. The companies' names, addresses, and phone numbers are listed on the CPF's website.[6] In February 2005, nine companies were listed. These procedures would increase price competition and reduce the scope for product differentiation.

The low commission in the United Kingdom comes at a cost in terms of service. The average annuity premium in 2001 was £24,000 (about $42,000) and the average commission estimated to be £360 (Cardinale et al., 2002, p. 14). The UK laws require the seller either to make a substantial investment in understanding the finances of the potential annuitant, in order to give him sound advice, or to simply execute the transaction and renounce the advisory role. According to Cardinale et al., UK insurance companies take the second course of action.

Both marketing and administrative expenditure can entail problems for the small annuitant, since both entail fixed costs. The UK example suggests that small annuitants pay for their small size not by a higher load, but by

[6] The CPF's website is www.cpf.gov.sg.

forgoing what one hopes would be good advice about the kind of annuity that best suits them given their personal and financial circumstances.

Another potentially important source of cost, and hence of load, is a provisioning requirement. Regulatory agencies typically require that reserves — over and above the technical reserves that fund the annuity — be maintained against investment and other risks. Since reserves earn a lower rate of interest than the discount rate used to value the insurer's obligations, a provisioning requirement entails an implicit tax on the part of the annuity provider's portfolio. Suppose, for example, that a company must provision 10 percent against 80 percent of the assets that fund its annuities. If the reserves earn a rate of interest that is 3 percent less than the discount rate, illustrative calculations imply that the premium would have to be raised by about $1\frac{1}{2}$ percent to maintain the insurer's profit margins. Impavido, Thorburn, and Wadsworth (2004) argue that provisioning, or minimum capital requirements constrain the annuity market unduly in some countries.

Price Variability and Price Competition

Data on annuity premiums are neither as consistent nor as reliable as would be desirable. Nonetheless, something is known about their behavior. One rather striking characteristic of the life annuity market is the range of the premiums that different insurers offer, particularly in the United States and the United Kingdom. In a study of the U.S. market Mitchell et al. (2001) found that the monthly pay-out per $1000 premium for a 65-year-old woman ranged from an average of $6.56 for the ten insurance companies in their sample (taken in 1995) offering the highest premiums to $7.76 for the ten offering the lowest. A dispersion of rates of this order persists today. A similar variation in premiums is evident in the United Kingdom, and can be seen at the websites of annuity sellers in both countries.[7]

What is surprising about this phenomenon is that the single immediate payment life annuity is, as financial products go, a plain vanilla wrapper. Given the age, sex, and domicile of the potential annuitant, it is defined by one number — the payment per dollar of premium — and perhaps also a

---

[7] For example, in its August 2004 report, *Comparative Annuity Reports* includes quotations from 40 different U.S. annuity providers for a life and ten year certain nominal annuities for 70- and 75-year-old men and women. In the case of 70-year-old men, the monthly income generated by a premium of $100,000 ranged from $753 to $676.

minimum and a maximum premium. There is no obvious relationship between industrial structure and premium variability. The UK market, which as of 2002 was dominated by five suppliers (Cardinale et al., 2002, p. 15), is quite concentrated. The U.S. market is less so, to judge by data reported by one of the annuity marketing websites. Specifically, in August 2004, at least 40 insurance companies were advertising life and ten-year certain annuities for 70-and 75-year-old men and women.

With such variations in premiums, it would pay to shop around, but their persistence implies that people do not. In the United Kingdom, the holders of a personal pension do not have to buy an annuity from the company that managed their pension, although most do. This behavior has suggested to some observers that annuitants do not understand an annuity's properties, although it may also reflect inertia and the effect of familiarity and trust of the pension sponsor. Put another way, potential annuitants may differentiate between otherwise identical annuities because they believe their future income will be more secure, whatever the terms of the contract, if it is provided by the company with which they are most familiar. Nonetheless, this extra confidence does come at a price.

The pricing model that this chapter introduced makes annuity premiums solely a function of the yield curve given potential annuitants' survival probabilities (which in turn depend on age and sex). That would mean that a major shift in the yield curve would entail a substantial change in premiums. If the yield curve were to shift up and down uniformly, the premium would depend on the sensitivity of the prices of bonds in the middle of the maturity spectrum to interest rate fluctuations.

Premiums do vary with the yield curve, but the general decline in interest rates that took place in the 1990s does not appear to have been fully reflected in the behavior of annuity premiums. Consequently, profit margins on annuities and similar products declined. Annuity premiums may also vary even when the yield curve is stable. Individual providers might wish to lower their margins to attract customers, in the hope of gaining market share, and increasing demand for other products they market.

CONCLUSIONS

A well-developed market for life or long-term annuities requires a well-developed government bond market with a complete maturity spectrum that is long enough to reduce the risk of unmatched distant liabilities to reasonable levels. Although, as Chapter 3 discusses, it may not be necessary to fund annuities 100 percent with bonds, substantial reliance on high quality bonds is necessary to minimize the risk of default. (This assumes that the rest of the insurance business does not cross-subsidize the annuity branch). A flourishing annuity market also requires some way of handling aggregate mortality risk.

The recent trends in a number of countries to a reduced supply of long-dated bonds and increased and more unpredictable longevity have between them increased the risks that life insurers face in underwriting annuities. Neither of these problems is insurmountable, although financial stability is a prerequisite for their solution. Financially stable governments can remedy the first problem by gradually increasing their reliance on long-term bonds. This is already happening, as the chapter noted. To judge from experience, governments that issue long-dated bonds do not have to pay a substantial premium in the form of higher interest rates to make this debt attractive to bondholders. Indeed, the trends in longevity would tend to increase the demand for it by insurance companies, and possibly other financial institutions.

Lengthening and deepening the government bond market poses a challenge for many emerging market countries. Some emerging market countries have made great strides in developing their bond markets. In some emerging market countries with fledgling annuity markets, however, the bond market remains undeveloped. In particular, the government cannot rely on long-term debt, unless it is indexed. Even in this case, there may be limits. Countries with a history of high inflation find it virtually impossible to issue debt that is both long-term and unindexed. The bondholder demands a hefty premium to hold the debt, and the higher that premium, the more likely it is that the government will default on the debt. When financial stability is finally achieved or regained, the market for these instruments can begin to grow again.

The problem of increasing longevity is less tractable for most countries than a limited supply of long-term bonds, unless the government is prepared to assume longevity risk by issuing an instrument like that proposed by Blake and Burrows. The solution of sharing longevity risk between annuitant and provider that Impavido, Thorburn, and Wadsworth advance is a second-best solution for the annuitant, although it is better than nothing.

If the private market is to replicate the essential features of the typical public pension system, it will need to invest in indexed bonds, which governments will need to provide, because businesses and financial institutions are not in a position to assume inflation risk. Indexed debt will not be free of risk for the government. Governments that have been unable to index public pensions may well have difficulty honoring their commitment to service indexed debt. This point needs to be borne in mind in the case of countries where a tradition of sound money and stable public finance has not yet been firmly established. It has less relevance for most OECD countries, however.

Finally, the discussion of Chapter 1 and 2 of demand and supply in the annuity market makes clear that a great deal is simply not known about the annuity market. Students of annuities have some idea of such important aspects of the market as the significance of administrative and sales costs, but their understanding is far from complete. Variations across countries in MW ratios could be better understood. The role and consequences of adverse selection in different markets is not totally clear. The data is lacking for a ready answer to a question like: what did the average annuitant pay for a single premium immediate life annuity in a given month of a given year (with or without a term certain feature), although in the United States, Chile, and the United Kingdom it is possible to calculate the range of premiums found in the market or offered by the large insurance companies. Better and more information on the market for annuities would probably make the market more efficient. The low commission on annuities in Singapore may owe something to the coordinating role the Central Provident Fund plays in the competitive process.

3

The Regulation of Annuity Providers

INTRODUCTION

In countries with established annuity markets like the United Kingdom and the United States, the annuity business is an integral part of the life insurance business, and it is not possible to isolate its operations from the other operations of the life insurance company. Consequently, the regulatory framework that applies to the life insurance business must also apply to annuities.

This chapter will survey the major regulatory issues that arise with the life insurance business in established markets. Most or all of these issues are relevant for countries with young annuities markets like Mexico and Hungary. However, there are obvious differences between the financial environments of the two groups of countries, and some regulatory issues are more important for the second group than the first. These issues are taken up in Chapter 4, in the discussion of the experience of individual accounts reform in Chile and other countries that have adopted a version of the Chilean model. This chapter begins by reviewing the rationale for regulation and the forms that regulation can take. It then describes the two standard approaches to regulation before turning to those aspects of life insurance regulation that are especially relevant for this study.

A word about the chapter's coverage of regulatory issues is in order. Financial regulation is a vast topic, even when it is restricted to the life insurance industry. The actuarial aspects of insurance regulation are particularly complex, and the literature on them is voluminous. The chapter's aim is the comparatively modest one of surveying the issues that would be of the greatest concern to public policy in the event of a major expansion of the private annuities market, be it because of mandatory annuitization with privatized provision under an individual accounts

reform, natural market growth or both. Hence, the chapter will cover the
more technical aspects of the subject in a general way.

THE RATIONALE FOR REGULATION

There are two principal rationales for regulating the life insurance industry.
The first is that, to use economists' terminology, the annuity market
and the market for other life insurance vehicles suffer, like most financial
markets, from the market failure known as asymmetric information. Life
insurance companies understand the properties of the products they sell,
including annuities, but most of their policyholders do not. Annuities
are complex and can take on many guises, and an annuitant is unlikely to
buy more than one or two in the course of his lifetime.[1] This means that
even a sensible and intelligent person will lack the time and expertise to
make an informed decision among different products and competing
suppliers. The sheer quantity of information on annuities available on
providers' websites may intimidate the potential annuitant. Some of these
websites provide clear and comprehensive information on annuities and
their role in providing secure retirement income, but how many potential
annuitants will visit them, let alone understand what they present, is
uncertain.

With a life annuity, the difficulty of choice is compounded by the need to
assess an annuity's merits against those of a wide and changing array of
other financial products. Despite the fact that some degree of annuitization
will enhance the welfare of many people, there is evidence, to which
Chapter 1 alluded that the annuity's provision of longevity insurance is not
fully appreciated. Other financial instruments lack the annuity's special
property of longevity insurance but are more liquid and have a more
flexible income stream.

As Chapter 1 has discussed, the life annuity's unusual character may
actually inhibit demand. If so, potential annuitants might be less vulnerable
to unscrupulous or over enthusiastic salespeople than they otherwise
would be. That said, a salesman would have an incentive to exaggerate the
merits of annuities with a guarantee feature, since it is the irrevocable
aspect of the purchase of an annuity that seems to deter potential

---

[1] Taylor (2004) reports on a survey of the UK annuity market that found that almost
two-thirds (over 60 percent) of those surveyed had purchased only one annuity of any
kind in their lifetime. Some 16 percent had purchased two and 13 percent had purchased
three annuities.

annuitants. The salesman might also misrepresent the loss of liquidity that the purchase of an annuity entails.

In any event, buying an annuity is a big decision, involving the outlay of what most people consider to be a large sum of money. If potential annuitants are quite ignorant of an annuity's properties and the costs of annuitization, then a case can be made for regulation of annuity sales. This argument is strengthened if annuitants, being at or near the end of their working lives, are especially vulnerable to the consequences of an ill-advised financial decision. If, for example, an elderly person is persuaded by a salesperson to annuitize a very high share of his wealth, he or she may have little available capital to fall back on. Too low a rate of annuitization, as Chapter 1 has discussed, is also a possibility. Mental frailty may also be an issue among older potential annuitants.

The second rationale for regulation stems from the way annuities are funded. Specifically, the incentive for insurance companies to adopt and adhere to prudent funding and pricing practices may be blunted by the peculiar timing of the payments involved in an annuity transaction. In the case of a single payment life annuity, a purchaser makes an up-front payment of her capital, but many years elapse before most of it is paid back. In a highly competitive and unregulated environment, this characteristic of annuities can give a life insurance company an undue incentive to under-price to gain market share, or to make unduly risky funding decisions, since without regulatory safeguards the company could conceivably encroach on its reserves for many years before the consequences of its pricing practices became apparent. Regulation may be justified if it prevents or at least reduces the likelihood of such practices.[2]

A third rationale for regulation derives from the potential for the financial difficulties of one insurance company to spread to the rest of the insurance industry, and even to banks and other financial institutions. This is especially true of the reinsurance side of the insurance business, which provides insurance for large risks to the industry itself (Das, Davies,

---

[2] Regulation may be good public policy even if the incentives for prudent pricing and funding behavior are reasonably strong. To draw an analogy with the regulation of food and drugs in the United States, the public may simply prefer to pay the extra taxes necessary for the additional assurance of product safety that regulation of these industries is thought to provide even if competitive forces give the industry powerful incentives to produce safe products. The example also illustrates a critical distinction between the food and drugs industries and annuity providers – the consequences of risky behavior (unsanitary practices and contaminated food, and inadequate testing and drugs that are ineffective or downright harmful) typically show up much faster with the former than they do with the latter.

84   *The Regulation of Annuity Providers*

and Podpiera, 2003). The risk of contagion is well recognized in the case of the banking industry, where deposit runs, even when they affect a bank that is fundamentally sound financially, can lead to runs throughout the banking system. This phenomenon results from a lack of full information on the part of depositors as to the condition of their banks (another example of asymmetric information), and can end in a generalized panic even if many depositors have full information. A well-informed depositor or policy-holder may know that a particular bank or insurance company is sound, but if everyone else is pulling their deposits out of the bank or canceling their insurance policies, it is in his interest to do so as well.

The financial structure of the typical life insurance company differs considerably from that of a bank, and so does its role in the financial system. In particular, the traditional liabilities of insurance companies do not serve as a means of payment, and have significantly longer maturities than bank deposits. Nonetheless, the possibility of contagion is more than academic. Because the financial condition of one life insurance company impinges on the conditions of the industry as a whole, the unsound financial practices of one company entail a social cost, or a negative externality, that justifies some regulatory presence. In addition, in the wake of the deregulation that has taken place in the United States, Europe, and Japan over the past 25 years, life insurance companies in these countries have become more bank-like on both the asset and liabilities side of their operations. On the assets side, they compete with banks in commercial lending and take on credit risk, and on the liabilities side, they offer products to their customers that are comparatively liquid, like guaranteed income certificates and variable annuities (Das, Davies, and Podpiera, 2003).

The argument for regulation based on consumer ignorance of the properties of annuities — as distinguished from ignorance about the financial soundness of the annuity provider — provides a rationale for measures to protect the consumer directly. These measures can assume a number of different forms. The relevant regulatory agency might wish to regulate the characteristics of the products the life insurance industry offers, the information it provides on them, and the terms of their contracts. For example, the legal component of the framework could include laws that require a cooling-off period, so that a decision made too hastily might be reconsidered in tranquility.

The regulatory framework would normally include a consumer education component, and there are two different approaches to consumer education. The first stresses the importance of providing clear, reliable, and full information in booklets, guides, and the like. Its premise is that the public provision of an adequate amount of information clearly presented is necessary to defeat the competitive pressures that might lead annuity providers and their sales representatives to mislead or bamboozle their customers. The second approach is based on the contrary premise that the issue is not lack of clear information, but rather the inability of ordinary human beings to process and act upon complex information however presented. This approach, which receives support from behavioral economics, implies that there should be restrictions on consumer choice, or measures that will direct or encourage consumers to make the prudent choices that they might otherwise overlook. This point is taken up again in Chapter 5.

The argument for regulation to curb unsound pricing and investing practices and that for regulation based on externalities could justify the regulation of many areas of the insurance business. These areas would include, but not be limited to: investment practices; actuarial assumptions; funding practices; pricing practices; capital adequacy, and provisioning; accounting procedures; qualifications of professional staff; insolvency procedures; policyholder guarantees; and corporate governance. This list could be easily expanded. Both of these last two rationales for regulation would also justify measures to promote transparent accounting, and the prompt dissemination of comprehensive information on a company's finances and operations, including its balance sheet and income statements. The presumption is that if companies are required to provide timely and comprehensive information on their operations, and are effectively penalized if they do not, they will confront a strong incentive to manage their businesses both prudently and efficiently.

APPROACHES TO REGULATION

The regulation of the business and investment practices of insurance companies is usually assigned to a central government agency rather than a subnational one. The exercise of this regulatory function belongs at the central government level because insurance is not a regional or local market. There are obvious economies of scale, and other economies related to risk-pooling, which tend to generate a national if not an international market. It is inefficient to establish what could be a large number of regional regulatory agencies to oversee a national market, particularly in a small country, or a country where the professional staff that a regulatory agency needs is scarce.

One part of the regulatory function is usually assigned to subnational governments, however — the apparatus of consumer protection. The difference in assignment makes some sense if consumer protection agencies are dealing with individual members of the public, while the staff of the agencies that regulate the business and investment practices of insurance companies is dealing with the companies themselves. Moreover, these agencies need specialized professional expertise in actuarial science and accounting and other fields that will not be necessary for the consumer protection function.

The United States is unique among the advanced countries in regulating the life insurance business at the state and not the federal (central government) level.[3] The federal government and its agencies play no direct role in its regulation.[4] Canada is a partial exception, in that regulation is shared between the federal government and the provinces. A number of countries with well-developed financial markets, including Canada and the United Kingdom, have consolidated the regulation of the insurance industry and other components of the financial sector in the hands of a single authority. This change in regulatory structure has been prompted by the liberalization of regulations that had compartmentalized the financial industry, the resulting blurring of the demarcation of the traditional activities of the different sectors of the financial industry, and the realization that many of the problems regulation confronts are systemic.

There are two basic approaches to the regulation of financial institutions: the application of direct controls (often termed compliance-based), and

[3] The McCarran-Ferguson Act of 1945 precludes the application of federal statutes to the life insurance business, unless they specifically relate to that business (General Accounting Office, 1999). Despite this decentralized regulatory framework, the National Association of Insurance Commissioners (NAIC), which is composed of the state insurance commissioners of the 50 states and 4 territories achieves some degree of uniformity of regulatory practice by drafting model regulations governing such areas as transactions between life insurance companies and their holding companies and affiliates, and encouraging state regulatory agencies to impose a regulatory framework of adequate rigor. Nonetheless, the quality of regulation and supervision is thought to vary from one state to another. The experiences of several life insurance companies in the late 1980s and early 1990s pointed to problems with the regulation of the industry, leading to efforts by NAIC to improve quality in lagging states (General Accounting Office, 1999).

[4] The Pension Benefit Guarantee Corporation (PBGC), the federal agency responsible for overseeing employer-provided pension plans, provides guarantees for the group annuities that pension plan administrators/sponsors purchase for their members, but not for individual annuities. Similarly, the Department of Labor's safest available annuity standard is designed to apply to members of employer-provided pension plans, and does not apply to individual annuities.

an indirect approach based on a system of incentives to promote prudent financial decision-making and a well-functioning regulatory framework. The direct approach requires the regulatory authority to intervene directly in the investment, pricing and other decisions an insurance company makes. It emphasizes compliance with specific rules that have been established to govern decisions in the various aspects of the business. In the case of the regulation of professional staff, for example, the direct approach could entail the agency's setting the qualifications for actuaries and other specialists. The indirect approach would rely on the disciplinary role of the market and the enlightened self-interest of the professional bodies concerned to ensure that their members are adequately trained and vetted. It will not work properly without a sound legal and commercial infrastructure.

J. Thompson (2003) has argued that the direct approach may be more suitable than the indirect approach for an insurance industry in a developing country, which lacks the institutions and market infrastructure necessary to make the indirect approach work. As a corollary, Thompson and others have suggested that, as a country's financial institutions develop, the regulatory approach should evolve from an entirely direct approach to a mixed approach that relies more and more on indirect mechanisms of control as time passes.

THE REGULATION OF INVESTMENTS

The investments of life insurance companies are normally regulated according to the prudent person rule (an indirect approach), or a framework of quantitative controls. The prudent person rule is often supplemented by limits on the share of a portfolio that may be allocated to a particular class or classes of assets, which mixes the two approaches. Given the importance of the investment function, this section will compare and contrast the two approaches at some length.

A regulatory framework based on quantitative restrictions – the direct approach – equates regulatory compliance with compliance with whatever quantitative restrictions are imposed on the allocation of the insurance company's portfolio. For example, insurers may be required to restrict their holdings of equities to less than 25 percent of the total market value of the portfolio, their holdings of real estate to less than 10 percent, and their combined holdings of equity and real estate to 30 percent.

Under the prudent person man rule, the company's investment policy is to be guided by the test of what a prudent person would do in the circumstances. The prudent person rule evolved from the Anglo Saxon law of trusts, and the literature on the subject cites as the major precedent a ruling by a Massachusetts court in 1830.[5] The New England court did not lay down specific guidelines. Instead, it enjoined trustees to exercise sound judgment, and to be guided by the decisions that men of judgment and intelligence would make when they sought to ensure the continued growth and safe investment of their capital. Effectively, the original rule sets out a social standard: prudent investing is the kind of investing that persons considered to be prudent would do. Davis (2001) argues that in practice, the key test of prudence is the way the process of decision-making is designed, and not its outcome. As Gordon Clark (2003, p. 4) puts it: "Fiduciary duty does not carry a guarantee for the value of assets; it is a behavioral imperative rather than a certain outcome."

The practical application of the prudent person rule in the United States and the United Kingdom is thought to have been overly conservative, in that it emphasized the preservation of capital over growth and income. The rule is also thought to have neglected the distinction between nominal and real values, thereby discouraging investment of part of a nominal pool of capital in assets that could serve as a hedge against inflation (OECD, 2002). The application of the rule also tended to judge the riskiness of a portfolio of assets by the riskiness of the individual assets of which the portfolio was comprised rather than the riskiness of the portfolio as a whole.[6] As a result, it may have discouraged the adoption of investment strategies that would have reduced risk without lowering the overall expected return.

To address this problem for U.S. employer-provided pension plans, the Employee Retirement and Income Security Act of 1974 (ERISA) set out a revised rule, sometimes referred to as the prudent investor rule, which explicitly embraces the basic tenets of modern portfolio theory. Specifically, the revised rule recognizes that the riskiness of the portfolio is not the sum of some measure of the riskiness of its individual instruments (OECD 2002, p. 53). It is acceptable for a portfolio to contain risky assets provided

---

[5] The case in question is *Harvard College v. Amory*, 9 Pick. (26 Mass.) 446, 461 (1830).
[6] In a study of the American banking system, Del Guercio (1996) finds that the stock portfolios of bank fiduciaries are by comparison with mutual funds tilted toward high-quality stocks. This she attributes to the banks' greater exposure to liability and the courts' interpretation of the prudent person rule, which emphasizes the qualities of individual stocks, and not their contribution to efficient portfolio diversification. She infers that if a similar pattern is evident for investments in other assets, diversification across asset classes may be inefficient. Risk may be higher than optimal given the expected rate of return, or vice versa.

the overall degree of risk does not exceed some reasonable level. To put it in more technical terms, a prudently invested portfolio should be on the risk-return frontier. In the particular case of insurance companies, the company's reserves should be large enough that it can withstand the losses that the asset composition of the portfolio could entail.

The revised version of the prudent investor rule does not specifically apply to insurance companies and other investors in a fiduciary capacity in the United States. For this reason, it is possible that insurance companies may adopt a somewhat more conservative standard in making their investment decisions. However, it is generally accepted in the United States and elsewhere that a judgment about the prudence of the investment portfolio of insurance companies has to take into account the match of maturities of assets and liabilities. In other words, the riskiness of the investment portfolio depends importantly on the maturity composition of the company's assets and liabilities, or more precisely on the relative duration of assets and liabilities.

In practice, modern portfolio theory does not provide hard and fast guidelines for asset allocation. The practical effectiveness of the prudent person rule requires some general agreement about what constitutes risky investing and what does not. In the specific case of life annuities, as Chapter 2 discusses, the bond-like character of the liability makes a strong case for allocating a large share of assets to high quality fixed-interest securities with a maturity structure that matches the stream of expected payments to the securities' income stream. Holdings of equities can be justified by the lack of long-dated bonds to match expected long-dated annuity payments.

In view of the considerable discretion that the prudent person rule gives organizations that make investment decisions for others, its regulatory effectiveness depends crucially on adequate internal control mechanisms, on corporate transparency and professionalism, and on an effective legal system. An insurance company that is liable to a lawsuit because of investment losses will want to have them attributed to bad luck — for example, a down market that could not have been anticipated — rather than bad judgment or incompetence. To make the case for bad luck convincingly, it will need to point to active and properly functioning investment and investment review committees, and to evidence that their practices were appropriately conservative, and that they were staffed by well-trained, competent, and honest professionals.

Corporate transparency, and in particular, full information on a company's balance sheet and off-balance sheet transactions, is supposed to create a disincentive to rash or fraudulent investing practices, particularly if shareholders are active and financially informed and industry analysts in investment houses and regulatory bodies carry out their responsibilities diligently. The legal system needs a well-developed set of procedures, legal and judicial expertise, and adequate resources if it is to adjudicate fairly and reasonably promptly the cases that are presented to it.

For many countries, these high standards of corporate governance and legal system performance set the bar very high. Some countries fall far short of attaining them. Corporate transparency can be an issue in any country, even in the United States with its highly developed capital markets, as the Enron debacle has made all too clear. Shareholders may lack effective control of managerial decisions, because of a lack of the specialized knowledge necessary for that control. In the particular case of insurance companies, shareholders' interests may not coincide with the interests of policy holders. The stock market, even in a country awash in financial information like the United States may not play an effective disciplinary role — if, for example, as is often claimed, it focuses excessively on the next quarter rather than taking the longer view, and is prone to fads. Keynes anticipated this concern when he wrote in *The General Theory of Employment, Interest and Money* that "investment based on genuine long-term expectation is so difficult today as to be scarcely practicable (1936, p. 157)."

Apart from the market's tendency to take the short rather than the long view, in the United States, industry analysts working for investment houses can and have been under pressure to downplay bad news (Shiller, 2000, p. 32). If a sizeable part of the professional analyst community were talking up the stock market, then actual stock values would probably be affected. This said, security exchange regulators have taken steps to reduce conflicts of interest, and it is hard to discern the impact of such conflicts on stock markets in the United States or in other OECD countries.

If there were some upward bias in the assessment of stock prices, most policy holders would have neither the time nor the technical background necessary to detect it. More generally, policy holders are not equipped to judge the soundness of the company's investment strategy. The effective application of the prudent person rule requires reliable and comprehensive information on company performance, on the basis of which appraisals of the worth of stocks may be made. The incentives that the securities industry confronts do not always ensure either that information is comprehensive, or appraisals unbiased. If nothing else, this underscores the importance of regulations that maintain the industry's incentives for honest and thorough assessment.

The great — perhaps the sole — advantage of the quantitative restrictions approach is that it does not make the same demands as the prudent person rule does on a country's legal or corporate infrastructure. Assuming that financial instruments can be clearly distinguished from one another, and that there is no difficulty in measuring total assets, determining compliance with the ceiling set for a particular asset class is no more than simple arithmetic and accounting.

Nonetheless, the quantitative restrictions approach has some potentially serious defects.[7] First, depending on its actual design, its restrictions may be either too loose or too restrictive. As an example of the first, a restriction of 35 percent of total portfolio on equities may not in practice be binding on an insurance company that should invest mainly in fixed interest securities, and may in fact encourage excessively risky investments. As an example of the second, a very low ceiling on equities or the prohibition of holdings of foreign securities may actually make the portfolio riskier than it otherwise would be. Similarly, prohibiting investments in derivatives; for example, options (puts) that guarantee a minimum sales price for an asset for a specific period might have the same effect.[8] Second, the approach typically imposes no restrictions on sub-groups (i.e. equity holdings in different sectors) even though variations in these holdings can substantially increase overall risk.

Third, the approach takes no account of the way the portfolio is funded, and the maturity composition of liabilities. Fourth, the approach makes no allowance for holdings where the risk is passed through to the policy-holder, for example, variable annuities in the case of U.S. insurance companies. Fifth, depending on the penalty imposed for non-compliance and on the way holdings are valued, the ceilings on portfolio shares can lead to excessive caution by portfolio managers as they try to ensure that the ceilings will not be broken. If, for example, shares are marked to market, and are volatile, the portfolio manager may prefer to maintain

---

[7] This section draws heavily on Davis (2001).

[8] Elementary portfolio theory casts the investment decision as one of ensuring that a given asset allocation maximizes the portfolio's expected return for the specified level of risk. Adding a constraint on portfolio allocation will reduce the expected return for a given risk level, or at best leave it unchanged. The potentially negative impact of quantitative restrictions depends on exactly how constraining they are. Restricting the share of equities to no more than 10 percent of total portfolio has quite different consequences from restricting it to no more than 40 percent, for example.

share holdings well below the ceiling that applies to them.[9] Sixth, the duty to comply with quantitative ceilings may detract from a search for the highest return for an acceptable degree of risk.

The putative superiority of the prudent person approach, at least in an environment of strong and effective financial regulation and supervision, has not made it the regulatory formula of choice in the case of insurance companies. Among the members of the OECD, only the Netherlands, the United Kingdom, and the United States rely on the prudent person approach (Davis 2001).[10] In the United States, the states may also impose ceilings on particular asset classes. In the state of Delaware, for example, a ceiling of 250 percent of capital and surplus applies to investments in shares, and a ceiling of 25 percent to real estate. Emerging market regulators typically rely on quantitative restrictions (Singh and Kong, 2005).

The quantitative restrictions that apply in OECD countries may in practice have little effect on a life insurance company's asset allocation strategy. In Canada, for example, the share in the total assets of life insurance companies of real estate and equity investments combined is limited to 5–25 percent. However, Canadian insurers are required to aim to match assets against their individual liabilities, with the result that equities are held primarily as an investment of surplus funds, implying that the limit on real estate and equity investments is not in practice constraining (IMF, 2004a, p. 93). In Japan, equity holdings of life insurance companies are limited to 30 percent and real estate holdings to 20 percent of the total portfolio. In neither country is there a ceiling on fixed interest securities. Whether these restrictions impose significant limits on the operations of life insurers may depend on the availability of long-dated bonds. If they are not available, then equities may be the best available hedge against long-dated liabilities, and a quantitative limit on equity holdings, if it is set too low, might result in an inefficient portfolio allocation.

Even if reliance on quantitative restrictions has little obvious effect on the allocation of investments across broad asset classes like stocks and bonds, the issue arises as to whether it has any influence on less observable aspects

---

[9] If the ceiling must be observed at the end of some stipulated accounting period, and penalties for non-observance are not particularly high, a company might simply follow its own asset allocation strategy until shortly before the reporting deadline. In this case, observing the limits on asset allocation amounts simply to end-of-period window dressing.

[10] The OECD includes the industrial countries as well as the Czech Republic, Hungary, Korea, Mexico, Portugal, Slovak Republic, and Turkey.

of investment strategy. It is hard to be definitive. Corporate governance is strong or reasonably strong in most members of the OECD; the transparency of corporate accounting and investing practices may vary, but must create reasonably strong incentives for prudent investing in most of them. It may be that the conditions under which a prudent person or prudent investor approach will work are also those under which a quantitative restrictions approach will work — or at least not hamper efficient portfolio allocation — provided that the restrictions are not set so stringently that they oblige a company to adopt an overly conservative investment strategy with little opportunity for portfolio diversification. If an insurance company has strong incentives to invest prudently, then the quantitative restrictions to which it is subject can be set to allow some leeway for changes in asset allocation when that it is appropriate.

Two general conclusions follow from this discussion. First, the prudent person or prudent investor rule is not likely to work well unless it is supported by a well-functioning legal system, and a culture that ensures the provision of adequate and timely information on financial markets and corporate finances and investment decisions. Under these conditions, however, a flexibly designed quantitative framework on portfolio composition might also work well. Second, a quantitative restrictions approach works better than the prudent person approach when these conditions are absent, and when the range of assets in which insurance companies may invest is very limited. These conditions are those found in developing or emerging market countries with capital markets that are still maturing.

REGULATION OF RESERVES

Valuation of Assets and Liabilities

An insurance company must maintain reserves over and above the technical reserves that back its liabilities — it must provision — because the return to its assets is uncertain.[11] For the company to have a good idea of the level of reserves it needs, and for regulatory agencies to have confidence in their assessments of solvency, a reliable balance sheet is essential. With life insurance companies' balance sheets, difficulties with valuation tend to be more severe on the liabilities than the assets side. Unlike the deposits that account for the major share of a bank's liabilities, most of

---

[11] The need to minimize the risk of contagion is another reason for maintaining reserves.

the liabilities of a traditional life insurer are not fixed in value. At the same time, there is typically no market for them, and their value cannot be easily determined by comparing them to traded securities with similar properties.

In the absence of market valuations, the value of liabilities such as a term life insurance contract or a life annuity will be determined using a more complex version of the actuarial method described in Chapter 2. That method requires estimates of life expectancy and interest rates, and typically in the past, in most countries the assumptions made for the interest yield curve were not frequently changed. A similar practice applied to asset valuation, where it could be argued that the long-term nature of the insurance business reduced the significance of period to period fluctuations in equity or bond prices. There was no such thing as marking to market. There is a move afoot in some jurisdictions to switch to market-based valuation where it is not already the norm. Some observers believe that it will lead insurance companies to adopt a more conservative portfolio strategy to reduce the impact of market-based volatility on their net reserves (International Monetary Fund, 2004a, pp. 99–101).

The introduction of new products with payout or redemption options has clearly increased the complexity of liability valuation. This increased complexity helps explain why there is currently no agreed international standard for liability valuation, although the tools provided by modern finance theory in principle make such agreement more likely.[12]

Solvency Evaluation

The lack of uniformity of valuation practices across countries poses a problem of international comparability of solvency measures or capital adequacy measures. This problem may be compounded by reliance on solvency indicators that do not adequately reflect solvency risk. In many countries, the insurance industry uses an indicator of solvency based on the relationship between total assets and some proxy for risk — like premiums. However, a surplus of assets over premiums or some other indicator of insurance risk may not be an adequate indicator of an insurer's exposure to solvency risk.

Even if all assets and liabilities were continuously marked to market, or revalued to reflect the market value of instruments with similar

---

[12] The American Academy of Actuaries has set out a general approach to valuing the liabilities entailed by life insurance products (American Academy of Actuaries, 2002).

characteristics, a measure of solvency that was based only on some measure of the excess of assets over liabilities would be seriously flawed. As an extreme example, suppose that a life insurance company, having invested 100 percent of the reserves it must set aside to meet its future obligations in triple AAA rated corporate bonds and government paper, shifts to a 100 percent investment in high-tech stocks. This would be an absurdly risky strategy even if there were no change to net worth. This kind of problem is not just a theoretical curiosity. In the 1980s, Japanese solvency regulations focused on the *level* of reserves relative to insurance obligations — which were proxied by premiums — but not on the *quality* or *degree of diversification* of assets.

These days, life insurance companies in a number of countries use complex models and simulation techniques to determine the level of reserves that they should maintain. Rather than attempting to emulate them, the chapter's exposition will revert to the simple model sketched in Chapters 1 and 2 and expounded more rigorously in Appendix 1 (see the Sub-section "Funding with a Risky Asset") to gain some insight into the need for reserves, and how reserve holdings should be related to the riskiness of an insurance company's portfolio and the maturity composition of its balance sheet.

To begin with, we assume again that the only risk an insurance company faces in providing annuities is the mortality risk of an individual annuitant. Life expectancies are known with certainty. In this hypothetical world, the insurance company could, as Chapter 2 has explained, fund its annuities with government bonds in such a way that the present value of its assets would always equal the present value of its future payments to annuitants. Assets and liabilities would be perfectly matched. Bonds would never have to be sold in a down market, or reinvested at rates of interest lower than those used to price the annuities. Apart from some reserves to cover the company in the event that the mortality rates of its annuitant pool were lower than those of the population at large, no reserves would be necessary.

Once investment risk is admitted, however, along with the possibility of funding the annuities with higher-yielding corporate debt, equity, and other financial instruments, the risk that the realized rate of return on the assets funding the annuities may be insufficient materializes. Provided the insurance company knew precisely the probability distribution of rates of return on its assets, it could determine the level of reserves it would have to hold to keep the probability that it would fail to honor its commitments to policy holders below some stipulated rate — for example, 1 percent.

This calculation is comparatively easy with a two-period model where it is assumed that the distribution of returns to risky assets is normal.

When the model is extended to cover many years, however, with many different kinds of assets, and liabilities with early repayment or cash out options modeling the appropriate level of reserves becomes very complicated. The introduction of aggregate mortality risk is a further complication. Whatever the degree of sophistication of the model used, these exercises need to distinguish between the probability of a failure of any size, and the expected size of the loss, since the severity and not just the likelihood of a loss have to be considered in formulating an investment strategy.

There is no internationally accepted standard of capital adequacy, and considerable cross-country variation in companies' provisioning practices and in regulatory provisioning standards. The International Association of Insurance Supervisors (IAIS) has prepared guidelines on solvency and capital adequacy requirements (IAIS, 2002, 2005), but as Das, Davies, and Podpiera (2003) point out, the guidelines are at a high level of generality. Das et al. note that in practice regulators rely on two models to assess capital adequacy: the fixed ratio model and risk-based capital models. European regulators prefer the fixed rate model, while Canada, the United States, Australia, and Japan prefer risk-based capital models. The United Kingdom has made substantial changes to its risk-based model, which will be discussed below.

There is a third approach, known as "risk or ruin," that has not been widely adopted. This approach requires the construction of a model that can calculate the probability of a company's failure over some specified horizon. Finland has applied this approach. Its complexity is an order of magnitude greater than the complexity of the first two approaches.

The fixed ratio model has the virtue of simplicity. It judges reserve adequacy by applying a specified ratio to some indicator of a specific risk to determine the level of reserves that should be maintained to provide an adequate buffer in the event that risk materializes. One commonly used indicator of risk in the life insurance business is the value of technical reserves.

The effectiveness of the fixed ratio model depends on how good its proxies for risk are. The fixed ratio risk indicator just described could be a good proxy for the effects of mortality risk — provided mortality risk grows proportionately with the value of technical reserves. (Select mortality risk in fact declines as the number of policies increases.) If an insurance company's business expands over time without changing the shares of whole life, life annuities, variable annuities, and other insurance products, and there is no change in the average longevity of the insured population, then exposure to mortality risk might also grow proportionately with its technical reserves. The fixed ratio model would prescribe that prudential reserves grow at the same rate, and provided its coefficient was well calibrated, its prescribed level of reserves would be appropriate. The composition of an insurance company's business does change over time, however, and the relative risk of each component could change as well.

The shortcomings of the fixed ratio model are more apparent in the case of investment risk. In particular, an indicator based on the level of technical reserves makes no allowance for the asset composition of the technical reserves, even though changes in asset composition can hugely affect risk. Hence, it cannot be a reliable proxy for investment risk. Business risk and its effects are more efficiently addressed by other means, such as measures that encourage adequate internal controls and accounting standards, and a transparent commercial environment.

The risk-based capital model also relies on specific ratios. Unlike the fixed ratio approach, however, it takes account of differences in risk among different kinds of insurance liabilities and different kinds of assets. Required capital is derived by applying a set of coefficients to the values of different classes of assets and liabilities and summing the results. Some versions of this method take account of the fact that holdings of certain assets may offset the risk entailed by certain liabilities (Das, Davies, and Podpiera, 2003). For example, if the value of bond holdings varies closely with the value of a particular insurance liability, like life annuity contracts, then the risk associated with the combined holdings is less than the sum of the separate risks.

The risk-based approach thus differs in two key respects from the fixed ratio model: its treatment of actuarial risk is more disaggregated, and it takes account of asset risk. In view of these differences, it is not surprising that European regulatory authorities, which have generally relied on the fixed ratio approach are moving toward a version of the risk-based model (International Monetary Fund, 2004a).

The risk-based model is superior on theoretical grounds to the fixed asset model because the reserves required by its application correspond more precisely to the risks faced by life insurance companies (Das, Davies, and Podpiera, 2003). Nonetheless, even the risk-based model's targeted reserves only approximate the level of reserves that would be derived from simple models of the probability distribution of an insurance company's earnings.

Risk-based capital models do not produce the same estimates of required capital as do more sophisticated techniques based on careful modeling of the various quantifiable risks that life insurers face, which is a shortcoming. However, risk-based models are much less complex than a fully articulated stochastic model. Moreover, their application does not require the amount of skilled professional time that the development and application of the more complex models do. Provided the capital requirements derived from them are a reasonable approximation to the requirements derived from far more complex models, their comparative simplicity may commend them to some regulatory authorities.

The discussion has focused on the possibility that methods of gauging reserve adequacy currently in use — especially the fixed ratio measure — may underestimate a company's needs to provision for solvency reserves. However, in the case of both methods described here, it is possible to require excessive provisioning for the risks entailed by one or more asset or liability classes. As Chapter 2 explained, provisioning increases the cost of doing business, since the return that reserves earn will normally be below the cost of capital to a life insurer. Too high a regulatory ratio amounts to an implicit regulatory tax.

The many different risks to which life insurers are subject and the variety of their products would all argue for a more complex regulatory approach, based on an intertemporal stochastic model that can be used to simulate the fluctuations in interest rates, asset prices, and loss experience (in the case of annuity providers, the losses that result from the underestimation of longevity) to which these companies are subject. Such models have been developed and are routinely used by life insurers in the larger markets. Different approaches are followed. One is stress testing, in which key variables such as interest rates are assumed to deviate substantially from their normal values, and the impact on income statements, liquidity, and the balance sheets of the company are then gauged. Stress tests can be based on a change to only one variable (or similar set of variables) like interest rates, and on simultaneous changes to a number of variables. Another approach is a Monte Carlo simulation, where all unpredictable variables are assumed to have some specified joint distribution, and the model is simulated a large number of times.

These insurance industry models can seve as valuable adjuncts to the less complex models the chapter has described. Primary reliance on the latter models can be justified as providing a basic test of solvency, which, should a company fail it, requires further and more intensive examination of the company's books. For risk-based capital models to work well, however, their parameters need to be set conservatively, so that those cases where a closer investigation would reveal that a company really has a solvency problem but passes the test, are rare. In the United Kingdom, insurance company regulation has been based for some time on a more complex risk-based model. As the following section explains, recent reforms have introduced a very comprehensive approach to solvency regulation and provisioning.

Lessons from Recent Reforms in the United Kingdom

The new regulatory framework for life insurers recently introduced in the United Kingdom substantially revises the regulations that determine the reserves that life insurers are expected to hold to deal with investment and other risks. The most significant changes apply to life insurers selling "with-profits" products. These products include savings and investment vehicles for which the insurer may give discretionary bonuses, which it would tend to do when markets were rising. Consequently, standard life annuities with or without a guarantee period are not included. The regulations determining the reserves of general insurers and reinsurers have also been revised.

The basic aim of the new approach − known as the twin peaks approach − is to ensure a more realistic and flexible assessment of the magnitudes and range of risks to which insurance companies are subject. It requires firms with liabilities associated with their with-profit business exceeding 500 million pounds (about 900 million dollars) to reserve an amount that is the greater of the amount that a somewhat modified version of the older approach would determine − the so-called regulatory peak − and the amount derived from a realistic accounting of liabilities and a capital reserve margin derived from comprehensive stress tests − the realistic peak. The twin peaks approach is optional for firms having with-profit liabilities of less than 500 million pounds. The UK Financial Services Authority (FSA) describes the underlying principle of the twin-peaks approach as a requirement that insurers hold resources adequate to an acceptable degree of certainty to meet both contractual obligations to policy holders and policyholders' reasonable expectations of future discretionary benefits (FSA, 2003, para. 3.36).

For the purposes of determining the regulatory peak, insurance companies continue to calculate the value of mathematical reserves, which represent the resources that insurance companies would need to hold to meet all their obligations to policyholders under a set of conservative assumptions about interest rates and asset returns, and which incorporate a margin for variations in the expected cash flows and the discount rate, or "margin for adverse deviation" (FSA, 2003, para. 2.11). The guidelines for determining the appropriate level of mathematical reserves are set out in an EU directive. However, mathematical reserves no longer take account of the estimated value of future discretionary payments. These are captured by the estimate of realistic liabilities that is calculated to determine the realistic peak, as explained below. The FSA has described mathematical reserves as representing a prudent actuarial assessment of contractual benefits (FSA, 2003, para. 3.54).

A resilience capital requirement (RCR) is calculated based on stress tests applying to holdings of equity, real estate, and fixed interest securities. The regulations require that capital be held if the effect of stressed market conditions is to cause a fall in asset values that exceeds the fall in mathematical reserves. Three stresses are calculated: one for fixed interest securities, one for equities, and one for real estate. The capital requirement is determined by the sum of the amounts determined by each test. The risk entailed by interest rate variation is captured by calculating the impact of a uniform increase or decrease in the risk-free yield curve of one-fifth of the long-term gilt (bond) yield. The required capital holdings are determined by which of the two perturbations of the yield curve entails the larger capital requirement. The stress for equities is a fall in stock market values that ranges from a minimum of 10 percent to a maximum of 25 percent depending on the recent behavior of the stock market and the gap between the earnings yield and the long-term gilt yield. The stress for real estate is a fall in values ranging from 10 to 20 percent depending on the relationship between the current values of real estate relative to the recent past − the higher the current value relative to its recent average, the greater the fall.

An additional margin called the long-term insurance capital requirement (LTICR), which equals about 0.4 percent of mathematical reserves, must also be maintained. The sum of the RCR and LTICR is the minimum capital requirement (MCR) for the purposes of the regulatory peak, subject to the minimum established by the EU's base requirement.

The starting point for a calculation of the realistic peak is a measure of realistic liabilities, which include estimates of the liabilities entailed by discretionary bonuses. These liabilities are no longer reflected in the calculation of mathematical reserves for the regulatory peak. Options and embedded guarantees are to be valued either by stochastic modeling or by relying on quoted options prices. Current modeling practice is to run between 2000−10,000 simulations (Muir and Waller, 2003). However, options and guarantees other than guaranteed annuity options (GAOs) continue to be valued deterministically (FSA, 2003, para. 3.31). Firms are expected to disclose the assumptions underlying the models, should options be valued in this way, but need not disclose details of their modeling exercises.

For the realistic peak, the risk capital margin (RCM) serves the function of the RCR. Its stresses for fixed interest securities, equities, and real estate are the same as those used in determining the RCR. In addition, the RCM includes stresses for credit risk (FSA, 2003, para. 3.77). For rated investment and non-investment-grade corporate bonds, the stress takes the form of an increase in the yield spread that varies inversely with the credit rating of the bond. In the case of non-rated corporate bonds, the stress depends on the insurer's assessment of credit quality. If the insurer has not assessed credit quality, a fixed charge of 10 percent of market value is applied. Similar procedures apply in the case of commercial mortgages and other non-rated assets, and in the case of reinsurer's concentration (the risk that a reinsurer may not be able to honor its commitments to the insurer). A stress is also included for persistency risk — the risk that policyholders will terminate their policies at a rate 50 percent less than assumed in the base line.

Under the twin peaks approach, insurance companies must maintain financial resources equal to or greater than the larger of the regulatory peak and the realistic peak. The regulatory peak is defined as the sum of mathematical reserves, the resilience capital requirement and the LTICR. The realistic peak is simply the sum of realistic liabilities and the RCM. When the reserves held under the regulatory peak fall short of the realistic peak, they must be increased to close the gap. The amount of additional capital required to bring the regulatory peak up to the realistic level is known as the with-profit insurance capital component (WPICC).

The twin peaks approach is a general framework for reserving. Its stress tests are more comprehensive than those of the approach it has replaced, and it is more sensitive to the relationship between discretionary payments and the state of the stock market than its predecessor. However, the new approach also requires that insurance companies make their own estimates of reserves, subject to general guidelines from the FSA. The basic rationale for this "second pillar" is that the twin peak framework will not capture all the risks that particular insurance companies may face. In particular, it may not take adequate account of longevity or mortality risks.

These individual capital assessments (ICAs), which apply to all life insurers, do not require that insurers apply specific stress tests with parameters whose values apply to all firms, as is the case with the procedure to determine the RCM. Instead, the ICA is expected to comprise a broad range of information on the firm's financial position, history, current business activities, a detailed review of the capital adequacy of the firm, and a risk assessment, with stress and scenario tests and identification of other pertinent risks. If the firm has relied on a sophisticated modeling approach, the ICA should also include a statement of the confidence level and modeling assumptions (FSA, 2003, para. 4.22). Although the FSA does not prescribe the parameters to be used in any stress test, it does require that stress tests be based on a confidence interval of 99.5 percent over a one-year period, meaning that insurers should have enough capital to meet their obligations 199 times out of 200.

These individual capital assessments are submitted for review to the FSA. There is no requirement to publish, however. This stage of the reform is still preliminary, and the FSA intends to review insurance company submissions over a period of two to three years. The FSA will issue an individual capital guidance, or ICG — its estimate of required capital — when it receives the results of a self assessment, which may or may not exceed the insurer's own assessment. If actual reserves fall short of the ICG, the insurer will be asked to take remedial action, or explain why the IGC could be revised downwards.

The twin peaks approach (and its second pillar complement) have not been in place long enough to permit a definitive or detailed assessment. Nonetheless, three general observations are relevant for both advanced and emerging market countries considering a similar reform. First, the system requires a highly sophisticated financial market place, and a highly developed financial market infrastructure. Because the items on insurance company balance sheets are not all traded, both regulators and companies must be able to apply and understand complex pricing models. Similarly, even if there can be some range in complexity of the models used in stress tests and simulations, the bar is set high. Second, the system requires the regulatory authority be given a large budget. The accountants, actuaries, and other financial professionals it hires have to be as good as their private sector counterparts, and, depending on the number and average size of the life insurance companies they regulate, their number may have to be large. Third, the approach requires that the regulator be given substantial discretion. The regulator's work does not begin and end with the application of a formula, be it simple or complex. In particular, giving a firm an individual capital guidance that implies its regulatory capital is insufficient even if it has satisfied the twin peaks approach will in some cases require a large dose of unquantifiable judgment.

PROTECTION OF ANNUITANTS IN THE EVENT OF THE FAILURE OF THE PROVIDER

Effective regulation does not imply that the regulated businesses should never fail. It is possible to design a regulatory apparatus that makes failure extremely unlikely, but doing so runs the risk of creating a cosseted and inefficient industry. Consequently, a sound regulatory framework has to provide for bankruptcy procedures. Typically, the procedures that apply to life insurers are common to business as a whole. At the same time, however, a government would normally want to protect annuitants from the incompetence or misjudgments of their insurers.

The guiding principle of bankruptcy law is that it should give the troubled company a reasonable degree of protection from its creditors, while at the same time preventing/discouraging the practice of asset stripping, where the company's assets are sold off to benefit shareholders and not conserved to satisfy the company's obligations to creditors. A related but very important additional principle is that resolution should be as speedy as the technical nature of the case permits. Quick resolution would be particularly important to annuitants, if the regular payment was a large share of their income.

Given the likely expansion of the private annuity market, it is important to consider the consequences of life insurance company failure for annuitants. As noted above, the assets that fund annuities are not treated like a private pension fund's assets; i.e. they do not constitute a separate entity that is distinct from the company's other assets, and they may be attached by the company's creditors.[13] In most countries, the annuitant is simply another creditor, and in fact his claim is subordinated to that of the bond holder.

Life insurance company failure has been rare. In the United States, some seven companies failed in the early 1990s because of excessive investment in risky real estate assets following the deregulation that took place in the late 1970s. At one of these companies, annuitants received only 70 cents of each dollar promised them (Reno et al., 2005, p. 82). Although the information on life insurance company failure in other countries is not comprehensive, failures in Japan and elsewhere in the 1990s have been attributed to a combination of the impact of financial deregulation

---

[13] In the United States, variable annuities are an exception to this rule. They are treated in the same way as mutual fund holdings. The difference in treatment reflects the fact that variable annuities are invested in the stock market, and only a minimum rate of return is guaranteed by the insurance company.

and swingeing changes in the economic and financial environment (Das, Davies, and Podpiera, 2003). In the United Kingdom, Equitable Life was required to stop taking new business when it began to have trouble honoring the contracts on with profit annuities when interest rates began to decline in the 1990s.

Some governments, like Chile, have established a formal guarantee to protect annuitants, while others have come to the rescue of policyholders on a case-by-case basis. In the United States, annuitants may make a claim against a fund administrated by the insurance companies located in the same state as the financially distressed company and financed by a pay-as-you-go based levy on financially sound companies. These state funds place a limit on the claim they will pay, which is currently $100,000 for most states (Reno et al., 2005, p. 81). The limit applies to the total of the claims a particular policy holder may have on a company. We return to the issue of the potential role and pitfalls of such guarantees in Chapter 7.

REGULATORY IMPLICATIONS OF THE GROWTH OF ANNUITY MARKETS: CONCLUSIONS

The growth of private annuity markets raises one overriding issue for the regulatory authorities in established annuities markets: will the current regulatory framework be up to the task of handling what may be a much bigger market? Here, we will draw some conclusions for regulations that apply mainly to established markets, leaving discussion of developing markets to Chapter 4.

First, the recent changes to the life insurance business, and in particular its entry into areas that were previously the preserve of the banks, raise a doubt about the ability of regulators to keep up with the pace of change. The consolidation of the regulatory function into one agency in countries like Canada and the United Kingdom is a response to this development. The more importance we attach to well-functioning annuities markets, the more concerned we need to be about the quality of the regulation of the life insurance industry.

Concerns over the effectiveness of life insurance regulation could be an argument for creation of specialized/dedicated annuity providers, particularly in smaller countries where regulatory effectiveness is more of an issue. This strategy has its own drawbacks, however. From the point of view of the regulatory function as a whole, increasing the number of financial institutions subject to regulatory scrutiny increases the regulatory workload. The skills required in the regulation of the life insurance business would encompass those required for specialist annuity providers. From the side of the financial industry, specialization may result in a less efficient deployment of the highly skilled professionals who are needed in both the annuities and the rest of the life insurance business.

Second, if sound regulation becomes more important with the growth of the annuity market that aging and other influences will bring about, it will become vitally important with mandatory annuitization and private provision. If the governments of countries with established annuity markets implement an individual accounts reform with mandatory annuitization and private sector provision of the annuities, they will almost certainly find themselves saddled with a formal or informal guarantee of the regular payments annuitants receive. Such a guarantee inevitably increases moral hazard, as Chapter 7 discusses at greater length. One possible consequence of a guarantee might be an attempt to cosset the industry, by regulating the terms of the annuities and the investments that fund them in such a way that the probability of default would be very low. In fact, some of the countries that have established individual accounts in the past 12 years have chosen to regulate closely the terms on which annuities are offered, as Chapter 4 discusses. Excessive regulation could effectively defeat the purpose of privatization.

Finally, the regulation of the distribution phase of an individual accounts reform should no more be treated as an afterthought than the basic design of the accumulation phase. It has been treated as such in more than one country. If the annuities are to be provided by private financial institutions, then some basic decisions have to be made about the regulatory framework that applies to them. In countries with well-developed financial systems, little change to the existing regulatory framework may be needed. However, the indirect approach to regulation may not work well in countries that are still developing the necessary financial infrastructure. In particular, quantitative restrictions on the investment portfolio may be preferable to reliance on the prudent person rule. The direct regulation of actuarial assumptions might conceivably be preferable to relying on the market or more indirect mechanisms, although the more direct approach probably limits the scope for genuine competition, and may foster inefficiency.

4

Experience with Individual Account Reforms

INTRODUCTION

This chapter reports on the international experience with individual account reforms to date. It describes the Chilean reform in some detail, because of its pioneering role and because we know more about it than we do about reforms elsewhere. The account covers the whole reform, but emphasizes the distribution phase, because that is the book's major concern. The chapter then describes and assesses variants of the Chilean reform that have been adopted elsewhere in Latin America and in Eastern and Central Europe.

THE CHILEAN REFORM[1]

Much has been written about the Chilean reform, both about its technical aspects and the politics behind its creation. The chapter will concentrate on its economic and administrative aspects.[2]

Chile's Individual Accounts System: Basic Features

Prior to the adoption of individual accounts, the public pension system in Chile was the main branch of a highly fragmented social security system. This trait, which the Chilean system shared with the systems of the other southern cone countries, Uruguay and Argentina, resulted from the system's piecemeal development. Initially, the employees of an industry like mining, who were able to act collectively to obtain benefits unavailable

---

[1] This section draws on a number of sources, including SAFP(2002), Baeza and Manubens (1988), and Rocha and Thorburn (2005).
[2] Diamond and Valdéz-Prieto (1994) is a thorough analysis of the economic aspects of the Chilean reform.

in other industries, would obtain coverage under a pension plan. Coverage was then extended gradually over many years to other industries and sectors.

As time passed, some consolidation of plans took place, but this was far from complete. In consequence, in 1979, on the eve of the establishment of the new system in 1981, there were some 32 separate pension funds, although most workers belonged to one of three comparatively large plans. As a result, both the conditions for eligibility for benefits and contribution requirements could vary from one plan to another, which must have impeded labor mobility between different industries and sectors. From the standpoint of administrative cost alone, the old system must have been highly inefficient.

The pension plans of which the old system was comprised were established as funded or at least partially funded plans. Like other South American plans, the real value of their reserves, which were held mainly in the form of government fixed interest securities, were eroded by unexpected inflation, and the financial position of the government did not permit it to recapitalize them. Unforeseen increases in longevity posed a further strain on the plans' finances. Consequently, replacement rates tended to be well below the rate implied by the plans' parameters. In Chile and elsewhere, systems that were generous on paper could not be so in practice. The obvious failure of the old system must have made a break from the past seem all the more attractive.

The Chilean individual accounts system is a defined contributions system in which members' accounts are managed by a private financial company called a pension fund administrator (*administradora de fondos de pensiones*, or AFP). Some 12 AFPs opened their doors when the new system started, but there are now six. The system has its own regulator, the Superintendency of Pension Fund Administrators (*Superintendencia de Administradoras de Fondos de Pensiones*, or SAFP). The SAFP is responsible for the supervision of all aspects of the system, apart from the supervision of the insurance companies that provide life annuities to retiring members. This latter task falls to the agency that supervises the insurance industry (*Superintendencia de valores de seguros*).

All new entrants to the labor force who are not self-employed are obliged to join the new system. The participation of the self-employed is voluntary. Persons already employed, and in principle covered by one of the many existing plans at the inception of the new system were given the choice of joining the new system, or remaining with their particular plan.

Because the contribution rate of the new system was less than the combined employer–employee payroll tax rate of the existing systems, older workers would receive an increase in take-home pay if they joined the new system. Whether because of that, or a loss of confidence in the old system and belief in the superiority of the new, many did. Membership jumped in the first year of operation to 1.4 million, or about 25 percent of the contemporary labor force, most of whom would have been older workers, and not new labor force entrants. As of March, 2002, the system had about 6.5 million active members, of which about 3.5 million, or 60 percent of the labor force, had contributed in December 2001. Some 70 percent of the labor force had made at least one contribution in the preceding 12 months. Contributors to the old system amounted to about 3 percent of the labor force as of the same date. Their number should dwindle to zero by 2020 at the latest, when the youngest contributors to the old system in 1981 will have retired.

The contribution rate to the new system was initially set at 10 percent, at which rate it has remained ever since. In addition to the 10 percent contribution, members pay what is termed an additional contribution to the AFP to cover disability and survivors' benefits and administrative costs and margins, which averaged 2.26 percent of the salary subject to the contribution in March 2002 and ranged from 2.09 percent to 2.55 percent, depending on the AFP. (These figures do not include additional fixed monthly charges for balance maintenance and contribution, and an annual percentage charge that vary from one AFP to another, and are waived by some.) (SAFP, 2002, p. 229)[3] The AFP the member has selected buys survivor and disability insurance from an insurance company. This coverage applies while they are active members of the system. Survivors' benefits for inactive members who have elected a life annuity take the form of survivorship rights to the annuity the member purchases when he retires.

Employers are required to withhold both the 10 percent contribution and the additional contribution from the employee's salary, and to remit them to the AFP that the employee has selected, where the 10 percent contribution is credited to the employee's account. Unlike some other individual accounts systems, the collection and allocation of contributions is not entrusted to a government agency. Wage and salary income subject to the contribution has an indexed monthly maximum that is expressed

---

[3] These figures do not include the commissions and other charges levied by the AFPs for the investment function, and deducted from the gross return the funds earn.

in *unidades de fomento* (UF), or development units and is indexed to the consumer price index. As of end 2004, the ceiling was 60 UF, or about 1790 dollars.

The participation of the self-employed in the new system is low, although it was also low under the old system (SAFP, 2002, p. 203). The Chilean government has taken measures to encourage the self-employed to establish accounts and contribute to them. It has also encouraged members to establish separate voluntary saving accounts with the AFPs. The funds that accumulate in these accounts may be withdrawn before retirement subject to certain restrictions, but they may also be combined with the funds in the individual accounts to finance a pension upon retirement. A law that came into effect in 2002 increased the classes of financial institutions allowed to handle voluntary contributions to include banks, mutual funds and insurance companies (SAFP, 2002, p. 61).

Until quite recently, contributors to the individual accounts, although they could switch costlessly from one AFP to another, were not entitled to choose the investments their account funded. Instead, they had a share of the single investment fund managed by the AFP. That investment fund was a legal entity separate and distinct from the administrator, with separate accounts and its own balance sheet. In 2000, the AFPs were authorized to offer two funds: one a balanced fund and the other a fixed interest fund. However, with the introduction of the multi-funds law in February 2002, each AFP may now manage five different funds that differ in respect of the share of higher-yielding risky assets they are allowed to hold in their portfolios. The funds range from a fund that can invest up to 80 percent of its portfolio in equities, with a minimum of 40 percent (Fund A) to a fund, with a zero limit on the share of equities and a high share of fixed income instruments (Fund E).

The SAFP applies an array of quantitative limits on the proportion of a fund's assets that may be invested in different classes of instrument (stocks, fixed interest securities, etc.). Initially, these restrictions were such that most of the single fund that an AFP managed was invested in indexed instruments issued by the Central Bank of Chile and the Chilean government and in instruments such as mortgage-backed securities. A system of quantitative restrictions, albeit a less complex one also applies to the portfolios of the life insurance companies that supply life annuities to retiring members. In addition, the regulatory framework creates a strong incentive for maturity matching, since shortfalls of assets from liabilities at any maturity require additional provisioning (Rocha and Thorburn, 2006).

Over time, the limits that apply to the funds that the AFPs manage have been relaxed. Limits on instruments and groups of instruments are now set for each of the five different kinds of funds that an AFP may manage. Limits on exposure to the financial sector and the foreign sector, to issues of particular companies, and to certain classes of companies as well as limits on related holdings apply to both the investments of the individual funds and their sum.[4] A risk-weighting system is applied to the value of securities, and a concentration factor as well as a liquidity factor are calculated and applied in the case of equity holdings by individual funds.[5] Holdings of foreign securities were not permitted until 1990. At present, a limit of 25–30 percent applies to these investments. The Central Bank of Chile establishes the precise limit within this range.

The regulation of investments continues to rely heavily on quantitative restrictions, but the range of assets that may be included in the portfolio of an AFP is much broader than it was 20 years ago. The system of limits, despite its complexity, gives the AFPs considerable latitude in practice in their portfolio decisions. The existence of separate limits for five different classes of funds means that investment strategies may vary from the conservative to growth-oriented.

The AFPs are subject to a rule intended to discourage sub-par investment performance. Specifically, AFPs are expected to achieve a rate of return that is no less than the lesser of: (i) 2 percentage points below the industry average for the past 36 months in the case of the more conservative funds (Funds C, D, and E), and 4 percentage points for the others and (ii) one-half of the average return for the same period. (In the case of an industry loss of 2 percent, AFPs would be expected not to incur a loss of more than 3 percent; i.e. 2 percent plus one-half of 2 percent. If a fund fails this rate-of-return test, then the difference must be made up from a reserve within the fund of excess profits, or from the AFP's own reserves. If an AFP lacks the funds to compensate for its below average investment performance, it will be subject to liquidation, and the accounts of its members will be transferred to other companies (SAFP, 2002, p. 82). This rule is thought to encourage herding behavior, since what counts

---

[4] The limits on holdings of instruments issued by a single issuer and those applying to instruments issued by particular sectors and other such limits that apply to the sum of the holdings of the five funds that each AFP manages are expressed as a proportion of the value of the instruments issued. The limit that applies to individual funds is proportional to the value of the fund. There are also limits on the share of a particular series of a securities issue that the five funds of a single AFP may hold.

[5] A government agency, the Risk Rating Commission, is responsible for risk rating. It is headed by the Superintendent of the SAFP.

for the survival of an AFP is its performance relative to other AFPs, rather than its performance as measured by some absolute or external standard.

The Bono de Reconocimiento (Recognition Bond)

When the new system was established, it was necessary to take account of, or recognize, the contributions to the old system of its members who were transferring to the new system. This was particularly important for those Chileans who had been working and contributing to the old system for some time. Broadly speaking, there were two ways of ensuring that contributory service under the old system would be properly recognized. The first would be to ensure that those who transferred to the new system were paid a pension under the terms of the old system that adequately reflected their contributory service. The second would be to credit the accounts established in the new system with a sum of money that could be used, along with contributions to the new system, to fund an annuity or some other distribution that would reflect the contributory experience with both systems.

The architects of the new system chose the second approach. Specifically, transferees to the new system from the old were entitled to a "recognition bond," (*bono de reconocimiento*) whose value varied with the number of years they had contributed to the old system and with their salary during those periods of contribution. The bonds began to earn interest at a real rate of 4 percent when the member left the old system to join the new. The bond becomes due when a member of the new system reaches the legal retirement age, is disabled, or dies. However, since 1987, it has been negotiable on the secondary market when a member becomes eligible for early retirement. In either case, the proceeds from the redemption or sale of the bond augment the balance in the individual account, and are used with the accumulated contributions and their earnings to fund a pension.

The Chilean experience demonstrates that the choice of a recognition bond as the means of acknowledging the acquired rights of members of the old system has momentous consequences for the development of the private annuity market, if the provision of annuities is privatized under an individual accounts reform. The large number of participants in the old system who became members of the new is estimated to have led to the issue of 1.2–1.8 million bonds in the past 24 years.[6] Liberalization of the

---

[6] García (1988, p. 281) reports three estimates of the number of bonds issued that range from 1.2 million to 1.8 million.

law in 1987 to allow recognition bonds to be sold on the secondary market contributed to a marked increase in the popularity of early retirement pensions.

Distributions for Retirement and Disability

To be eligible for the regular retirement pension (*pensión de vejez*), a male member must be at least 65 years old, and a female must be 60 years old. Once these ages are reached, a pension may be drawn at any time. There is no claw-back if the members continue to work, and apart from a few specialized occupations, no restrictions on working while drawing a pension. An early retirement pension (*pensión anticipada*) may be drawn, provided the value of the pension equals or exceeds a specified minimum value and achieves a specified replacement rate, as explained below.

Until recently, both the regular and the early retirement pension had to take one of the following forms: a series of programmed withdrawals; an income for a specified period combined with a deferred life annuity with regular payments that begin when the specified period has elapsed (*renta temporal con renta vitalicia diferida*); and an immediate life annuity.[7] However, a law passed in 2004 has broadened a member's choice by allowing him to draw a pension that combines a fixed and a variable component, and to combine a life annuity simultaneously with a programmed withdrawal. The annual payment for all pensions, apart from the variable component of the variable annuity introduced in 2004, must be indexed in UF.[8] Under all these options, the state guarantees a minimum pension for those members who have contributed to the new system for at least 20 years.[9] The immediate life annuity and the programmed withdrawal options are by far the most popular, accounting for over 85 percent of the total stock of pensions by number as of March 2004 (Table 4.1).

---

[7] The value of the payment made during the period before the deferred annuity begins to make payments is determined by applying an interest rate to the balance in the individual account that is a weighted average of the average real rate of profit of similar funds and the rate of interest that determines the value of the premium for life annuities. In consequence, it can change every year.

[8] Once the annual payment is determined, it is paid in twelve equal monthly installments.

[9] There are also a minimum survivors' and a minimum disability pension, which require shorter periods of contribution. Their values are a fixed proportion of the standard minimum pension. The minimum pension has risen substantially over time. At present, it is about $130 per month for people who are under 70 years of age. A limited amount of social assistance is available for those who lack this length of service and lack the means to finance a minimum pension.

Table 4.1. *Chile: share of life annuities and programmed withdrawals by class of pension as of March 2004 (in percent except where indicated)*

	Life annuity			Programmed withdrawal	Number of pensions
	Immediate	Deferred	Total		
Men	54.2	11.6	65.8	34.2	401724
Normal retirement	34.4	6.0	40.4	59.6	72992
Early retirement	70.8	20.9	91.7	8.3	187402
Disability	35.8	10.8	46.6	53.4	24923
Widows	36.8	0.2	37.0	63.0	55999
Orphans	53.5	0.2	53.6	46.4	60398
Parents	24.8	0.0	24.9	75.1	10
Women	39.8	12.1	51.9	48.1	104162
Normal retirement	28.3	7.8	36.1	63.9	55733
Early retirement	65.8	22.4	88.2	11.8	32889
Disability-total	31.9	10.1	42.0	58.0	8515
Widows	33.3	1.6	34.9	65.1	63
Orphans	18.4	0.0	18.4	81.6	6947
Parents	33.3	0.0	33.3	66.7	15
Total	51.3	11.7	62.9	37.1	505886
Normal retirement	31.8	6.8	38.5	61.5	128725
Early retirement	70.1	21.1	91.2	8.8	220291
Disability-total	34.8	15.8	71.8	28.2	33438
Widows	36.8	0.2	37.0	63.0	56062
Orphans	49.5	0.1	49.6	50.4	61095
Parents	24.8	1.2	37.0	63.0	6275

Memorandum item:
  Percentage share of early retirement in total retirement

Men	72.0
Women	37.1
Total	63.1

Note: Excludes about 7000 temporary pensions
Source: SAFP

Guaranteed annuities are an option, and a popular one, with more than 80 percent of total annuities issued being guaranteed for various periods.

With a programmed withdrawal, the funds in the member's account with the AFP remain there. The AFP continues to manage the account, and the member draws down the accumulated balance in the account at a rate that is determined by his or her sex, age, and family situation. It is adjusted once a year. Members with dependents draw down their account at a lesser rate than those without dependents, because a part of the balance is reserved to finance survivors' pensions. This arrangement implies that if the member lives long enough or earns a low average return on the balance in the account, he will exhaust the balance. At this point, provided he had contributed for 20 years, both he and his survivors would be eligible for minimum pensions.

For a given year, the maximum permissible withdrawal is calculated by determining the value of the regular payment of a hypothetical annuity that the balance in the account could fund. The calculation uses the same mortality table used to calculate the technical reserve requirement for an annuity, but applies a synthetic formula for the discount rate that is a weighted average of the life annuity discount rate, and the average rate of return of the AFP industry (Rocha and Thorburn, 2005, p. 64).

Because the synthetic discount rate would normally exceed (or not be less than) the one used for a life annuity, the initial payment will exceed the regular payment of the life annuity that could be purchased with the same capital. The monthly withdrawal is recalculated once a year based on revised life expectancies and a revised discount rate. However, the combination of the way the discount rate is calculated and the fact that life expectancy does not decline *pari passu* with age means that unless a member has very good luck with his investments, he will exhaust the balance in his account over a period about equal to his life expectancy at retirement. For example, if a 60-year-old contracts a programmed withdrawal, and has a life expectancy of 15 years, the annual withdrawals will typically dwindle to close to zero by the time he is 75.

Since the value of the payment under the programmed withdrawal depends on the investment performance of the AFP, the member bears both investment and longevity risk. These risks are mitigated, however, for qualifying members by the state-guaranteed minimum pension, which kicks in when the funds in the account are exhausted. This feature means that a programmed withdrawal could appeal to people whose annuity income would not be significantly higher than the minimum pension, since the state's safety net reduces the potential loss from a bad investment experience, while the programmed withdrawal initially makes a higher payment than the life annuity. The safety net also mitigates longevity risk. Because the balance may be bequeathed, it should appeal to people who believe their life expectancy is short or have a strong bequest motive. Of course, it will also appeal to people who are short-sighted.

Pensioners who have chosen a programmed withdrawal are required to maintain the balance of their funds in one of the three most conservative of the five funds their AFP offers. This provision is intended to prevent an excessive capital loss, with could have serious consequences for older persons, given the limited time left to them to earn, save, and recoup the loss. At the same time, it mitigates the moral hazard that arises when some one nearing retirement expects to receive a pension that is close to the minimum. In such a case, the consequences of gambling with the funds in the account for a high return are less severe than they would otherwise be.

In the case of a life annuity, the member withdraws his funds from his account, and purchases the annuity from an insurance company. A married member is required to purchase a joint annuity, which also provides for small payments to minor children should he pre-decease them. The value of the pensions paid to survivors is a specified proportion of what is known as the base pension, which is a specified proportion of the base wage — the average wage of the last ten years before retirement. For example, the widow of a pensioner receives a pension equal to 49 percent of her deceased husband's base salary. If the funds in a member's account are not sufficient to purchase a life annuity with a regular payment that at least equals the minimum pension, the member must opt for a programmed withdrawal.

Survivors' pensions for the family of active members are financed from a combination of the balance in the member's account and the insurance that the member's AFP contracted on his behalf. If the funds in the account alone are insufficient, the insurance company must make up the difference. As a result, a member who dies while active may have no funds left in his account to bequeath. Only members who have no families will routinely be able to bequeath the funds in their account at their death to a beneficiary of their choosing. A special provision is also made for workers who die in a work-related accident. Under all pension options, a member can withdraw in a lump sum the difference, if any, between the balance in the account and the sum required to finance a pension with a value equal to the greater of 120 percent of the minimum pension and 70 percent of his average taxable wage over the previous ten years.

The state extends a limited guarantee against the failure of an annuity provider. Specifically, in addition to guaranteeing the amount of the minimum pension, it extends a guarantee for 75 percent of the amount by which the regular payment exceeds the minimum pension up to a maximum of 45 UF, or about $1340 monthly. Given that the average value of a Chilean pension is about $750, this ceiling is comparatively generous.

It does not appear that the regulatory framework has had a significant impact on annuity premiums in Chile. The price of an annuity will be a function, as we have discussed, of the mortality rates embodied in the life table used by the insurance company, the interest rates used to discount future payments, and the implicit tax entailed by the regulatory regime. In Chile, life insurers are free to use a proprietary life table, or to adapt some other table for the pricing of life annuities. They are required to use the life table stipulated by the SAFP to calculate the level of their technical reserves. Since life expectancy has increased substantially since this table was constructed, it can be argued that companies have been under-provisioning, although this effect might have been offset by the discount rate used. A more up-to-date mortality table has recently been published. (Rocha and Thorburn, 2006, p. 94).

Rocha and Thorburn estimate MW ratios in Chile. They find that, despite considerable variation by age, sex, and size of premium of the annuitant, MW ratios tend to exceed one. This suggests to them either that intermediation costs are low, that insurance companies are adopting relatively aggressive pricing strategies or that they are expecting interest rates to rise. Although it is not possible to infer confidently from these results that provisioning requirements have not been excessive, they suggest that they have not imposed an onerous tax. These relatively high estimates of the MW ratio are all the more surprising given that in other countries, the MW ratios estimated for indexed annuities are typically below those estimated for nominal annuities. Rocha and Thorburn attribute this apparent anomaly to the dominant role of indexed instruments in the Chilean financial system. The relatively high level of MW ratios may also reflect the relatively large number of insurance companies selling annuities – some 15 as of 2004.

Middlemen (insurance brokers) have played an important role in the market for life annuities in Chile. Data from the SAFP show that sales commissions amounted to about $3\frac{1}{2}$ percent of the total premium in the early 1990s. They rose to close to 6 percent in the late 1990s before declining quite steeply to around $2\frac{3}{4}$ percent in 2001–2003 (Larrain Ríos, 2004). There have been instances of collusion between the broker and the member to increase the share of the funds in the account that the member could withdraw as a lump sum. In one instance, the account holder received a sum that was worth far less (measured at any reasonable discount rate) than the income stream he gave up (Palacios and Rofman, 2001). The law was changed recently to prevent brokers from taking such blatant advantage of their clients, and a temporary cap of $2\frac{1}{2}$ percent was placed on commissions. There have also been reports of sales representatives sharing their commissions with their customers, perhaps because they were not at liberty to lower them to under-price the competition. The SAFP has also introduced an electronic bidding system to facilitate comparison shopping for annuities to reduce their cost. The system allows a member on the verge of retirement to seek quotations from a number of insurance companies without requiring a personal visit, or the intercession of an agent.

Since the inception of the Chilean system, it has been possible to retire prior to the ages of 65 and 60, if the accumulated value in the retiree's account is sufficient to fund a pension that satisfied a minimum income condition and a replacement income condition. Until 2004, these conditions required that the would-be retiree be able to contract for an annuity with an income equal to or greater than 110 percent of the minimum state-guaranteed pension; and equal to or greater than 50 percent of the average taxable income of the last ten years of contributions. If these conditions were satisfied, the retiree could also opt for a programmed withdrawal.

The early retirement pension has proved very popular. Of about 349,000 pensions in the form of programmed withdrawals or life annuities for regular and early retirement being paid as of March 2004, some 63 percent were for early retirement (Table 4.1). Of these, only about 10 percent took the form of programmed withdrawals – the rest were in the form of either immediate life annuities or deferred annuities. This preference among those who retire early for the life annuity probably reflects the fact that many would not be able to take advantage of the minimum pension guarantee, because they have less than 20 years of contributions. In these circumstances, choosing a programmed withdrawal would leave them without any insurance against longevity risk. Those who opt for early retirement tend to earn higher incomes than those who wait, perhaps because the lower paid are less likely to satisfy the minimum income requirements for early retirement.

A deferred annuity may be attractive to many because it can be designed so that the payments are front-loaded. Specifically, the member contracts with and pays an insurance company for an annuity that will begin in 1–2 year's time and then may draw down the balance during the intervening period. In addition to satisfying the minimum replacement and income requirements, the value of the withdrawals in the first two years may be as much as twice the annual income from the annuity (but no less than one-half).

Many of the people who opted for the early retirement pension have apparently done so in order to supplement their income from work and/or surmount economic hardship, and did not intend to leave the labor force, according to a survey commissioned by the Superintendency (Larrain Ríos, 2004). Concern that people opting for early retirement could be headed for a straitened old age — since by stopping their contributions and opting for an early pension they could be substantially reducing the share of working life income that the pension would replace — has motivated changes to the eligibility requirements. Specifically, in February 2004 legislation was passed to raise the minimum income level in stages to 150 percent of the minimum pension by August 2008, and the minimum replacement ratio to 70 percent by August 2010. The measurement of the income base used in the replacement ratio calculation has also been changed to stiffen the requirement.

By at least four different yardsticks, the Chilean reform has been very successful. First, the rates of return earned by the AFPs in the 1980s and most of the 1990s were very high, in spite of the fact that the funds of AFPs were held mainly in indexed government securities. These high rates were largely the result of special circumstances, but the fact that this indexed debt was always honored points to the overall sound management of the Chilean economy. Second, the reform has had an important beneficial side-effect: it has stimulated the development of domestic capital markets (Holzmann, 1997). Third, the supervisory body, the SAFP has been exemplary in its provision of information on the system's functioning. Fourth, on one fundamental test of the distribution phase — that pensioners receive their pension in full and on time — the Chilean system scores brilliantly. There are no reports of delays, and no general failure to pay retired members their due. This record owes something, like the success at the accumulation phase, to the sound management of the economy.

Set against these successes are some disappointments, and some problems in need of fixing. Coverage is still well below 100 percent of the eligible population — although coverage in Chile is broad compared with its neighbors — and the self-employed have not shown much interest in participating. The minimum pension guarantee encourages participation by lower wage earners for only the twenty years it takes to become eligible for it. The commissions and fees that the AFPs levy for managing and investing the accounts have been very high, so that while the gross real rate of return on the funds they manage has been estimated to have averaged 10 percent since the system's inception, the net return is three percentage points lower (Rocha and Thorburn, 2006, p. 16). The programmed withdrawal option probably suits some people well, but not others, because of the lack of full longevity insurance and the decline over time in the annual benefit. Finally, although Chileans are now much more knowledgeable about their options, there remains an issue regarding informed choice, which is clearly recognized by the Superintendency.

As we have seen, the Chilean Superintendency has taken action to address these shortcomings, including both changes to the parameters of the system and institutional reforms like the establishment of electronic bidding for annuities. The large share of the informal and agricultural sectors in Chile's economy puts a limit on the rate of coverage of the system that is below the rates achieved in the industrialized countries, but a conventional pay-as-you-go (PAYG) system would not be any more successful in this respect.

OTHER LATIN AMERICAN SYSTEMS

Of the eight other Latin American countries that have adopted some variant of the individual accounts system, Bolivia, El Salvador, and Mexico have followed the Chilean example of requiring new entrants to the labor force to join the new system. Bolivia has gone one step further, by requiring older workers to forsake the old system and transfer to the new one. Elsewhere, in Colombia, Peru, and Uruguay (if income is below a specified level), new workers are given the choice between the old system and the new, and in Argentina they are given a choice between the old PAYG system, and what is in effect a carve-out − a combination of a PAYG and the new individual accounts system (Table 4.2). Costa Rica is unique in the region in having voluntary add-on individual accounts.

The distribution phase of the individual accounts component of the other Latin American reforms has been modeled more or less closely on the Chilean system. About half of the countries have used the recognition bond as the instrument to handle past contributions to the old system, and have followed Chile's example of fixing the rate of interest payable on it in real terms. Argentina and Uruguay are exceptions: rather than issuing a recognition bond, they increase the pension a member of the new system receives to reflect his service under the old. As a result, the annuity markets in these two countries will be smaller than they otherwise would have been.

The choice of distribution options is typically similar to that in Chile. All systems offer a life annuity, and all of these are indexed, except for the

Table 4.2. *Basic features of Latin American systems (emphasizing the distributional phase)*[a]

	Argentina	Bolivia	Chile	Colombia	Costa Rica	El Salvador	Mexico	Peru	Uruguay
Form of system	Mixed: PAYG/IA	Individual accounts	Individual accounts	Mixed PAYG/IA	PAYG with voluntary IA	Individual accounts	Individual accounts	Mixed: PAYG/IA	Mixed: PAYG/IA
Choices for new workers	Choice of PAYG or PAYG with IA component	Mandatory	Mandatory	Choice of PAYG or IA[b]	IA supplements PAYG and is voluntary	Mandatory	Mandatory	Choice of PAYG or IA	Mandatory depending on income
Treatment of past contributions	Reflected in public pension	Reflected in public pension	Recognition bond	Recognition bond	Not relevant	Recognition bond	Contributions to former DC plan transferred to IA	Recognition bond	Reflected in public pension
Source of disability/ survivors' insurance	Private insurance	Private insurance	Private insurance	Private insurance	Public, with optional private coverage tied to IA	Private insurance	Public (social security institute)	Private insurance	Private insurance
Minimum rate of return on contributions	Relative guarantee	No guarantee	Relative guarantee	Relative guarantee	Relative guarantee	Relative guarantee	No guarantee	Relative guarantee	Guaranteed rate of return

Form of pension:

Programmed withdrawal	No	Yes	Yes	Yes	Yes	No	Yes
Immediate life annuity	Yes	Yes	Yes	Yes	Yes	Yes	Yes
Deferred annuity	No	Yes	No	Yes	No	No	No
Lump sum	No	Yes	Yes	Yes	Yes	No	Yes
Minimum pension	Yes	Yes	Yes	Yes	Yes	Annual cash benefit for citizens aged 65	Yes
Early retirement	No	Yes	Yes	Yes	Yes	Yes, but for IA-financed part only	Yes, but for IA-financed part only

[a] Some countries with very recently introduced individual account systems are not included

[b] Contributors are allowed to switch systems every three years

Sources: Devesa-Carpio and Vidal-Meliá (2002); Holzmann and Linz (2005); Palacios and Rofman (2001); and Mackenzie, Gerson, and Cuevas (1997)

Argentine annuity.[10] Similarly, compulsory disability and survivors' insurance is provided by private insurance companies everywhere but Mexico and Costa Rica, and most countries have a guarantee on the relative return earned by the equivalent of the AFPs. Every country but Bolivia has a minimum pension, although Bolivia does have an annual social assistance cash benefit payable at age 65 without any other eligibility requirements.

Insurance companies have a monopoly of annuity provision in every country but Argentina, where completely separate institutions were established to annuitize distributions from the individual accounts that the reform of 1994 established. In Argentina, the companies providing annuities may not invest in stocks or real estate. Similar limits apply to the insurance companies in Peru. All the countries follow the Chilean example and leave the regulation of the insurance companies that supply the annuities to the insurance regulator (in Colombia, the bank superintendency is the regulatory authority).

As used to be the case in Chile, the regulatory authorities of Argentina, Colombia, and Peru require insurance companies to use the life table that the regulatory authority stipulates in pricing annuities (Palacios and Rofman, 2001, p. 12). The mortality rates of the regulatory table are significantly lower than the rates in the national tables, which means that premiums must be higher than they would be if the national life tables were used, and may well mean that profits would exceed the level that would prevail in an unregulated market. Any degree of adverse selection or implicit taxation of reserves would attenuate this effect, however. The restriction may also increase the incentive for nonprice competition, and thus increase advertising and other sales expenses. The regulatory authorities in the three countries, unlike Chile's SAFP, also require life insurance companies to use the specific interest rates the authorities stipulate in calculating the present value of their reserves. In Argentina, the retirement insurance companies must also rely on a stipulated interest rate in pricing their annuities. This means that price competition in the Argentine market is expressed solely through variations across companies in the commission they charge on their annuities.

Regulation of the discount rate used to calculate reserves and premiums may have some unexpected consequences. In the case of Argentina, for example, it appears that an increase in market interest rates will not be

---

[10] When the reform was implemented in 1994, the Argentine peso was rigidly pegged to the U.S. dollar under a currency board arrangement. This "anchor" was intended to keep the rate of inflation in Argentina at U.S. rates.

reflected in the premiums annuitants pay, whether the increase is temporary or permanent, because the rate used to calculate the premium has not changed. In practice, the premium may be effectively lowered or raised by changing the sales commission, although this would mean that the commission would have to include an element of profit.

In the case of Argentina, Colombia, and Peru, the limit on the interest rate used to value reserves means that, if an increase in market interest rates is reflected in lower premiums, it will be necessary to increase the ratio of prudential reserves to premiums to ensure that provisioning for annuities is adequate. The relatively low rate of interest used to determine reserves combines with what may be conservative mortality assumptions to produce a conservative estimate of reserves (i.e. more than is likely to be necessary).

The pension reforms in the Latin American countries that followed Chile were implemented in 1993–1997, or 12–16 years after the pioneer. Consequently, the total number of retirees under the new systems, and the number of annuitants, is small, and reform has not had much impact on the size of the annuity market in any of the countries, which was small to begin with. In Argentina, the effect of the comparative immaturity of the system on annuity markets has been compounded by the decision not to issue recognition bonds. Members who retired in 2003, for example, would have been contributing to the new system for less than 10 years. Even at a contribution rate of 11 percent, the balance in the account of the average member of the new system would be modest. By mid 2003, of some 46,000 retirees under the new system, only 5 percent had chosen a life annuity from a retirement insurance company (SAFJP, 2004).

The currently small scale of annuity markets in Latin America, apart from Chile, may not be an issue if they can be expected to develop rapidly. Some national markets will develop more rapidly than others, depending mainly on the coverage of the new system, the average age of its members, and the treatment of acquired rights under the old system. In Chile's case, coverage is comparatively broad, and the choice of the recognition bond approach helped jump-start the annuity market, as Palacios and Rofman put it. In the other countries, it will be critical for annuity providers to be large enough to achieve low administrative and distributive costs and avoid costly nonprice forms of competition. In countries like Costa Rica and Uruguay, however, a small population will limit the absolute size of the annuity market, while in Bolivia the size of the market may be limited by the low rate of coverage of the system's population, and comparatively low incomes.

EASTERN AND CENTRAL EUROPE

The reforms of pension systems of Eastern and Central Europe are even more recent than those of Latin America (Table 4.3). The Polish reform is the oldest of the group, and it dates from 1999. The Latin American experience has undoubtedly influenced the European approach to reform. However, the new European systems differ in important ways from the Latin model. First, reform in Eastern and Central Europe has been based on or inspired by the three pillar model that the World Bank began recommending in the mid 1990s. The individual accounts component is the second pillar, and does not completely replace the old state PAYG system. Kazakhstan, in the former Soviet Union, is an exception that proves the rule: its basic structure is modeled closely on Chile. Second, in Poland and two smaller countries, the reform divides potential members into three age groups: the youngest must join the new mixed system; the oldest must stay in the old system; and only the middle group (in Poland, those born between January 1, 1949 and December 31, 1968) has a choice between the two. In other countries, membership in the new system is mandatory for people below a certain age, and optional for others. Third, disability and survivors benefits typically continue to be provided by the state.[11]

Fourth, the introduction of the new system was typically combined with a parametric reform of the old system that reduced benefits — a step that would have been necessary with or without an individual accounts reform, given the budgetary costs of aging populations. In Poland, the old PAYG system remains, but has been transformed into a notional defined contributions system and the first pillar of the new system. Fifth, there tends to be less choice for members regarding the form their distributions may take. In particular, only Estonia permits programmed withdrawals, and under more restricted conditions than is typical of the Latin American systems. Hungary is among the few countries that allow lump-sum withdrawals under certain conditions. Finally, the coverage of the systems in Eastern and Central Europe is broader than those of Latin America, mainly because of the greater importance of industry and the organized sector in the economy.

The recent vintage of the new Eastern and Central European systems may explain in part why the distributional phase of the reform is still to be worked out, or is incomplete in most countries. In Poland, for example, a law that would regulate the distribution of the funds that accumulate in the

---

[11] As a result, the accumulated balance in the account of an active member who has just died is not used to defray the cost of the benefit to survivors, as it is in Chile.

individual accounts has not yet passed through the legislature, and various options remain on the table (Fultz, 2002). Among a number of issues to be resolved is whether annuities will be unisex or discriminate between men and women. Another is whether a monopoly of annuity provision should be conferred on insurance companies or specialized providers, as in Argentina. A third issue is whether the annuity payment will be guaranteed. Chlon (2002) notes that since the retirement age for women is 60, and participation in the new system is optional if not mandatory for everyone born on or after January 1, 1949, some women could retire and draw annuities beginning in 2009. Consequently, less than three years remain to work out these important aspects of the distribution phase in Poland.

In Hungary, the distribution end of the recent reform is more advanced. Some degree of annuitization is compulsory, and the annuity itself may be provided by either the pension fund (the company that manages the individual accounts) itself, if it chooses to do so, or by a life insurance company. Annuities may take one of three forms: single life, joint lives (which may include spouse and children), and a certain life. Hungary also allows inheritance, without conditions, of any remaining funds in the account upon the death of the account holder. If the pension fund provides annuities, it must offer a choice between a life annuity and at least one of the other two. Special rules apply to determine the technical reserves for annuities should the pension fund be the supplier. It would be very difficult to ascertain whether these requirements are more onerous than those that would apply to insurance companies; it is not clear why they should differ. The annuity is to be unisex, and indexed to consumer prices and wages with equal weights on each. Funding these annuities will require the insurer to take on inflation risk as long as there are no indexed financial instruments in Hungary. Unisex annuities, when the private sector supplies them, raise some basic social issues and pose certain technical difficulties, which Chapter 7 will tackle.

The Hungarian system provides a wider choice of distributions than its neighbors do, since in addition to the annuities just described, it allows a lump-sum withdrawal of the whole balance if the contribution period is 180 months or less. It also allows account holders to withdraw that part of the accumulated balance that exceeds twice the amount necessary to fund a prescribed annuity on two lives (Augusztinovics et al., 2002, p. 44). If the balance falls short of this amount at retirement, the government tops it up.

The distribution phase of the individual accounts system that Croatia has introduced is still more developed. The system offers a broader menu of annuities – simple life, joint life, certain and life, and joint certain and life,

Table 4.3. *Basic features of Eastern and Central European systems (emphasizing the distributional phase)[a]*

	Bulgaria	Czech Republic	Croatia	Estonia	Hungary	Kazakhstan	Latvia	Poland
Form of system	PAYG with IA	PAYG with voluntary IA	PAYG with IA	PAYG with IA	PAYG with IA	Individual account	PAYG (NDC) with IA	PAYG (NDC) with IA
Membership choices[b]	Mandatory for workers born after 12/31/59	IA supplements PAYG and is voluntary	Similar to Poland	Mandatory for young, optional for older workers	Mandatory for persons covered by the PAYG system as of 6/30/98 or later if aged 42 or more	All must join new system	Similar to Poland	Oldest: old system Youngest: new system Middle group (born between 1/1/49 and 12/31/68) may choose
Source of disability/survivors insurance	Mixed	Public, with optional coverage through IA	Mixed	Mixed	Public	Public	Public	Public

126

Minimum rate of return on contributions	No	No	Yes – relative to average rate of return	No	Yes – relative to long-term interest rate	Yes – relative to average rate of return	No	Yes – relative to average rate of return
Form of pension:								
Programmed withdrawal	No	No	No	Yes	No	Yes[c]	No	No
Immediate life annuity	Yes	Yes	Yes	Yes	Yes	No	Yes[d]	Yes
Term annuity	Yes	No	No	No	Yes	No	No	No
Deferred annuity	No	No	No	No	No	No	No	No
Lump sum	Yes	Yes	No	No	Yes	Yes	No	No
Minimum pension	Yes	Yes	Yes	Yes	Yes	Yes	Yes	Yes
Early retirement	No	Yes	Yes	No	Yes	Yes	Yes	No

[a] Some countries with very recently introduced individual account systems are not included
[b] In all the European systems, new labor force entrants must join the new system
[c] These are the options now available, before annuity providers open their doors
[d] Accumulated balance in individual account may be transferred to NDC
Sources: Anusec and other (2003); Kritzer (2001/2002), Chlon (2002), Fultz (2002), and The Social Security Administration (various dates)

with some restrictions depending on marital status and age; all four are indexed. The government decided to establish dedicated annuity suppliers — pension insurance companies — on the grounds that this approach would prevent the annuities business from being used to cross-subsidize the rest of the business of life insurers. They also believed that separate companies would facilitate effective supervision (Anusec et al., 2003). The asset allocation of the pension insurance companies' technical reserves is subject to quantitative restrictions that set strict limits on holdings of equities and real estate. The law also sets a limit of 5 percent on the commission that the companies can charge when the annuity is purchased. Finally, annuities are fully guaranteed.

SIMILARITIES AND DIFFERENCES BETWEEN LATIN AMERICA AND EUROPE

For all the social and economic differences between the countries of South and Central America, and Eastern and Central Europe, their individual account systems share two fundamental features. First, in nearly all of them, account holders have no access to the funds in the accounts prior to retirement. Hungary is an exception, and Chile a limited exception, since in Chile's case the balance in the account may be bequeathed, but only when the account holder has no family members who qualify as survivors. Second, distribution takes the form of a life annuity or some-thing approximating a life annuity (a programmed withdrawal) in all of them. The range of options is greatest in Chile and Hungary. However, in Chile, a lump-sum distribution of part of the account balance is allowed only when the rest of the balance is sufficient to fund an annuity that satisfies both a minimum income and a minimum replacement rate criterion. Together, these criteria are quite strict. These two features mimic two standard features of a public pension system: the provision of a life annuity, which ensures a stream of some income throughout post-retirement life, and a concern for financing retirement that excludes the use of the funds the system raises for other purposes.

One notable difference between the Latin American and European systems is the treatment of disability and survivors' benefits. In Europe, this component of the old public pension system was maintained in most countries. Had Chile wished to maintain the old system, it could not have eliminated the payroll tax. Instead of paying for insurance, as members do now, they would have continued to pay a much reduced payroll tax in addition to the 10 percent contribution for the AFP. From a purely administrative point of view, it would make little sense to rely on a mixed system of financing, where part of the disability and survivors' benefits is financed by a payroll tax and part by insurance payments. The treatment of disability and survivors' pensions in an individual accounts reform is taken up again in Chapter 7.

PART TWO

Individual Liberty versus Security in Retirement, and the Government's Role

INTRODUCTION

The designers of an individual accounts pension reform must make a huge number of technical decisions. But two basic issues of political economy and philosophy underlie all of them. The first is whether to place restrictions of any kind on withdrawals from the accounts. The second, assuming that restrictions are imposed and take the form of a requirement to purchase an annuity or some other financial product that provides for phased withdrawals, is who should supply the product: the public sector, or the private sector.

The regulation of distributions from individual accounts raises basic issues of political philosophy: the proper domain of state action, the bounds of individual choice, and the appropriateness of paternalistic government. Similar issues arise with the regulation of distributions from employer-provided pension plans and tax-favored individual retirement savings and personal pension plans. As the introduction noted, the defined contribution plan is superceding the defined benefit plan in a number of the larger industrial countries. Typically, withdrawals from these plans are lump sum. The growing importance of defined contributions plans is creating an important public policy issue: whether to impose restrictions on distributions to prevent an excessive rate of dissaving, or modify the tax system to the same end.

The question of whether annuities, if mandatory, should be publicly or privately provided raises similar philosophical issues. It also raises some basic economic issues — such as the significance of market failure in the private annuity market — as well as a host of regulatory and administrative issues. The diehard libertarian or his opposite, the diehard statist, might each of them be content to decide the merits of mandatory annuitization and private provision of annuities on philosophical grounds alone. An informed decision must be based, however, on a careful examination of the considerable practical social, economic, and administrative implications that reform would entail. This short chapter addresses the issues of political philosophy that an individual accounts reform raises, and outlines the basic economic and administrative principles that should guide decisions on whether to privatize annuity provision or not.

THE CASE FOR RESTRICTIONS ON WITHDRAWALS AND MANDATORY ANNUITIZATION

The basic argument for restrictions on withdrawals from individual accounts rests on the premise that these funds are replacing, in part or in whole, the benefit that the public pension would have provided. Annuitization or similar restrictions on the rate of withdrawals are then justified by the same arguments that justify the provision of the public pension in the form of an annuity.

There is little disagreement that the publicly provided retirement benefit should take the form of a pension (i.e. a regular flow of income rather than a lump sum or small number of lump-sum withdrawals). Nonetheless, it is worth reviewing the two standard rationales for this position. The first is that many people have a great deal of difficulty in making sensible decisions about saving and investment, particularly when they involve determining how rapidly to encroach on a sum of capital to finance consumption over many years.

The complexity of the financial decisions involved in saving for retirement and in managing assets during retirement, combined with the natural tendency to elevate present over future pleasure, can make it hard for people to save enough for retirement, and can predispose them to draw down the funds they have saved at too rapid a rate once retired. The skills involved in developing and sticking to a short-term personal or household budget are rudimentary in comparison with the skills involved in successful retirement planning. The first requires merely learning from experience, basic arithmetic, and some degree of self-control. Even so, it poses a challenge for many people. The second is much more complicated. In particular, the calculations involved in turning a lump sum into a stream of income that maintains its real value over a long period are beyond most people. The fact that about one in ten American families lacks even a bank account (Reno et al., 2005, p. 39) suggests that even in a country like the United States, financial sophistication should not be taken for granted. In the United Kingdom, a recent survey found that only a small minority of either sex understood that when the general level of interest rates rises, bond prices must fall (Gardner and Orszag, 2004). The same survey found a disquieting degree of uncertainty about the amount of saving participants needed to undertake to secure an adequate income in retirement.

The argument that economists sometimes advance, that people do not have to understand financial mathematics to make sensible economic decisions any more than they have to understand differential equations to throw a baseball, has much more validity when it applies to choices among different alternatives today than when it applies to a choice between less consumption now and more consumption twenty years from now. We can learn from experience whether we like jam today more than we like marmalade today; it is much harder to know how much jam we should be willing to give up today to have jam tomorrow (i.e. in old age). The inability to learn by doing about how much we should save might not cause us to under-save systematically, but would leave all those people who erred on the wrong side with too little savings for retirement.

Ignorance about what the future holds for us makes it tempting to discount it at a very high rate, which would mean that people would not simply make mistakes in their retirement planning, but systematically under-save. Warner and Pleeter (2001), in a study of a group of U.S. Department of Defense employees offered a choice by a downsizing program between an annuity and a lump-sum payment in the early 1990s, found that the average discount rate implied by the choice of the group's members exceeded 17 percent. If this were the rate that guided most people's saving for retirement, their standard of living would suffer a drastic decline when they stopped working. Posner (1995) argues that a "multiple selves" model of the human being can help explain the "rather meager provision that most people make for their future (91)," as well as the observed tendency for discount rates to decline with age. In effect, we do not save for old age because we see ourselves when old as a different person. This effect could be mitigated if, as Posner (70–72) conjectures, the discount rate declines with age.

Another source of both under-saving during working life and excessive dissaving during retirement is problems of self-control. Retired people can understand intellectually that they are running through their retirement nest egg too rapidly, but find ways of rationalizing their behavior and downplaying its consequences. Belt-tightening, like starting a diet, can always be put off until tomorrow. Distinguishing in practice between

excessive discount rates and lack of self-control is difficult, but they have
similar effects. It is also true, as Chapter 1 discussed, that many people can
suffer from the opposite problem in old age: they can be excessively
cautious in drawing down their savings. But the annuitization of the
retirement benefit mitigates both problems.

Pinker (2002, p. 303) makes the case for paternalism from the
perspective of evolutionary biology: "But economists repeatedly find
that people spend their money like drunken sailors. They act as if they
think they will die in a few years, or as if the future is completely
unpredictable, which may be closer to the reality of our evolutionary
ancestors than it is to life today. If so, then allowing people to manage their
own savings ... may work against their interests. Like Odysseus approaching the island of the Sirens, people might *rationally agree* (italics added) to
let their employer or the government tie them to the mast of forced
savings."

Many studies provide evidence that would appear to refute the standard
economic model of the life-cycle saver rationally allocating consumption
over the course of his/her life. Burtless (2004) surveys work in this area
and concludes that in the United States, the evidence is overwhelming
that many people enter retirement with little or no liquid assets.
In addition, other studies, making an indirect test of the hypothesis of
the rational saver find that pension plan members can be remarkably
ignorant of the basic properties of their plans: in one instance, a high
percentage of participants in a defined contributions plan could not
identify their plan as such.

Other studies, taking a different angle, have tried to assess directly
whether the assets of households at retirement are adequate for
consumption in retirement. Gustman et al. (1997) found that about
80 percent of the retired participants in a health and retirement study had
enough wealth, and that the shortfall for the remaining households was
typically not large. In a comment on this study, Burtless (2004) notes that
most of these households were receiving both social security benefits
and an employer-provided pension. Consequently, the finding has little
relevance for the significant minority of employed Americans who lack an
employer-provided pension. Finally, Engen et al. (1999), which differed
from earlier studies by taking account of uncertain earnings and mortality
rates, found that the hypothesis of the rational saver could not be rejected.
Burtless, commenting on this study, notes that by including housing wealth
in the measure of personal wealth, it may have overstated the wealth
effectively available to defray living expenses in retirement. This could be

the case if the increase in house prices is fully reflected by an increase in expected rents.[1]

The evidence, as might be expected, is not clear-cut. Nonetheless, it seems prudent to conclude that a significant minority of people in any country could have problems with planning or self-control that would prevent them from saving enough during their working life, and cause them to dissave excessively when retired.

The second rationale for restrictions on withdrawals is that they mitigate a problem of free riding. Even if people are not short-sighted, lump-sum payments to the retired who are poor could encourage them to spend excessively, if they knew that they would become wards of the state, and receive a minimum social assistance pension. This is a real problem in Australia, as Chapter 1 explained. Similarly, Chileans with a relatively small balance in their individual account who qualify for a minimum pension have an incentive to choose a programmed withdrawal over an annuity, because the initial payments will be higher and the minimum pension the state will pay when the funds run out provides a safety net. These arguments would justify not simply mandatory annuitization, but mandatory annuitization in the form of an indexed pension, since that is the standard form the social security benefit or public pension assumes. Both sets of arguments justify restrictions on withdrawals from individual accounts during the holder's lifetime, and more generally, they justify limiting the property rights that might otherwise adhere to individual accounts.

The argument for paternalism is less compelling if the funds from the individual accounts are supplementing or topping up a state pension that is already generous. This would not be the case with any of the plans advanced recently for the United States, since the replacement rate that social security provides drops off considerably as a contributor's income rises. It might conceivably apply to reforms in other countries, particularly if the individual accounts component is an add-on, and the introduction of individual accounts is not accompanied by a substantial reduction of the public pension.

As Chapter 6 will discuss, the issue of mandatory annuitization can be viewed from a more individualistic angle. We may grant the arguments that many people are short-sighted, and that annuity market problems have

---

[1] An increase in the expected cost of renting means that some, if not all of the capital gain from the sale of a house would have to be set aside to pay for the increase in rent. The size of the capital gain in this situation will depend on the life expectancy of the seller. A person with only a few years to live can pocket most of the gain.

resulted in many people having a less than optimal share of their wealth in the form of annuities. But we should also grant that some people nearing retirement may have a high share of wealth in annuitized form (e.g. a generous employer-provided pension) at retirement. For them, the case for annuitization of any amount of the balance in their account is weak. Similarly, the special circumstances of some people — e.g. the dying — argue for little or no annuitization.

A case by case determination of the share of funds in an individual account that should be subject to mandatory annuitization is, unfortunately, completely impracticable. It also raises the issue of parity of treatment, both perceived and actual. For example, simply explaining the technical basis for the decision to allow a person to make lump sum withdrawals instead of requiring annuitization could prove very difficult. It could also have political complications, depending on the way the determination of the appropriate share of the funds in an individual account to be withdrawn in a lump sum was made. As an example, in the United States people who receive a pension (annuitized income) from their employer tend to have higher incomes than people who do not participate in employer-provided plans, whether defined contribution or defined benefit plans (Gale and Orszag, 2003). The perception that the better off could do what they like with the balance in their individual account while the working poor were required to annuitize could fuel a popular judgment that the annuitization criteria were unfair, and not even sensible.

Finally, problems with the annuity market might justify compulsory participation in a public pension scheme even if all citizens were far-sighted and rational. Compulsory participation could allow the state to provide annuities at a lower cost than private financial institutions, because universal participation would mitigate adverse selection. That said, the case would have to be made that public provision was more efficient than mandatory annuitization with private provision.

REGULATION OF WITHDRAWALS FROM DEFINED CONTRIBUTION PLANS

The case for regulating withdrawals from defined contribution plans offered by employers or set up by the contributor himself is less strong than the case for regulating withdrawals from individual accounts. The retirement income that defined contributions plans will provide comes on top of the public pension and the individual accounts annuity, if there is one. The public pension and the income financed by the individual account are the cornerstone of a retired person's safety net, particularly for a person who has been one of the working poor. The employer-provided pension or personal pension is less important, particularly in countries like France, Italy, and Germany where the public pension now offers most contributors a high replacement rate.

Nonetheless, in the United States and in the United Kingdom, employer-provided pensions, which increasingly take the form of defined contributions plans, normally provide a substantial share of retirement income, particular for employees in the middle to upper income ranges. The state has some interest in encouraging, if not compelling, plan participants to make sensible decisions, not simply about how contributions are invested, but also the pace at which they will be withdrawn upon retirement (and depending on the form of the distribution, the way the balance of accumulated contributions and their earnings is invested during retirement).

The paternalistic school of thought might take the view that the compulsory annuitization of some part of the funds in such private plans could be justified. Whatever the philosophical merits of this position, it suffers from the drawback that, because the plans are voluntary, compulsory annuitization could encourage potential plan participants to save in other ways. In the case of employer-provided plans, compulsory annuitization would encourage employees or their unions to give up compensation in the form of employer contributions to pension plans for higher take home pay, and to press employers for lower employee contribution rates. In the case of personal plans, forced annuitization might simply divert personal savings to other investments that, unlike individual retirement accounts (IRAs) in the United States and registered retirement savings plans (RRSPs) in Canada, did not benefit from special tax treatment but would not be subject to forced annuitization. That said, the Netherlands annuity market has been stimulated by making annuitization of distributions a condition for favorable tax treatment of the savings vehicles.

There is an intermediate position between compulsory annuitization and laissez-faire, which Sunstein and Thaler (2003) have termed libertarian paternalism. Its premise is that people do not act like the rational economic man of the textbooks when they make economic and financial decisions, particularly decisions about how to allocate saving among competing investments. On the contrary, they make bad financial choices sufficiently often that it is socially justifiable and not an infringement on personal liberty, to use various means to encourage, but not oblige them to make prudent decisions.

The position of libertarian paternalism is buttressed by the empirical work of the behavioral finance school (much of which only confirms common sense). In particular, recent studies have found that choices about financial investments are strongly influenced by the way they are presented – the framing effect; that increasing the range of options from which a choice is to be made can have a paralyzing effect on decision-making; that people avoid making the right decision when it involves recognizing a loss; that people are prone to inertia; and that the rules of thumb ("decision heuristics") on which people routinely rely when they make financial decisions can be seriously misleading. These impediments to sound decision-making would aggravate the consequences of the tendency to under-saving already noted, but even if that tendency were not present, they would cause households to take on unnecessary risk for a given expected rate of return, or alternatively, to be overly cautious.

As one example, in the United States, defined contributions plans can offer the participating employee facing a decision on how to invest his contributions, a choice among hundreds of mutual funds. Recent research on choosing among a very large number of alternatives found that increasing the options seemed to diminish the chooser's satisfaction with the outcome, and to encourage indecision (Schwartz, 2004). Given how costs increase with the number of alternatives – and the apparent attendant anxiety the decision maker feels about the increased likelihood of making the wrong choice – some limitation on choice might be beneficial.

Even when the choices are more limited, recent research suggests that the way choices are framed significantly influences the outcome. Benartzi and Thaler (2001) found that when defined contribution plan members were offered a choice of investing their contributions in a number of different mutual funds, they tended to allocate their contributions among them in equal parts. With four funds to choose from, they would tend to put 25 percent of their contributions in each, regardless of the riskiness or speculative character of the funds. Consequently, if two of the four funds were aggressive growth funds, they would be choosing a portfolio with 50 percent of its assets invested in high risk stocks.

In light of these tendencies, libertarian paternalism argues not for compulsion, but for default rules that would encourage generally prudent decisions. In the case of a defined contributions pension plan, the default setting for the investment of plan contributions could be a relatively conservative portfolio. For example, if the choice were limited to mutual funds, the default setting might be no more than 50 percent of the portfolio in equity funds of any kind, and no more than 20 percent in aggressively managed growth funds. Asset allocation could also vary with age: some mutual funds in the United States are structured this way.

A similar approach could be taken to guiding the decisions regarding withdrawals of retiring employees. Mitchell and Utkus (2004) point out that at present in the United States, the default value for defined contributions plans is a lump-sum withdrawal. Instead, the employer could recommend that at least two-thirds of the accumulated funds be used to buy a group annuity, whose premiums the employer would negotiate for its retiring employees. Employers would have an interest in ensuring their employees made relatively conservative decisions during the accumulation phase of the plan, and at the distribution stage. Sponsors of defined contribution pension plans in Canada and the United States are fearful of being sued if they offer investment advice to plan members and investment performance is poor. A somewhat more paternalistic and less liberal approach would be to encourage plan contributors to precommit to a minimum rate of annuitization when they first begin contributing, or perhaps at a specified number of years before the statutory retirement age.

The practice of libertarian paternalism may well become widespread in countries like the United States and the United Kingdom, given the increasing importance of defined contributions plans, the incentive that employers may have to avoid lawsuits, and a general recognition of the prevalence and risks of excessive spending. The legal aspects of this issue are beyond the book's scope, but it looks to be an encouraging development.

PUBLIC SECTOR VERSUS PRIVATE SECTOR PROVISION

The same basic issue of political philosophy that arises with mandatory annuitization arises with the issue of public versus private sector provision. The issue arises with privatization in general. The libertarian takes the extreme position that the state should confine itself to the provision of the most basic public goods, such as law and order – goods that the market cannot profitably supply, if the libertarian recognizes any goods as such – and basic regulation of the marketplace. At the other extreme, the statist would ignore the arguments that economists advance for the greater efficiency of private sector provision of marketable goods and services, and argue that the provision of annuities that provide most of the income of many retired people is too important to be left in the hands of the private sector.

The most common choice of countries that have introduced an individual accounts component to the public pension systems of their countries has been privatization, albeit, as we have seen, privatization subject to a heavy degree of regulation; that it is common does not automatically make it the right solution.

The economist's method of tackling the question would be to start from the working hypothesis that the provision of marketable goods or services, including financial services like annuities, would normally be carried out more efficiently by the private sector than the public sector, at least in the absence of market failures. He would then investigate whether the particular industry in question was affected by any market failures. If that was the case, he would ask whether the effects of these failures could be adequately mitigated by a special regulatory framework, or whether public sector provision was necessary to deal with them. Most economists maintain that even if an industry is affected by market failures, the effective remedy would be a well-designed regulatory regime, or taxes and subsidies that helped align private with social benefits, and not public sector provision (i.e. public sector enterprises or financial institutions manufacturing, providing and/or marketing the goods or services in question).

An assessment of market failure should also recognize that annuity provision involves three basic functions. They are: administration (ensuring regular payments, keeping accounts, policing fraud, etc.); actuarial tasks (estimation of mortality rates and related calculations used as a basic input into pricing); and investment. Conceivably, one or two of these functions might be candidates for privatization, even if the whole business were not.

The list of potential or actual market failures with private annuities would clearly include asymmetric information and adverse selection. Asymmetric information, as Chapter 3 explained, is an issue both because of the unusual characteristics of annuities, and the difficulty annuitants (and other policyholders) would have in acquiring adequate information about the soundness of a particular life insurer.

Adverse selection is obviously problematic: its effects on the size of the annuity market are uncertain, however. It arguably reduces the demand for annuities by the poor, and thus has a distributional impact. Compulsory annuitization should in principle lower average premiums because it would lower the life expectancy of the pool of annuitants. It would not, however, drive private providers out of the market.

A third possible market failure might be the failure entailed by a decreasing cost industry. The annuity business does not fall in this category, although there are obvious economies of scale, both with respect to risk pooling, and administration. Provided the market is sufficiently large, it should be able to accommodate many suppliers without raising the average cost of annuity provision (i.e. the costs of record-keeping, actuarial services, payments, etc.) excessively. However, as long as the public pension system remains in place, it may be less expensive for the government to administer the provision of annuities and assume responsibility for the actuarial function. This leaves aside the question of whether or not the entire public pension system should be privatized. A fourth market failure is entailed by the costs of choice among many alternatives. If it really is as great as some recent authors suggest, there may conceivably be a case for restrictions. That would clearly involve regulation of the industry; whether it would involve public sector provision is less clear.

There are two final rationales for public sector provision. The first is predicated on the failure of government regulation. For example, assume that a guarantee on the regular payment that annuity providers made to annuitants is considered an essential social policy. If that guarantee cannot be extended without creating excessive incentives for risk-taking by the providers, there is a case for public provision. The second rationale also involves regulation. If the regulatory apparatus necessary to ensure adequate performance of annuity providers is sufficiently costly, public sector provision may be less expensive than private provision.

Before turning to the more technical issues that are covered in the chapters that follow, we should consider two possible arguments in favor of private provision. First, there is a political economy argument to the effect that placing money in the public sector's hands, even if it is in trust, will only increase its size. This argument is advanced against reforms of the public pension system that entail pre-funding – i.e. building up a surplus as a means of financing the increase in pensions that aging will entail. In the American setting, some economists maintain that diverting payroll taxes from social security, as happens under a carve-out reform, would increase national saving by reducing government expenditure. (The popular phrase is "starving the beast.") This argument does not rest on a market failure as such, but on a failure of the political process. A second argument is the importance of beneficial spin-off effects for the development of a country's broader capital market from the development of a private annuity market. As Chapter 4 noted, there is evidence for these effects in Chile. The positive spin off argument is, of course, of relevance for emerging market countries, and not for countries that already have well-developed capital markets.

6

Policy Issues with both Public and Private Sector Provision of Mandatory Annuities

INTRODUCTION

This chapter begins by elaborating on the general arguments that Chapter 5 advances as to why general rules, and not individual preferences should govern the extent of annuitization of account balances, and considers what form distributions should take. It then turns to address various issues that mandatory annuitization entails for the safety net. These include the merits of a guarantee on annuity balances, the distributional effects of a carve-out reform, and the implications of reform for family benefits and the disability pension. This chapter also briefly discusses some legal issues that arise with the creation of individual accounts, since they have a bearing on family benefits. This chapter concentrates on those issues that could arise with mandatory annuitization regardless which sector provides the annuities. Chapter 7 addresses the additional issues that private provision entails.

THE SCOPE FOR RESPECTING INDIVIDUAL PREFERENCES

Most people could benefit from the annuitization of at least part of their wealth when they retire. The question is how much. The case for annuitization is the strongest for people who either have little annuitized wealth to begin with, or would have problems managing their expenditure without the discipline that annuitization provides. As Chapter 5 argued, the case is weak for an account holder whose wealth is already highly annuitized. It is also weak for some one who is relatively well off and able to manage a budget. A policy of liberalized withdrawals would also benefit people whose life expectancies were much less than the average for their age cohort. For the dying, this policy would be a great blessing. The case for annuitization is also less compelling when the individual account is added as a supplement to a public pension system that is relatively generous.

In an ideal world, there might be some way of tailoring the extent of annuitization to personal circumstances. For example, each account holder, as they approached retirement, might receive several hours of basic financial planning counseling free of charge from a competent and honest financial advisor. (They would be much in demand.) The advisor's most important task would arguably be recommending an appropriate degree of annuitization. Based on that recommendation, the government agency responsible for the public pension system and individual accounts would decide what part of the funds in the retiree's account could be withdrawn in a lump sum, and what part might be annuitized.

In practice, this imaginative proposal would face insurmountable problems. For example, those account holders who wanted to minimize the share of the balance in their account that was annuitized would oppose the agency's proposal. An appeals process or a formal right to a second opinion would be necessary to reduce complaints from account holders that they were the victims of bad advice. The appeals process could be very costly, and even its decisions would seem arbitrary to many.

The advisory process could also entail a basic principal-agent problem. Financial advisors would be under pressure from account holders to recommend the lowest rate of annuitization their financial situation would justify. To ensure objective and competent advice, the responsible agency would have to engage in quality control. In practice, quality control might end up relying on the application of general rules that would defeat the purpose of individualized advice.

A less costly way of considering personal circumstances in determining the share of an account holder's balances to be annuitized could be based on selected objective indicators of wealth and the share of it that was annuitized. These indicators might be derived from such sources as personal financial statements, income tax returns, and statements from the sponsors of employer-provided pensions. Even this approach would be burdensome administratively, as well as prone to gaming (e.g. artificially increasing the share of annuitized wealth by buying a annuity with a short term) or to fraud. The second approach would also be vulnerable to charges of unequal or discriminatory treatment, since in the absence of simple rules, it could be difficult to explain why one account holder was obliged to annuitize the entire balance of her account, while another was allowed to make substantial lump-sum withdrawals. In sum, an individualized approach to determining the extent of annuitization of the balance in an individual account would not be feasible. It would be very costly, or simply unworkable.

RULES TO DETERMINE THE EXTENT OF ANNUITIZATION

If a policy tailor-made to individual account holders is not feasible, then a general and rules-based approach needs to be followed. But what rules? A rule of full annuitization would be simple to apply. However, it would undoubtedly leave some persons over-annuitized. In addition to people with substantial employer-provided pensions, this group would include people with a strong bequest motive. If the bequest that a person wished to leave was particularly large, then they might wish to annuitize only a small part of their wealth. The impact of over-annuitization on bequests can be at least partly undone by acquiring a life insurance policy, as Chapter 1 discusses. In fact, if both annuity and life insurance are actuarially fair, the impact of over-annuitization can be completely undone by acquiring life insurance (see the section "Life Insurance" in Appendix 1). In practice, the lack of actuarial fairness of life insurance and life annuities means that mandatory annuitization would still entail some loss of welfare.

Granted the great difficulty of making the right judgment about what degree of annuitization is appropriate for a particular person, it is possible to develop relatively simple general rules based either on rules of thumb about the appropriate relationship between income in retirement and working income, or on the replacement ratio provided by the public pension system before reform. Chile is an example of the first approach.

An important difference between the annuitization rule in Chile and the rule that most public pension systems with an individual accounts component would apply is that the rules for these systems would need to take account of the benefit paid by the public system in determining the degree of annuitization of funds in the individual accounts. The extra administrative burden this rule would entail should not be great, particularly if the regular annuity payment financed by the individual account can be combined with the benefit from the public pension system in a single pension payment.

In the case of a carve-out reform, the rule could require that the account holder annuitize enough of the accumulated funds in his account so that the sum of his reduced pension and the annuity payment would equal the benefit he would have received under current (pre-reform) law. If the sum of the public pension and the regular payment fell below the income implied by the replacement ratio, the balance in the individual account would be entirely annuitized. A severe shortfall due to poor investment performance raises the issue of the need for a guarantee, which is discussed below.

If a further reduction in the public pension was needed to address a solvency problem with the public system, the replacement schedule, which would be used to determine the share of the funds in the individual account to be annuitized, taking into account the income from the public pension, would have to shift downwards. The new schedule could be interpreted as the schedule that would have prevailed under a conventional reform of social security in which individual accounts played no role.

The reform of a public pension system could also be the occasion to revisit the relationship between the pension and income during working life. Public pension systems typically replace income according to a declining schedule — the ratio of pension to income declines as income rises — and either the public pension system or another agency provides a minimum pension once an age criterion is satisfied. One possible alternative to a declining replacement schedule with a minimum income is a simple minimum income rule. Under such a rule, the sum of the public pension and the annuity from the individual account would only have to equal or exceed some stipulated income level: for example, 75 or 100 percent of a specified poverty line or some other income level deemed a socially acceptable minimum. Any funds left in the account after this rule has been satisfied could be withdrawn as a lump sum.

The difficulty with relying on a minimum rule income alone is that it could leave people whose income is about average or greater under-annuitized: the replacement ratio falls off drastically as income rises. As long as public pension systems, with or without an individual accounts component, are intended to provide more than simply a rudimentary safety net for the elderly, this option has to be discarded. Nonetheless, the introduction of an individual accounts reform could in principle be accompanied by a change in the shape of the curve describing the relationship between the public pension and income at retirement.

THE CASE FOR EXEMPTIONS

The terminally ill cannot be accused of shortsightedness for preferring a lump-sum or liberalized withdrawal scheme to a life annuity. Abstracting from administrative and other complications, a strong case can be made for exempting the dying from mandatory annuitization; for allowing them early access to the funds in their account; and possibly for allowing retired persons with terminal illnesses the right to shift from the regular payments of a life annuity to an accelerated withdrawals scheme.

In the United Kingdom, there already exists a market for enhanced annuities. Enhanced annuities are intended for persons with serious and life-threatening illnesses and short life expectancies, and for impaired lives — people like smokers, who are not necessarily seriously ill, but have life expectancies shorter than average.

Nonetheless, a policy to liberalize withdrawals when the account holder is dying does have some potentially undesirable implications, and could prove complicated to administer.[1] Relaxing the normal rules for the dying would increase the average life expectancy of the pool of mandatory annuitants. Annuity providers would not be able to offset the financial impact of these early deaths against the costs entailed by those annuitants who live longer than average. Consequently, the exemption would increase the average cost of the annuities funded by individual accounts, with the size of the increase depending on how strictly the criteria for exemptions were set. If annuity provision were privatized, the government might wish to subsidize the extra expense directly, rather than allow average premiums to increase. A rule to liberalize withdrawals from individual accounts for the dying could lead to demands to convert social security or public pension benefits or acquired rights into a lump sum to provide an additional benefit.

Under either public or private provision, the administrative requirements of the policy would not be trivial. In the case of people whose illness developed after retirement, a privately provided annuity would have to specify the annuitant's rights in the event of terminal illness. There is an obvious incentive for fraud if the balance of the individual account were large, or if the public pension system's rules were liberalized to allow lump-sum distributions.[2] The criteria for eligibility and their application would inevitably seem arbitrary.[3] If the dying are given special dispensation, why exclude the chronically ill? There is also the issue of the form the withdrawals should take: a lump sum seems acceptable under the circumstances, but phased withdrawals that exhaust the balance in an

---

[1] There is an important difference between the way the British market for enhanced annuities functions, and the way a generalized policy of exemptions to the dying would function. The former is based on a voluntary bargain between insurer and policy holder; the latter would require special regulations (for example, a procedure to determine whether a sick person was sick enough to qualify for liberal treatment).

[2] A similar incentive for fraud exists now with disability benefits. With disability benefits, however, there is no large up-front lump-sum payment.

[3] For example, how short would an individual's life expectancy have to be for her to be deemed terminally ill? The complications that would arise if the medical prognosis proved to be inaccurate would need to be considered as well.

account over a short time are also attractive. Despite these potential pitfalls, it can be argued that the plight of the seriously ill and dying calls for a more liberal treatment even if it entails extra costs to society.

The dying are not the only people who could make a case for liberalization of withdrawals, but the case for special treatment for other groups is weak. Anyone facing large unexpected expenditures – for example, an individual with high medical bills – could argue that she was also a deserving case. These exceptions would entail administrative complications similar to an exemption for the dying, which would multiply as the grounds for exemption were broadened. Administering and policing a policy with many exceptions would be costly and the policy would be vulnerable to abuse.

More important, and in contrast to an exemption granted to the dying, these additional exemptions appear to court a serious risk of moral hazard. The more liberal the withdrawal rules become, the less incentive workers have to save to defray life's unexpected expenditures and to finance retirement. Unless contribution rates were substantially raised, these perverse incentives would defeat the main purpose of a public pension system. The Singaporean system has a generous withdrawal policy, as Chapter 1 noted, but its contribution rates are very high.

THE FORM OF THE ANNUITY

The standard public pension benefit is an indexed life annuity, and it is natural to consider requiring the mandatory annuity to take this form rather than another. Other annuities, like the variable annuity, have similar features, however, and their relative merits are considered below. There is also the issue of choice. There are certainly grounds for restricting choice among different forms of annuities. Some choice might be welfare enhancing, however, given that any restriction on withdrawals that ensures they will last for a long time already gives the annuitant a fair measure of protection from over (or under) spending.

Indexed Annuities, or Real versus Nominally Fixed Payments

Indexation is an important property of a pension. Inflation, even at low rates, can substantially lower the real value of a nominally fixed pension or a life annuity over the course of retirement. It is hard for anyone, even some one who is financially sophisticated to create and maintain an inflation-proof portfolio of assets. Stocks are often thought to be a good hedge against inflation, at least in the long run. Bodie (2001) argues that they are not, because they are more risky in the long term, and their real values vary more than many believe. When inflation is low and reasonably stable, the holder of a nominal annuity can protect himself to some degree by saving part of the annuity payments to supplement the regular annuity payment as the cost of living rises. The rate of return to such saving will be less, however, than the conditional rate of return of the annuity.

Moreover, this homegrown approach to inflation insurance requires self-discipline as well as some financial expertise, and it remains vulnerable to unexpected inflation. An unexpectedly high rate of inflation can result in substantial unforeseen declines in real income. If, for example, a person has a planning horizon of 15 years, during which period he assumes that the annual rate of inflation will be $2\frac{1}{2}$ percent, while inflation actually averages 4 percent, the real value of his annuity payment is reduced by 20 percent over the period.[4] An indexed annuity, whether provided by the state or the private sector, thus provides valuable protection against inflation.

Governments could easily supply directly an indexed annuity financed with the funds from individual accounts. The account holder would simply exchange that part of the balance he was required to annuitize for the government's annuity. It would also be feasible for annuity providers to do so, provided, as Chapter 2 discusses, that governments developed a thriving market in indexed debt. This allows the private sector to lay off inflation risk on the government.

The evidence from studies of the money's worth (MW) ratio of indexed annuities in the United Kingdom suggests that inflation insurance they provide comes with an extra cost of about 5 percent of the premium (Brown et al., 2001a). This could reflect the fact that indexed debt trades at a premium relative to unindexed debt, which would be the case if investors valued the inflation insurance that indexed debt provides.[5] If this is the case, then the governments that issue indexed debt might reduce the costs of debt service by relying more on it. The greater share of indexed debt in total public debt would increase the return on it and make it a more

---

[4] For additional discussion, see the section "Dealing with the Uncertainty of Inflation after Retirement" in Thompson (1998).

[5] The current yield on an inflation indexed security will be less than the yield on a nominal security, because inflation will raise the nominal value of the coupons and the principal of the indexed security over time. It is possible to calculate the constant rate of inflation that will equalize the yield of nominal and inflation-indexed securities of equal maturity if both are held to maturity. This rate is known as the break-even rate of inflation. The evidence the chapter refers to implies that the actual rate of inflation normally falls short of the break-even rate.

attractive investment. James and Song (2002) have argued that the extra cost of indexed annuities also reflects the fact that nominal annuities can be backed by equities as well as bonds, whereas indexed annuities have to be backed by an indexed asset, which are limited for the moment to government bonds. Gaps in the maturity spectrum of indexed public debt would also raise the cost of indexed annuities. Markets for indexed securities tend to be less active and less liquid than markets for fixed interest securities.

It may be that governments can provide indexed annuities less expensively than the private sector. If the balances in individual accounts are transformed into indexed annuities by the government, the operation eliminates the private sector middleman and the attendant costs of intermediation. With private sector provision, the government issues the indexed debt, which insurance companies then acquire. All of this has a cost, and is unnecessary with public sector provision.

A case can be made for nominally fixed over indexed annuities. Doyle and Piggott (2002) carry out simulation exercises in which they compare the lifetime utility achieved by investing in different annuities. In such an exercise, a nominal annuity has the advantage that, as compared with a real annuity, its payments are front-loaded, and hence discounted less. One counter-argument to this view is that after the fact people will find that they would have preferred an income stream that was constant and not declining in real terms. Another is that if people wish to tilt their consumption forward, they can do so even if the pension they received is indexed in real terms by running down their financial assets. Conversely, maintaining a level of consumption that is constant in real terms is harder with a nominal than with an indexed annuity.

Variable Annuities, or Fixed versus Variable Payments

As Chapter 1 described, the variable annuity market in the United States, at least its accumulation phase, is far larger than the market for fixed annuities, and the market for individual life annuities in particular. Variable annuities have certain features in common with indexed annuities. Part of their return may be fixed in nominal terms, but part is variable, and depends on the return to the underlying investment. Once the annuitization phase begins, the annuitant may be guaranteed a fixed nominal return plus a specified percentage of the gain in the capital value of the underlying investment. The annuitization period can be for life, or for a fixed period. A variable annuity may also have a minimum return that is adjustable, but not reversible.

Unlike an annuity with a fixed nominal return, a variable annuity based on an investment in the stock market will be partially correlated with inflation. However, the correlation with inflation from year to year, or even over longer intervals is not high. This means that a variable annuity is not a good hedge against inflation. Even when inflation is stable or prices are completely stable, there is no guarantee that the real value of the regular payment will be preserved. A variable annuity is superficially more attractive than an indexed annuity because its initial payments, like the payments of a nominal annuity, are higher in nominal terms. However, this feature probably appeals most to people who would tend to discount the future excessively.

Phased Withdrawals

Phased withdrawals are a compromise between a lump-sum withdrawal and a life annuity. They can take many different forms. In Chile, for example, the programmed withdrawal is, as Chapter 4 explained, made a function of life expectancy, and recalculated every year. A phased withdrawal might also aim to make constant nominal payments over a period related to life expectancy at retirement. If, for example, a retired person's life expectancy were 18 years, a particular phased withdrawal formula might assume a pay-out period of 25 years, on the grounds that 90–95 percent of the members of the person's age cohort would have died within that time.

A phased withdrawal scheme raises the issue of what happens to the balance of the account if the account holder dies after retirement. This depends critically on what happens to the benefits a public pension system normally provides to spouses and survivors. Chile does not provide separate benefits for family members, as Chapter 4 discussed, and in consequence, some of the money in the account is set aside for them. If separate benefits are maintained, there may be leeway for relatively liberal inheritance rules. The implications of reform for family benefits are discussed more fully below.

Compared with a lump-sum withdrawal, phased withdrawals, depending on the formula used to determine the annual payout, impose some discipline on people who have problems with self-control and financial management. The degree of discipline depends on the period over which the withdrawals take place and whether withdrawals are front-loaded or in equal installments. They can also provide access to capital if the account holder has some control over the rate of withdrawal. However, they are inferior to life annuities both as a control or commitment mechanism, and as a means of longevity insurance. If their payments are not indexed, they provide no insurance against inflation. This being said, phased withdrawals, as Chapter 4 discussed in the Chilean setting, are superior to life annuities when the annuitant has a short life expectancy or a strong bequest motive.

One final argument for phased withdrawals is that if a decision has been made to privatize the distribution phase, but the insurance industry is not yet ready to provide competitively priced life annuities, phased withdrawals, provided the withdrawal period is sufficiently long, may be an acceptable temporary substitute.

Conclusions Regarding the Choice of the Form of Annuity

Chapter 1 addressed alternatives to annuitization, pointing out that the more risk people could stomach, and the greater the return to conventional financial instruments, the less the share of wealth that should be annuitized, and the later in life annuitization should take place. Even if we limit the choice to different kinds of annuity, it is clear that some annuities are better suited to some people's circumstances than others are. Some people would be better off with an indexed annuity, others with a nominal annuity. Others might be better off with a variable annuity, and still others, particularly those who knew their life expectancies were relatively short, with phased withdrawals (depending on the withdrawal period).

A policy conceived for the general citizen of any country should not assume that he or she is a financial rocket scientist. Variable annuities make serious demands on financial expertise, and could pose a challenge for self-control, since the excess returns of good years need to be saved to smooth consumption expenditure in the lean years. They are an imperfect hedge against inflation. Phased withdrawals make less of a demand on financial expertise, but unless they are indexed provide no inflation insurance. Given the level of most people's financial sophistication, the lack of inflation insurance from the private sector, and the importance of some longevity insurance, there is a strong case, if only one form of annuity is to be offered, for requiring the purchase of an indexed annuity.

It might be argued that once substantial restrictions are imposed on the speed of withdrawals from individual accounts, the exact form of the annuity is a second order issue. Perhaps the choice between an indexed annuity, a nominal annuity, a nominal annuity with a variable component or a phased withdrawal scheme could be left to the individual annuitant. However, the same issues that would arise if an account holder were free to choose how rapidly to run down his balance at retirement would also apply when the choice is restricted to the form the annuity should take. Shortsightedness could bias the annuitant in favor of a nominal annuity, and issues of control arise with nominal annuities, variable annuities, and perhaps with phased withdrawals. The extra choice would also increase the costliness of the system, whether annuities were provided by the public or the private sector.

SAFETY NET ISSUES

Guarantees on the Balance of Individual Accounts

The introduction of an individual accounts component in a public pension system has weighty implications for the social safety net. Investment risk would be an issue for any account holder, but the poor are particularly vulnerable to a bad financial market performance. Even if stock and bond market returns were predictable, the adoption of individual accounts has distributional implications. Investment risk for the poor at retirement can be mitigated by guaranteeing the balance of the account or the income from the annuity that the balance could fund. However, setting appropriate limits on a guarantee is no easy matter. An unconditional guarantee could entail serious moral hazard.

A guarantee that automatically tops up the account balance to some stipulated minimum level, or to the level necessary to purchase the minimum annuity the law requires could court a serious moral hazard problem. If an account holder's balance is likely to fall short of the guaranteed amount, he confronts a strong incentive to engage in risky "double or nothing" investing (gambling for redemption). The incentive arises because, if he loses, he is no worse off than he would have been had he adopted a more prudent investment strategy, and if he wins, he can win big. To avoid such gaming, or ensure that it not generally attractive, the guarantee should be defined conservatively. This means that, in practice, it protects only the low-paid.

In a proposal for reform of U.S. social security, Feldstein and Samwick (2000) have suggested that the guarantee be defined with reference to a combination of broad market index funds. The amount of the guarantee is determined by making a calculation of the hypothetical balance that would have accumulated in the account had it been invested in these index funds in the proportions specified by the guarantee policy (for example, 60 percent of an S&P500 index, and 40 percent of a corporate bond portfolio). A fall in the combined social security benefit and annuity payment below the benefit specified under current law resulting from the poor performance of the stock and bond markets would be guaranteed; additional losses would not be covered.

Depending on the shares of bonds and stocks in the reference portfolio, even this policy might encourage some account holders to invest more of their account balance in the stock market — invest less conservatively — than they otherwise would. It effectively reduces the risk of loss from investments that are more speculative than the reference portfolio and increases their average rate of return.[6] It does not, therefore, eliminate moral hazard entirely. Samwick (1999) presents estimates of the cost of this guarantee that imply that the risk to future taxpayers of extending it is very small. Bodie (2001), taking the contrary view, and applying options theory, argues that this kind of guarantee could be very costly.

A less costly approach would guarantee the achievement of a level of income equal to the old-age benefit provided by a country's social assistance program. In the case of the United States, this benefit is well below the poverty line — so that the guarantee would be unlikely to prove expensive.[7] The policy would effectively leave most contributors to social security completely exposed to investment risk, since even a very bad financial market performance would not reduce the combined social security and individual accounts annuity below the benefit.

To avoid this outcome, the rule might instead be that guarantees should be large enough that the sum of the reduced public pension and the annuity payment should equal the public pension benefit under current law,

---

[6] Suppose for the sake of illustration that investing in the broad market earns a rate of return of 13 percent with a probability of 0.65, and a loss of 3 percent with a probability of 0.35, for an average return of 7.4 percent. Investing in growth stocks can result in a gain of 22 percent with probability of 0.65 or a loss of 10 percent with probability of 0.35, for an average return of 10.8 percent. We assume that both classes of stocks are positively correlated (their markets are up, and down, at the same time). Suppose further, that the implicit return of the current social security system is 1 percent. Investing in the broad market with the guarantee means that the risk of a loss is replaced by the risk of small gain of 1 percent. This increases the expected return to 8.8 percent. The potential loss from investing in growth stocks is reduced to 6 percent from 10 percent, and the expected return is increased to 12.2 percent. The Feldstein-Samwick proposal does not, to be fair, directly subsidize gambling. The compensation the account holder receives is the same whether he invests in the benchmark portfolio or the more aggressive portfolio. However, the compensation is paid when the aggressive strategy entails a loss.

[7] The U.S. Supplemental Security Income Program (SSI) provides a basic safety net for those elderly and disabled people (adults and children) who are ineligible for social security benefits. Its maximum monthly benefit as of January 1 2005 was about $600 for individuals and $850 for couples.

or a somewhat reduced but proportional benefit, with a cap applying at some level of income that was deemed to provide the minimal socially acceptable standard of living in retirement. This would ensure, up to a specified income level that workers would not do worse with individual accounts than they would have done under the current law. The higher the multiple of the poverty line used as the cap, the greater the risk of moral hazard unless restrictions on asset allocation like those proposed by Feldstein-Samwick apply. The potential welfare cost entailed by investment risk would have to be weighed against the danger of excess moral hazard in setting the cap.

Other Design Issues with Implications for the Social Safety Net

An individual accounts reform in the form of a carve-out can have substantial consequences for the social safety net that is built into or complements the typical public pension system. These consequences arise even when the population is not aging, because a carve-out reform will require a reduction in the average pensions that will be paid to the current working generation. Were there no reduction, contributors would receive the same public pension they would have received without reform, plus the income funded by the balance in their individual account. When population aging and other influences confront the public pension system with a solvency problem, and increases in the payroll tax are ruled out, then an additional reduction in average pensions is required. This additional reduction needs to be apportioned among the regular retirement pension, the disability pension, and family benefits. Leaving family benefits and the disability pension for the next section, we first consider the impact of reductions in the regular retirement pension on the distribution of retirement income among able-bodied participants in the system.

After the reform is implemented, contributors who are retiring will receive a reduced public pension plus the income from the annuity that their individual account will fund. Consider the impact of a proportional reduction in the public pension that is the same for all contributors regardless of income level, and assume that the implicit rate of return to the contributions to the public system declines as income rises. (We abstract from differences in the life expectancies of contributors at different levels of income.) If, in addition, the rate of return to individual accounts does not vary with income level, the proportional reduction of the public pension can be expected to lower the combined return on the payroll tax and individual account contributions of the low paid relative to the combined return enjoyed by the better paid. If the reform has been phased in, then the difference between the rates of return of the old system and the new, mixed system should be very small initially – since the annuity that can be financed by contributions after just a few years will be very small – but will grow over time.

In the particular case when the financial return to individual account contributions equals the implicit return to the payroll taxes of a contributor earning an *average* wage, it will be below the implicit return of those contributors earning below the average. As a result, low-income earners will be absolutely, and not just relatively, worse off because of the introduction of individual accounts. If low-income earners invest more conservatively than they need to, as some observers have conjectured, they will be still worse off.[8]

It follows that safeguarding the *relative* position of the poor will require such a measure as an increase in the replacement rate of the public system at lower incomes relative to those at higher incomes. For example, the public pension, instead of being reduced across the board, could be reduced in a way that preserves benefits for the low-paid. The introduction of guarantees on the minimum balance in the individual accounts might serve a similar purpose.

Family and Disability Benefits[9]

The benefits that public pension systems pay to family members and the annuities and other financial instruments available on the private market, as earlier chapters have discussed, have a superficial functional similarity. A joint annuity offers protection to the surviving spouse of a couple, for example. Life insurance can serve the same function as survivors' benefits. There is a crucial difference between the publicly provided benefits and the protection sold by private markets, however. In the private market, a decision to buy a joint rather than an individual annuity increases the premium per dollar of regular income. Under the typical public pension system, a single man is entitled to the same pension as a married man with the same earnings history, but the spouse and dependents of the married man will receive additional protection in the form of spousal and

---

[8] Penner and Cove (2002) assess the evidence that women invest more conservatively than men, and conclude that there is no clear-cut difference in strategy.

[9] This section sets out in general terms the implications of an individual account reform for family benefits. Reno et al. (2005, chapters 6 and 7) has a detailed discussion of the issue in the American setting.

survivors' pensions. The public system, unlike the private system, is not actuarially fair, in that the expected return to all pensions (ordinary retirement, survivors' and spousal pensions) combined is higher for a family with one income earner than the expected return to the ordinary retirement pension of a single person with the identical earnings history.

The introduction of individual accounts has important implications for family benefits, and for the distribution of benefits between families and single persons (or between large and small families), and among family members. First, when the sum total of all pension benefits of current contributors must be reduced, a decision must be made on how to allocate the reductions across the different classes of pensions. Second, a decision to introduce individual accounts raises the basic issue of the property rights associated with them. That in turn has implications for the treatment of survivors' benefits, and benefits for divorced spouses.

Family benefits need not be affected at all by the introduction of individual accounts. This is not to say that some legislative or administrative regulations might not have to be changed. For example, family benefits are often expressed as a specific percentage of the ordinary retirement pension. If that is reduced, then the percentages used to determine the family benefits will have to increase to keep them unchanged. These are merely superficial changes.

In deciding on how a reduction should be shared across the various family and disability benefits, one point to keep in mind is what the appropriate group of beneficiaries should be: is it the family or the individuals of which it is composed? Is a reduction in survivors' benefits acceptable, for example, because on average it will be offset by gains in the sum of the ordinary retirement pension and the annuity financed by the individual account? To answer that question positively, we have to assume that changes in the distribution of benefit income within a family have no effects on the intra-familial incidence of the consumption that the income finances. For many families, this is not plausible.

There are many possible solutions to this problem of division within the family. Some of them are more Solomonic in their wisdom than others. It might be best to assume that, unless there are compelling reasons to lower family benefits that are unconnected with the individual accounts reform, the basic goal of policy should be either maintaining them, or if they are reduced, putting a compensatory mechanism like insurance in place.

The discussion will assume that a country planning either to introduce an individual accounts component into its system or fine-tune a system already in place has already decided on what the appropriate level and general form of family benefits should be. The introduction of an individual accounts reform could be the occasion for a reform of these benefits, but this potentially important issue is not addressed here.

To illustrate how different solutions to the problem of maintaining family benefits might work, we assume that the public pension system prior to reform is a simple pay-as-you-go (PAYG) system with a payroll tax rate of 10 percent. Unlike any such real world system, it is in a steady state, its current revenue equals its current expenditure, and it is also actuarially balanced (meaning that the present discounted value of expected outlays equals that of receipts). The system pays regular retirement benefits as well as disability and survivors' benefits — in which we include spousal benefits for convenience — in the proportions shown in the table, which have been chosen purely for the sake of illustration.

Selected parameters of a hypothetical PAYG public pension system (in percent except where noted otherwise)

Rate of payroll tax	10
Carve out percentage	2
Share of family benefits in total	40
Share of disability pension	10
Share of ordinary retirement pension	50
Internal rate of return for average household (equals return of individual accounts)	5
Internal rate of return for a single person ((50+10)/100 times 5)	3

The reform will be a carve-out, with 2 percentage points being diverted to the individual accounts. For every $10 billion in pensions of all kinds the systems pays, $5 billion are for ordinary retirement, $1 billion are for disability, and $4 billion are for family benefits. We assume that a working single person has the same chance of benefiting from a disability pension as one who is married with a family.

The simplest solution is to keep family benefits and the disability benefit unchanged. This requires that the regular retirement pension be reduced by 40 percent. The present value of the regular retirement pension a single person receives is reduced from $5 for every $10 of contributions to $3. However, assuming that the $2 invested in individual accounts earns the same return as the return of the old system as a whole, and taking no account of the greater risk attached to the income that the individual account will generate, single people are no worse off. The system prereform is designed to benefit people with families and survivors, and that aspect of it is not changed by the reform.

Another possible solution is to lower all classes of benefits proportionately, and institute compulsory insurance for disability and survivors' benefits. Without some kind of insurance, this solution would lower the expected pension of single people by less than the first solution, leaving them better off and families worse off. To prevent a decline in family welfare, an insurance system could be implemented, whereby a percentage of the contribution to the individual account finances family benefits to complement those that the state provides. This solution is a hybrid of the standard approach of public pension systems and the Chilean approach. As such, it entails administrative duplication. Two bureaucracies, one in the public sector the other in the private sector (insurance companies) are responsible for disability and survivors' benefits.

A more radical solution would also lower family benefits proportionately, but would require contributors with families to buy joint and survivor annuities as well as disability insurance. This third solution introduces an element of actuarial fairness. Contributors with large families would effectively have a smaller retirement pension, and single contributors would have a larger one. Whether such a solution is genuinely fair, let alone politically feasible in any country is debatable. An extreme variant of this solution would make the system of family benefits completely fair actuarially; this is what would happen if the state benefits were eliminated, and contributors required to buy joint and survivor annuities that reflected their family situation. However, the extreme variant would require a larger carve-out, because the payroll tax rate would be reduced by 5 percentage points.

Like the second solution, the moderate variant of the third solution would entail duplication of administrative resources. It would also entail a large redistribution of benefits from large to smaller families and from families to single people. The impact of this approach might be mitigated by being phased in gradually. However, gradual or not, this solution raises a basic issue about the purpose of a public pension system, and the competing claims of social solidarity and individual fairness.

Issues Related to Family Benefits and the Legal Status of Individual Accounts

The legal status of the individual account has a bearing on the design of the reform of the family benefit system. If account holders have rights of property with respect to their accounts that are similar to those associated with a savings account, then the rules and restrictions on the inheritability of regular financial assets would apply to the individual accounts as well. Similarly, the balance in the account may be subject to division between holder and his spouse in the event of a divorce according to the applicable laws in the relevant jurisdiction. Reno et al. (2005, p. 15) also raise the possibility that the balances of individual accounts might be attached by third parties.

In the American setting, Perun (2002, pp. 286–288) sets out a number of basic issues that the design of an individual account should address with respect to the inheritability of the balance of the account and the rights of divorced spouses to a share of the balance. In the case of inheritability, the basic issue is whether the balance should be inheritable only by the spouse, by the spouse and children, or by anyone at all. In the case of divorce, the questions are: whether the divorced spouse should have rights to one-half (or some other statutorily determined share) of the accumulated funds; or whether her rights should be decided by a judge. Perun poses these questions with the U.S. legal system in mind, but similar questions would be raised in countries with a different legal tradition.

A treatment of these legal issues is well beyond the book's scope. Nonetheless, there are important issues of economic and social policy at stake. One key issue is whether the survivors' benefits will decline because of the individual accounts reform, a possibility we have already addressed. Whether or not restrictions are placed on the potential beneficiaries of the balance of the account can make a material difference in some cases to the adequacy of survivors' benefits. If beneficiaries are restricted to family members, the family benefits of the public system have not been changed, and the accumulated balance in an account is substantial, then average benefits are effectively boosted. This being said, placing restrictions on inheritability would be a haphazard way of supplementing the family benefits that the public pension system provides. Either the standard public pension approach or insurance would be more effective, since the amount of the pay off would not depend on the number of years the account holder had been making contributions. The cost of the insurance could be reduced by giving the insurer first call on the balance of the account, as happens in Chile.

Divorce raises complicated legal and administrative issues for an individual accounts system in which the accounts are effectively treated as personal property. One important economic issue that arises is whether any benefits a divorced spouse obtains from a claim on the individual

162   *Policy Issues with both Public and Private Sector*

account should be offset against the benefits that the public pension system pays. One particular issue that arises in the United States is that a spouse could have a claim on the balance in an individual account without having the right to a spousal benefit. This could occur because a marriage must have lasted at least ten years before a divorced spouse has the right to a pension based on her spouse's retirement pension.

In other OECD countries, a flat rate benefit for divorced spouses is common, although a few countries have adopted a splitting system, where the credits or accrued benefit each spouse has earned under the public pension system are split between them (Thompson and Carasso, 2002). A similar approach might be applied with individual accounts. This would entail a transfer from the account with the larger balance to the account with the smaller balance. In fact, if the accumulated funds in the individual account were not split, and the public benefit of the nonworking or lower-earning spouse were reduced, the total benefit that the spouse would receive would decline.

Allowing inheritability and treating accounts like other property for the purposes of family law may have macroeconomic consequences. Suppose that the structure of family benefits is not changed, or that if family benefits are reduced, the reduction is compensated by an insurance arrangement. If account holders have property rights – and Perun (2002, p. 286), speaking of the U.S. case, considers it a virtual certainty that they will – then the funds in the account will be spent earlier than they would had individual accounts not been created. At present, when a contributor dies before retirement, his family receive benefits, but there is no notional individual account with a balance for them to inherit. With the introduction of individual accounts, family members will continue to receive the standard benefits if the law is unchanged. However, they, or some other beneficiary, will receive a share of the account balance. The same will occur with divorce. With the typical reform proposal for U.S. social security, the impact of this extra inheritance on aggregate spending is probably small. With a Chilean-style reform, however, where 10 percentage points of salary are placed in the individual account, the effect would be more marked.

7

Policy Issues with Privatization of the Provision of Annuities

INTRODUCTION

The private provision of mandatory annuities raises a host of issues. The chapter begins by tackling one of particular importance: the impact of reform on the average premium per dollar of regular income. The experience of Chile and subsequent reformers does not provide much guidance on the likely change in annuity prices that results from reform, because these countries did not have private annuity markets of any size prior to the introduction of individual accounts. Consequently, the chapter relies on a simple analytical framework that can be used as a rough guide to how great that impact might be. The chapter then addresses the issue of the overall level and variability of premiums with private providers, as well as the implications of premium differentiation by sex/gender and other characteristics. Finally, it takes up the merits and potential pitfalls of guarantees to annuity providers, tax matters, and the basic administrative aspects of mandatory annuitization.

THE LEVEL AND VARIABILITY OF PREMIUMS

Premium Level

Mandatory annuitization with severely limited exceptions would require that virtually every member of each age cohort buy an annuity of some size as he or she retired. Because voluntary annuitants have a longer life expectancy than the rest of the population, such universal mandatory annuitization would lower the average life expectancy of the annuitant population. In a competitive annuity market, premiums should vary with the average life expectancy of the annuitant population as a whole. As a result, universal annuitization should tend to lower the average premium per dollar.

By making four simplifying assumptions about the mandatory and voluntary annuity markets, a simple formula can be derived to gauge the impact of mandatory annuitization on premiums. First, the amount of the balances in individual accounts that must be annuitized in a given year is known. Second, the voluntary life annuity business is unaffected by the requirement, in the sense that voluntary annuitants continue to buy annuities — including any annuity they are required to purchase — generating the same regular income, even if the premium per dollar changes. Third, the premium for the enlarged population of annuitants is determined as the discounted expected value of annuity payments plus a load factor that is not altered by the reform. Fourth, insurance companies cannot distinguish between voluntary and involuntary annuitants.

With these assumptions, it can be shown (see Appendix 1, section "Adverse Selection") that the post reform premium per dollar for a given age cohort of retirees will be a weighted average of the premium per dollar that members of each group of annuitants would pay if that group represented 100 percent of the annuitant population. The relative weights are determined by the average regular payment each group receives times its number at the time of annuitization. If the group of voluntary annuitants is dwarfed by the group of conscript annuitants, and the average annuity payment each group receives is the same, the post reform premium per dollar will be lower than the pre-reform dollar by an amount that reflects simply the difference in life expectancies of each group. The weights will also depend on the treatment of contributions to the state system prior to the reform. If a recognition bond is issued, then the average regular payment funded by the balance in the individual account will be greater, and the premium per dollar lower. Finally, the formula's estimate of the decline in the premium per dollar should be conservative if the expansion in the market's size lowers the average costs of annuity providers, and hence the load factor.

The speed with which a policy of mandatory annuitization with private provision affects premium values, and the ultimate size of the effect, will depend on various features of the reform. Apart from the treatment of acquired pension rights under the public pension system, the most important of these are: how quickly the new regime is phased in; the size of the individual accounts component of the system relative to the size of the now reduced public system; and the rules that determine how much of the balance of an individual account must be annuitized.

A reform where all contributors, regardless of their age, participate in the individual accounts system, could cause an increase in demand for annuities almost immediately, although the size of the balances accumulated in individual accounts would be very small, to the point that annuitization might not be practicable. If workers who are middle-aged or younger join the system, but not the older workers, then some time will elapse before the reform affects annuity demand. With no recognition bond, a full working lifetime would have to pass before the demand for annuities by each successive age cohort of retirees reached its steady-state level. The stock of outstanding annuity contracts would grow rapidly, with the rate of growth leveling off once all cohorts were contributing to the new system throughout their working lives.

Apart from these transitional issues, if his/her income were modest, an account holder might contribute for 35 years without accumulating a sizeable balance. This is particularly true if the individual accounts reform was a carve-out, where only two or three percentage points of the payroll tax would be diverted to the individual account. For example, if a worker earned an average of $25,000 in current dollars for 35 years, of which 2 percent was diverted to her individual account, where it earned a real rate of return of 3 percent, the accumulated sum would amount to about $31,100 in current dollars. Many individual accounts would accumulate even smaller amounts. The smaller the average balance subject to mandatory annuitization, the less would be the impact on premiums.

Premium Variability

Premiums can vary substantially across providers in the same market, as Chapter 2 discussed. Mandatory annuitization with private provision might be expected to reduce the dispersion of prices by increasing the number of actual and potential annuitants who would engage in comparison shopping. Mandatory annuitization already applies in the United Kingdom, where it still pays to shop around, but this may reflect special features of the British market, and in particular the fact that the institution investing and managing the contribution is also allowed to sell annuities.

Premiums also vary substantially over time, but this is less puzzling. Given the way premiums are funded, they can be expected to vary with the general interest level and the shape of the yield curve. Even if an individual account holder can predict quite accurately the accumulated balance in his account at retirement age, he will not be able to predict the ratio of income to premium accurately until very close to the date at which he locks into his annuity.

The practical significance of interest rate fluctuations depends on their amplitude. Fluctuations in short-term interest rates are normally larger than fluctuations in medium- and long-term rates, with the result that substantial fluctuations in short-term rates may not have much effect on annuity premiums. Fluctuations in short-term rates, if they are expected to be temporary, may have no effect on premiums, particularly if insurance companies prefer to maintain relatively stable premiums. Interest rate volatility is more of a concern the greater the share of retirement income that the individual account is expected to generate. It may also be more of a concern to the elderly poor, given their vulnerability to unpredictable income swings. Some possible remedies are discussed below.

Despite the abundance of data on current annuity premiums in countries with well-developed financial markets, the times series data set for premiums is less comprehensive than might be expected. In the United States, there is no readily available consistent time series with an average premium per dollar of annuity payment covering the past twenty years, although data do exist for a more distant period. Mackenzie and Schrager (2004) use an indirect method based on a sample of data on the yield curve for U.S. Treasuries to make estimates of how much premiums could be expected to vary over time. They do not find that the variability of premiums attributable to movements in the yield curve is huge. Nonetheless, the premium paid for the same stream of income could vary substantially between two cohorts of retirees. In addition, the yield curve sample covered the period 1992—2002, which was a period of comparative financial stability for the United States.

The problem of premium variability can be mitigated by making the rules that govern withdrawals from individual accounts more flexible. One approach would be to allow purchases of annuities to be deferred, with programmed withdrawals from the individual account during the interval between the date at which the account holder was first eligible to purchase an annuity and the actual purchase date.[1] Deferring purchase of an annuity would at least allow the account holder to benefit from an increase in interest rates in the years immediately following the date when he would normally annuitize. The strategy would not guarantee him any given premium rate, however.

---

[1] The withdrawal schedule could be designed to approximate the monthly payment of an annuity that the account holder could afford, with the premium based on reasonable assumptions about interest rates and life expectancy. For example, the yield curve used to calculate the premium could be based on average values over the past 30 years, taking account of the decline in inflation that has taken place over that period. A deferred annuity has to address the issue of the consequences of the death of the annuitant before payments start. These are similar to the consequences of the death of an account holder during working life.

Another strategy would be to allow the purchase of a deferred annuity some years before retirement (effectively advanced purchase). Specifically, in a period when interest rates are relatively high, the account holder could contract with a life insurance company to provide a life annuity with the start of payments being deferred until the account holder was eligible for withdrawals. Deferred annuitization lengthens the period between the insurance company's receipt of the premium and the expected date of the last annuity payment. By increasing the gap between the maturity of the longest-lived bond and the date of the last annuity payments, it increases the insurance company's interest rate risk. Blake (1999) notes that deferred annuities in the UK have proved to be very expensive, but the evidence on this point is lacking.

A third strategy for people nearing retirement would be to protect themselves to some extent from the consequences of interest rate fluctuations by following a home-grown immunization strategy. This would entail their holding a diversified portfolio of bonds whose value would vary with the present discounted value of their expected income in retirement. However, complete immunization, as Appendix 1 explains, is generally not possible. Maturity matching would be a problem for the same reason that it is a problem with deferred annuities. Perhaps more importantly, the practicality of the typical person carrying out such a strategy is in question. Advice would undoubtedly be available in many countries, but it would not be cheap. The availability of bonds at different maturities in small lots could also be an issue.

Neither early purchase with deferred annuitization nor deferred purchase, singly or in combination, nor home-grown immunization would ensure that retirees from different age cohorts would all obtain the same income per dollar of premium. This lack of equal treatment of different cohorts does not result from deliberate discrimination. Nonetheless, it might not be very popular if people found it hard to understand (or simply unacceptable) that the same amount of savings did not give everyone title to the same income. This said, the issue has apparently not arisen in Chile or the UK although the voluntary character of the British system may make interest rate variability more acceptable.

PREMIUM DIFFERENTIATION

In pricing annuities, life insurance companies differentiate between males and females. In the United States and United Kingdom, a life annuity would cost a 65-year-old woman 10 percent or so more than it would cost a man. The potential also exists for differentiation based on socio-economic, cultural, and racial characteristics.[2] Public pension systems do not differentiate in this way, since the old-age retirement benefit typically depends only on a contributor's earnings history and age, and not on his/her sex. Similarly, employer pension plans in most countries may not differentiate based on the sex of the plan member — only salary history and length of participation in the plan determine the value of the pension.[3] Consequently, the average lifetime benefit a woman receives, be it from social security or an occupational pension, will be greater than that of a man with the equivalent earnings history.

Whether or not premium differentiation by sex is seen as fair or unfair depends on the emphasis placed on wealth versus income as an index of material wellbeing, which may in turn depend on the importance attached to social solidarity. The traditional approach of solidarity — men subsidizing women — can be justified on the grounds that the burden on women of having to accumulate more savings during their working life or work longer because they will live longer during retirement should be shared by society at large. It can also be defended as a way of mitigating the discrimination that women have experienced at the work-place. The contrary view might argue that the fact that women typically enjoy longer life means that equal pensions increase their lifetime income and consumption, creating an unjustified disparity between the way they are treated and the treatment that men receive.

If the purpose of a public pension system is to achieve some minimum income level during the retirement years, however, then what is relevant is that income level, not the expected capitalized value of the postretirement income stream. Reliance on private sector annuities might compromise a woman's achievement of a minimum income level in retirement. The seriousness of this consequence of premium differentiation is mitigated to the extent that the private annuity supplements a public pension benefit that ensures a basic level of income support that is the same for both men and women.

---

[2] Insurance companies in the United States do not differentiate premiums on racial lines (for example, by charging African Americans a lower premium than the population at large based on their lower life expectancy). Such a practice could not withstand a legal challenge.

[3] In 1983, the Supreme Court of the United States ruled that the Civil Rights Act requires that employer-provided pension plans use unisex life tables in calculating pensions. The ruling follows from the applicability of the Civil Rights Act to the employment relationship, and does not apply to individual annuity contracts.

One solution would be to bar the use of the sex of the applicant as an index in annuity pricing, so that male and female annuitants of the same age would be charged the same premium. If life insurers provide the annuities, this restriction would pose a technical problem both for them and for public policy. Life insurance companies that are successful in obtaining as their clients a share of men higher than the share of males in the retired population as a whole will have higher profits than those companies with a disproportionate number of women. If the premium life insurance companies charge per dollar of lifetime income stream is high enough to allow them to earn a normal profit on annuities for women, it will be more than enough to earn normal profits on annuities sold to men, since the competitive premium for male annuitants would be less than that for women. The break-even unisex premium will be somewhere in between.[4]

Hence, life insurance companies would have an interest in discouraging female applicants, if they could do so legally, and in encouraging male applicants instead. Life insurance companies could be required to accept applications for annuities from women, but any insurance company with a share of women higher than the average would, other things being equal, earn below average profits. How great a problem this would be in practice is uncertain. It might lead companies to adopt a passive attitude to female annuitants, while competing through nonprice means − if that were legal − for male annuitants.

Observance of a law forbidding differentiation by sex in premium-setting could conceivably be facilitated by an industry pooling arrangement. The arrangement might work as follows. Life insurance companies with more men than women would contribute an amount to the pool that would be a function of the premium differential, any difference in average annuity size, and the difference in the numbers of male and female annuitants. Life insurance companies with more female than male annuitants would draw from the pool, with their drawing being determined in the same way.

The development of genetic tests raises the further issue, as Walliser (1998) points out, of what limits should apply to life insurance companies' use of normally confidential or sensitive personal information in pricing their products. The issue is particularly important for life insurance, but could also become important for life annuities.

---

[4] The unisex premium per dollar should be a weighted average of the premium per dollar for men and for women, with the weights depending on the relative numbers of men and women.

A related issue is differentiation in pricing by size of annuity. Small annuities could be more expensive per unit of income, since some administrative costs are a function of the number of policies rather than their total amount. The evidence on this point is not conclusive, although Finkelstein and Poterba find that the money's worth (MW) ratios of very small annuities in the United Kingdom are lower than those of bigger annuities. Quotations from the websites from U.S. annuity providers do not distinguish between large and modestly sized annuities. The quoted premiums may not necessarily equal final effective transactions prices, however. As Chapter 2 pointed out, UK annuity providers offer less service to small annuitants than they do to larger ones. A law forbidding price differentiation between small and large annuities might also lead insurance companies to discourage applications for modest annuities.

Finally, if a rating system were to develop for mandatory life annuities like the one used for life insurance, issues might arise as to the perceived fairness of the variations in premiums it would bring about. Premium differentiation might well benefit groups in countries that are seen as disadvantaged, which might be a plus. The notion of two people with the same earnings history receiving different pensions might be perceived as inequitable, however.

GUARANTEES FOR ANNUITY PAYMENTS

If annuitization is mandatory, it is reasonable to suppose that the public will expect their annuity payments to be guaranteed by the government even if the provision of the annuity is privatized. A guarantee need not be a formal component of an individual accounts reform for a government to be seen as having a moral responsibility, either to enact one or to provide an informal guarantee. It would undoubtedly face great political pressure to do one or the other.

A formal guarantee could take the form of an insurance arrangement, under which a central government agency could partially or wholly insure payments to annuitants in the event of the failure of an annuity provider. An informal guarantee could take the form of a tacit understanding to bail out financially troubled annuity providers, or at least ensure that annuitants received their payments on time and in full. The practice regarding guarantees on annuity payments differs among countries that have implemented an individual accounts reform, as Chapter 4 describes. Peru has no specific guarantee, while Chile has a partial guarantee. Poland is considering a full guarantee.

A guarantee, especially a formal one, that the annuity contract will be honored creates a potentially serious moral hazard problem, one that is possibly more serious than the moral hazard created by a guarantee on the minimum value of the funds in an individual account, which Chapter 6 analyzed. A guarantee that annuity payments will not be reduced or interrupted by the financial difficulties of the provider creates an incentive for the provider to offer excessively generous terms (i.e. relatively low premiums) to attract customers, since they will suffer no loss even if its investment experience is unfavorable. If the provider is lucky and things go well, the annuity payments are honored. If things go badly, the taxpayer becomes the annuity provider's partner and shares in the loss.[5] The long time between the initial payment by the annuitant and the time when most of the payments to the average annuitant have been made creates an incentive for similar behavior, as Chapter 3 noted.

A generous guarantee on annuity payments is analogous to a poorly designed deposit insurance scheme. Excessively generous deposit insurance creates incentives for depositary institutions to offer unrealistically high rates of interest and make risky investments, because insurance reduces the incentive deposit holders have to monitor the performance of financial institutions and withdraw their funds from institutions in difficulty.[6]

The incentive to excessive risk-taking is reduced to some extent if the regulations on provisioning require extra capital to compensate for duration mismatches, or an excessively risky asset portfolio. Another possibility is to levy risk-based premiums on the insurance industry, as has been proposed for defined benefit pension plans in the United States.

If the coverage of a guarantee cannot be reduced, the extent of mandatory annuitization of the balances in individual accounts may have to be limited to contain the potential damage from moral hazard.

---

[5] Retired or soon to be retired persons who are subject to mandatory annuitization bear part of the loss in their role as taxpayers. However, they benefit on balance from the policy, whereas the general taxpayer, who is on average younger, loses.

[6] Deposit insurance was once justified as a means of preventing unnecessary and destructive runs on the banking system, which could — and in the United States in the 1930s did — result in the bankruptcy or closure of essentially sound institutions. The banking system was seen as a public good, and deposit insurance as a means of discouraging massive cash withdrawals that entailed large negative externalities (the collapse of the clearing and credit system). Subsequent experience made clear that deposit insurance could have some highly undesirable side-effects in the form of the incentives to excessive risk-taking that the text discusses. The generous deposit insurance provided to deposit holders of savings and loan (S&L) institutions in the United States in the late 1970s and early 1980s contributed, along with deregulation, to the subsequent S&L crisis. Gillian Garcia (2000) is a comprehensive survey of the issues related to deposit insurance.

Current best practice with deposit insurance is to limit the guarantee so that only small depositors are fully protected, and to rely on the kind of supervisory framework that Chapter 3 described, whose general lines apply to both banks and insurance companies. A full guarantee on mandatory annuities that targeted a generous replacement ratio without the support of a strong regulatory framework would be folly. Whatever the regulatory framework, however, a very generous guarantee would increase the incentives for annuity providers to take excessive risks.

TAXATION OF ANNUITIES

The taxation of individual accounts raises particularly complex issues. The difficulties stem in part from the inconsistent way in which most countries tax capital income and saving. In principle, a broad-based tax system can tax either income or consumption. The classical personal income tax model treats income that is saved exactly as it treats income that is spent or consumed. The taxpayer may not deduct contributions to savings plans or his net purchases of financial assets from his taxable income, and the income these plans earn is taxed as it accrues or is realized. A consumption tax, as the name implies, is intended to tax only consumption. It effectively taxes income if and only if it is consumed, not when it is saved.

In practice, most OECD countries do tax income fairly comprehensively, but deviate to some extent from the classical income tax model by giving special tax treatment to the income that funds certain savings vehicles, and sometimes the income these vehicles generate, to encourage saving. In particular, saving for retirement tends to be encouraged by permitting before-tax contributions (contributions that reduce taxable income) to certain savings vehicles subject to certain limits and conditions, and deferring taxation on both interest and principal until the owner starts to make withdrawals. Provided the taxpayer is in the same tax bracket when distributions are made as he was when the contributions were made, this consumption-tax approach equates the net of tax return to the gross return to saving, instead of introducing a "wedge" between them, as the classical income tax does.

The annuities that are voluntarily purchased may be funded from either before-tax or after-tax income. If they are purchased with after-tax income, then only part of the regular income they generate will be subject to taxation under a classical income tax system. Specifically, the part of the income deemed to be interest income is taxed, while the part deemed to be a return of principal is not. The regular payments of an annuity purchased with before-tax income, like the contributions to a saving plan that were deductible from income tax, would be taxed in their entirety.

Broadly speaking, there are four approaches to treating distributions from individual accounts − which we assume take the form of an annuity or phased withdrawals − for tax purposes. The first is to treat them as if they were still a part of the public pension. Treating distributions in this way entails combining them with what remains of the public pension benefit, and then taxing the combined benefit in the same way it would have been taxed had there been no individual accounts reform. If the public pension has been given preferential conventional tax treatment − as is the case in many countries − that treatment continues to apply.

The second approach taxes individual account distributions according to the classical income tax model. The third treats individual accounts like existing tax-favored voluntary saving plans (these could include both employer-provided defined contributions plans and private plans like the IRA in the United States). The second and third approaches could result in a change in the net of tax benefit postreform, even if the combined pretax benefit did not change. The fourth approach is eclectic: for example, a simplified version of the conventional tax treatment of voluntary annuities.

Taxing individual accounts like a tax-favored savings scheme implies either that contributions would be deductible from taxable income and distributions fully taxable − as noted above, this is the more common approach − or that contributions would be taxable and distributions would be fully exempt. This treatment of individual accounts is not strictly necessary, since contributions to them are not voluntary, and since giving them special treatment will not encourage additional savings. Special treatment could be justified, however, if the contributions to the individual accounts had been deductible from taxable income when they were financing the public pension system (i.e. in the case of a "carve-out" individual accounts reform). This would not be the case with U.S. social security, if the contribution to the individual accounts were financed from the employee's share of the payroll tax, since that part of the contribution is not deductible from the contributor's taxable income.

The contributions to and distributions from individual accounts could be taxed according to the classical income tax model. To tax annuity income like income from after-tax saving, it is necessary to separate the interest and principal components of annuity payments. In the case of a simple life annuity, the method used in the United States involves subtracting from the income the annuity pays each month an amount that is equal to the premium divided by the number of months of the annuitant's deemed life expectancy upon annuitization. For example, if an annuitant's life expectancy at age 65 is deemed to be 216 months (18 years), the premium would be divided by 216, and the result subtracted from the monthly payment. The difference is then multiplied by 12 to give annual taxable income. Once the annuitant's life span surpasses its expected value − 18 years in this case − the payment is fully taxed.

The tax calculation assumes in effect that the annuity provider pays back the premium in equal installments over a period of 18 years. This is only a rough approximation of the patterns of the blend of interest and principal repayments in an 18 year certain annuity. The initial payments made under an annuity contract are largely interest; as with a mortgage, the principal component increases over time. The tax treatment of annuities varies considerably across countries. Brown et al. (2001a) discuss U.S. tax issues in more depth.

The tax treatment of annuities has an obvious influence on the development of the voluntary annuity market. Although the distribution phase of a voluntary annuity is in some respects analogous, and serves a similar purpose to the pay-out phase of a funded private pension plan, its tax treatment tends to be distinctly less favorable than that accorded to a private pension. Among OECD countries, pension plans typically either allow a deduction of contributions from taxable income (i.e. the employee's contribution is deductible from his taxable income, and the employer's share is deductible from taxable profits) or they exempt the pension, and they typically do not tax the income of the pension plan either as it accrues or as it is realized (King 2004).

Although giving an individual accounts system the same treatment as a tax favored savings vehicle like the IRA in the United States or the RRSP in Canada is not necessary to encourage savings, it has the obvious appeal of symmetry and consistency, and would obviate the need to distinguish between the principal and the interest component of distributions. Conceivably, the public pension system could be treated the same way: i.e. employer and employee contributions could be exempt from corporate or personal income tax, and pensions taxed like other income. Existing retirees might have to be grandfathered to avoid a swingeing increase in their tax burden, however. The revenue effects of such a tax reform could be considerable in many countries, and would have to be very carefully assessed. A reform along these lines would have to be phased in gradually.

ADMINISTRATIVE ASPECTS OF PRIVATE PROVISION

Ensuring the smooth introduction of private sector provision of mandatory annuities will require very careful preparation. This will be particularly true if the system offers annuitants a broad range of choice among different annuities, and if a guarantee on annuity payments is provided. Successful reform will require the establishment of new systems or programs and procedures for the monitoring, control, and regulation of the annuity market and its providers. The most important of these systems and procedures are listed below, with a brief summary of their functions.

All reforms involve issues of sequencing. In the case of an individual accounts reform, it appears that all of these components of the regulatory apparatus would have to be in place before a single account holder withdrew his funds to purchase an annuity. Arguably, at least the broad outlines if not the details of the administrative side of the reform should be worked out before individual accounts are even established.

Educational Programs

These programs would inform account holders of their rights and responsibilities regarding annuitization, and provide them with adequate and clear information regarding the choices they needed to make. One basic design issue with educational programs would be the relative responsibilities of industry and government. The respective responsibilities of the concerned government agency and annuity providers in supplying prospective annuitants with information would have to be clearly delineated. In Chile, the responsibility lies with the pension funds (AFPs), under the oversight of the SAFP.

The educational program would have to target prospective annuitants some years before they were eligible to receive distributions from the individual accounts, or even earlier if the balances were inheritable under certain conditions. If a choice was allowed among different forms of annuities, the educational program would be charged with ensuring that the merits and drawbacks of each form were *very* carefully explained. The program would have to provide guidance in choosing not only among different forms of annuities, but also in choosing between immediate and deferred annuitization, if that were an option. One key issue is whether, when there was a choice, to establish default values or make explicit recommendations, or simply rely on the educational program to guide annuitants in making their choices. The evidence with default values applying to investment choices suggests that they could have a significant and salutary influence on annuitization decisions.

Notification and Registration Systems

A notification system would be needed to inform prospective annuitants of the deadlines for important decisions well in advance of the decision points. Its deadlines would need to be coordinated with those of the educational program. Similarly, a registration system for mandatory purchases of annuities, and — depending on whether the payments process could be self-policing or not — a system to record and monitor payments to annuitants would have to be created.

Regulation of Eligible Annuity Providers and their Products

A system would need to be put in place that ensured that annuities were purchased only from eligible institutions, and these institutions would have to be adequately vetted. The vetting might be handled automatically by the agency responsible for regulating life insurance companies, if the annuities were to be supplied only by them. A system to verify that annuities conformed to the model prescribed by law would have to be developed.

Guarantee Administration

Arrangements for the administration of a government guarantee, if there was one, applying to the minimum balance in an individual account upon the retirement of its holder would have to be designed and implemented. Some of the guarantees of this type are comparatively simple, as Chapter 6 noted, but some proposals are more complex and would be harder to explain. Similar arrangements would be necessary for a guarantee, if one were extended, on the payments of annuity providers in the event that insurance companies were unable to honor their commitments.

Procedures for Exceptions to Mandatory Annuitization

Finally, rules would need to be implemented to determine the conditions under which a person could be exempt from the requirement to purchase an annuity (if exemptions were permitted), and procedures to vet applications for exemptions. These procedures could perhaps piggyback on existing procedures for determining eligibility for a disability pension.

8

Conclusions and Recommendations

The book began by posing three basic questions. What should the policy toward distributions from individual accounts be — in particular, how restrictive should the rules applying to annuities or distributions in other forms be? Should annuities, if they are mandatory, be supplied by the public or the private sector? How can markets for voluntary annuities be made more efficient, and their effective regulation ensured? This concluding chapter proposes answers for each of them.

POLICY ISSUES WITH EITHER PUBLIC OR PRIVATE PROVISION OF MANDATORY ANNUITIES

Distributions before Retirement and Bequests

Chapter 4 noted that countries that have adopted individual accounts, whether to complement or replace an existing pay-as-you-go (PAYG) system, have taken the position that individual accounts do not enjoy the same legal status as holdings of other financial assets. Specifically, they are not endowed with the same complement of property rights. Instead, existing individual accounts systems treat individual accounts exclusively as a source of income for retirement. In virtually no country are withdrawals allowed while the account holder is still alive, whether they are intended to finance an education or the purchase of a house, pay medical bills, or tide the account holder over a spell of unemployment. In Chile, the balance in individual accounts at the death of the holder is inheritable, but only under certain conditions. Singapore's CPF is a prominent but unique exception to this general rule of restrictions on withdrawals prior to retirement, because the provident fund exists for purposes other than simply financing its contributors' retirement.

177

In contrast with international practice, advocates of individual accounts in the United States often stress their private property aspect. Reno et al. (2005) and Perun (2002) contend that in the American setting, a restrictive interpretation of individual accounts – i.e. one that emphasizes retirement security – is likely to be modified and made more flexible as time passes. This view rests in part on the fact that no financial instrument now available in the U.S. market is subject to the kind of restrictions that apply in the individual account systems the book has surveyed. The possibility that the restrictions initially imposed on distributions from individual accounts may be progressively relaxed is one that countries contemplating an individual accounts reform would do well to consider.

The international practice notwithstanding, a case can be made on compassionate grounds for allowing the dying exceptional access to their accounts before retirement. Further liberalization of access, however, will either jeopardize the primary purpose of the individual accounts as sources of retirement income, or require additional financing. The CPF in Singapore could not function without a high contribution rate. Whatever their merits on social grounds, liberalized access rules can seriously complicate the administration of individual accounts, and they may have macroeconomic consequences. A system where account balances may be bequeathed without any restrictions will boost aggregate consumption and lower saving, unless there are offsetting changes to family benefits or reductions in some other expenditure programs. Similarly, a system that allows early withdrawals in hardship cases will likely reduce the pension ultimately received by the beneficiaries of the policy, and conceivably increase the government's expenditure on social assistance or minimum pensions. Neither of these effects may be very large – among other things, the impact of allowing bequests depends on the mortality rate of account holders during their working lives, and the poor, who will have small accounts, have higher mortality rates than the rich – but they have to be considered.

Distributions after Retirement: How Much Annuitization?

What share of the balance in individual accounts should be subject to annuitization depends on the replacement rate that the public pension system offers, and on whether the income from the individual accounts is supplementing the public pension (as in an add-on reform) or partly replacing it (as in a carve-out reform). If the replacement rate is high to begin with, and the individual accounts reform is an add-on, the case for annuitization is weak. (It might be argued that if the replacement rate is indeed high, then a cut in pensions over certain income ranges might be called for.) If, however, the public pension serves mainly as a social safety net for the poor or less well-paid, and the reform is a carve-out, the case for the mandatory annuitization of the balance in individual accounts is strong. The simplest solution in this case is 100 percentage annuitization. Most countries will fall in between these two extremes.

Tailoring the rate of annuitization to individual circumstances is not feasible in any country. Erring on the side of over- rather than underannuitization is the council of prudence if we are particularly concerned with providing longevity insurance. A Chilean-style rule that imposes a minimum income level and replacement rate and allows what remains of the accumulated balance after these conditions are satisfied to be withdrawn as a lump sum is a feasible option. The public pension — which will be reduced by a carve-out reform, and may be further reduced by the need to stabilize the finances of the public pension system — and the annuity funded by the account should be combined in applying the rule. The administration of this rule is easier if the public sector pays out both pensions, but is still feasible if the private sector is supplying the mandatory annuity.

Distributions after Retirement: What Form of Annuity?

Like the optimal degree of annuitization, the optimal form of the annuity varies from one person to another. (Strictly speaking, they would be determined together.) As simulation exercises can demonstrate, a variable annuity, despite its higher risk, could be more welfare-enhancing as a component in the portfolio of a retired person than a fixed nominal or indexed life annuity would be, depending on the person's wealth, taste for risk, financial acumen, and life expectancy. Similarly, depending on the rate at which a person discounts the future and the rate of return to saving, a nominal annuity may be more welfare-enhancing for some than an indexed annuity. However, the issue is not what would be best for particular individuals, or even a particular class of individuals but what would be best for the general population or its most vulnerable members. An indexed life annuity has some obvious advantages over either a variable annuity or some form of programmed or phased withdrawals: the demands it makes on financial management skills and self-control are clearly less rigorous; and the inflation protection it provides is not readily available in another form, because most financial markets do not now offer indexed life annuities. Moreover, mandatory annuitization can be expected to lower the cost of annuities provided by the private sector, making them more attractive in comparison with conventional financial assets than they otherwise would be.

Social Safety Net Issues:
Account Guarantees and Redistributive Concerns

Providing generous guarantees on individual account balances is potentially dangerous and an unsound policy. If a guarantee is provided, it should be strictly limited, and designed in a way that minimizes moral hazard. It will be important that the government not be seen as the implicit guarantor of individual balances no matter how large. If it did come to be viewed in this way, a manageable formal guarantee might become a costly, unmanageable informal scheme. A limited formal guarantee should remain a limited guarantee.

The reduction in the benefit that the public pension system provides that will take place with a carve-out reform, depending on how it is carried out, could undo some of the progressivity that is built into the structure of the typical public pension system. Broadly speaking, there are two ways of avoiding this outcome: making the benefit reduction progressive in proportional terms (i.e. raising the proportional reduction in the benefit as income increases), or offering some sort of guarantee that ensures the poor receive a minimum income. The first approach tries to adjust the public pension in a way that is fair to people across the whole range of incomes. The second emphasizes protecting those at the low end of the income scale. Which of the two approaches is preferable depends in part on the degree of progressivity built into the existing system. For example, if progressivity is limited to the lowest income ranges, then the two approaches will give similar results.

Social Safety Net Issues: Family and Disability Benefits

The designers of an individual accounts reform must decide whether to retain family benefits in their present form. If they do decide to retain them, they must then decide whether and by how much to reduce their amounts. A carve-out requires that aggregate pension benefits be reduced, and the reductions allocated in some way across the regular retirement pension, the disability pension, and family benefits (survivors' and spousal benefits). In principle, some of the disability and family benefits could be financed from the individual account, just as the life annuity that the individual account funds is expected to make up for the reduction in the regular retirement pension. The simplest way of protecting family benefits, however, in the case of a reform where individual accounts do not replace the public pension entirely, is to retain the public system's family benefits as they are, with appropriate adjustments in parameters if necessary to maintain their value. Any satisfactory alternative would require that transfers among family members compensate for any decline in family benefits. This is simply not a realistic assumption.

One approach to protecting family members that might satisfy this requirement would be moving to a system of actuarially fair joint and survivor annuities. This approach would, however, substantially change the orientation of the typical public pension system, where the emphasis has not been on actuarial fairness, but on providing some measure of protection to the vulnerable. The distribution of income among families of different sizes would also change. Finally, the establishment of individual accounts has implications for the position of divorced spouses, particularly if they have a claim on the account balance.

ISSUES WITH PRIVATE PROVISION OF MANDATORY ANNUITIES

Premium Variability

Mandatory annuitization is bound to lower average premiums in the annuity market, but its effects on premium variability are less certain. In the United States and the United Kingdom, annuity premiums vary substantially across providers and they vary over time. In a competitive market, variations along both dimensions are normal and desirable. Nonetheless, annuities need to be efficiently priced — the value for money ratio should be as high as is consistent with a reasonable profit for providers — and competition should not take costly and wasteful forms.

To foster an efficient annuity market, countries could consider establishing a publicly run online information center that would ensure that potential annuitants receive adequate and reliable information on competitive premiums. This center could supply information on both mandatory and voluntary annuities. It would be easier for annuitants to use if they do not have to choose among an unlimited number of annuity providers. In large markets, an issue would undoubtedly arise if some suppliers were excluded. Nonetheless, some solution to that problem could undoubtedly be worked out. A related issue is the question of whether listing means endorsement.

By restricting the choice of the form of annuity, as the book has recommended, the information the center provides will be easier to understand. The government could require that the choice be made online, although it need not discourage contacts between sales representatives and potential annuitants. These arrangements, together with the increased size of the market, might lower the variation in premiums across providers, and presumably would assist annuitants in obtaining better value for money.

Unless the government steps in to subsidize, or fix, annuity premiums, variation in premiums from one year to the next is an ineluctable consequence of private provision. To the extent that a country's financial environment is stable, so that neither nominal nor real interest rates fluctuate markedly, then one basic source of instability of the premiums of both nominal and indexed annuities will be removed. Variation of annuity premiums can also be mitigated by allowing both deferred annuitization and early annuitization, and by a strategy of do-it-yourself immunization. Such tactics do not eliminate the possibility of premium variability, or even place a ceiling on the premium per dollar of regular income.

Group Purchases and the Administrative Function

Both the administrative burden and the cost of annuities might be greatly reduced by a system of group purchases of annuities. In addition to reducing costs, group purchases would effectively deal with the problems posed by a unisex premium, since the government could determine the gender composition of all the groups.

A group purchase arrangement might work as follows: the government could group annuitants of a given age cohort in sub-cohorts of some minimum number, using a selection procedure that would ensure that different sub-cohorts would have the same average life expectancy. It would then invite bids from life insurance companies. The economies of scale entailed by grouping might reduce the cost of annuities substantially. This could be particularly important for small annuities.

Premium Differentiation by Gender or Other
Personal Characteristics

Private providers of voluntary annuities differentiate premiums by gender. Differentiation based on health is uncommon, but is practiced in the

British market. Differentiation on health and on other grounds may well develop in other markets, if the regulatory framework permits it, as the market for private annuities develops. Such differentiation could be considered undesirable when the purchase of the annuity is mandatory. In the case of those female annuitants whose working life has been spent in low-paid jobs, differentiation could reduce an already modest retirement income. The importance of this issue depends in part on the relative generosity of the public pension postreform. If the annuity financed by the individual account is topping up a generous public benefit, discrimination between the sexes is a less serious matter.

Discrimination on other grounds might actually improve the lot of the low-paid, if their premiums per dollar declined. That said, the fact that a policy of compulsory annuitization would result in the same amounts of money buying annuities with differing regular income streams might raise questions in the minds of those annuitants who ended up with the short end of the stick. Discrimination might seem inequitable to this latter group, even if it seemed fair to other groups.

Guarantees on the Regular Annuity Payment

A full guarantee on the income from mandatory annuities supplied by the private sector would be bad public policy. If there is a guarantee, it has to be limited, in line with best practice in insuring bank deposits. The small annuitant should be favored over the large one. At the same time, the desirability of a partial rather than a full guarantee on payments by annuity providers makes effective regulation of the insurance business all the more important. The topic of regulation is taken up again in the chapter's final section.

Administrative Aspects

The key to a successful introduction of mandatory annuitization, particularly with private provision, will be careful preparation. Both the costs of preparation and the costs of the system when up and running will depend critically on how much choice annuitants are allowed: the less choice, the less costly the system will be. Aside from its role in keeping costs down, restricted choice appears to contribute to well-informed choice by annuitants among the options open to them, so long as the substantive choice they enjoy is reasonably broad.

PUBLIC VERSUS PRIVATE PROVISION: A SUMMING UP

Chapter 5 noted that the provision of annuities involves three basic functions: the administrative function, the actuarial or underwriting function, and the investment function. The question at hand is whether, in the event of mandatory annuitization, it might be more efficient for the public sector, rather than the private sector to perform one, two, or perhaps all three functions.

At a minimum, the public sector might perform the administrative function if a country decided to privatize both the investment and underwriting functions. Specifically, the government agency responsible for the administration of the public pension system could be assigned responsibility for all record-keeping and payment functions, and related tasks. Administration by the responsible public agency (the Social Security Administration in the United States) would have the advantage that the agency could use its existing accounting and payments systems.

The life insurance companies would market and sell the annuities, and would continue to perform their traditional functions of underwriting risk and investment. When they had sold an annuity, they would notify the agency, which would then make monthly payments on the annuitant's behalf until his or her death. The insurance company would make a monthly transfer to the agency on behalf of all its policyholders. This arrangement should entail some savings, since account holders would receive one check, not two, every month. Because the insurance companies would continue to bear longevity risk, they would have a strong incentive to obtain accurate and prompt notice of policyholders' deaths. Retaining the administrative function in the public sector might reduce administrative costs, but to do so it would be essential that the responsible public agency be efficient and apolitical. The arrangement would have the added advantage of facilitating the collection of annuity market statistics, which is an important public policy goal in its own right.

Privatizing the underwriting function would, as the discussion to this point makes clear, have some definite drawbacks. Some of these could be effectively mitigated, but others would prove recalcitrant. One serious concern with private provision is value for money. However, mandatory annuitization itself would reduce average premiums, and a group purchase scheme might reduce them further. Another concern, and one that may not be so readily addressed, is the variability of average premiums per dollar of regular income from one age cohort of retirees to another. A third concern would be the ability of the private sector to offer an indexed life annuity, as most public systems do. Indexed annuities, if offered by the private sector, will require the prior development of a large market for indexed government debt, with a full maturity spectrum and adequate supplies at each maturity. Developing this market would take some time. Finally, privatization would require extensive preparation before even the first annuity contract was signed, as Chapter 7 has emphasized. The greater the range of choice offered to account holders, the more elaborate would the preparations have to be.

Apart from the variability of premiums, the potential problems with privatization just listed appear to be manageable. However, a guarantee, particularly on payments to annuitants would be a more serious problem. In particular, mandatory annuitization is almost certain to oblige a government to extend a formal or a de facto guarantee on the payments made by the provider, even though such a guarantee entails a serious risk of moral hazard. Minimizing the degree of mandatory annuitization would ease the task of regulation and reduce moral hazard because it will reduce the amount of income at risk, but could also result in a serious degree of underinsurance against the risks of longevity and inflation. The issue of excessive price competition flagged earlier should not arise if a government agency is responsible for underwriting and pricing of annuities.

These are the problems with privatizing underwriting. What are the advantages? One potential benefit of privatizing the underwriting function might be lower premiums. After all, the market would be more competitive. However, the normal benefits of competition do not have the relevance for a public pension program that they do for other marketable goods and services. The public provision of such goods is normally considered undesirable because employment and other production decisions become politicized, and because the market does not act as a goad to greater efficiency. However, the scope for efficiency gains in the underwriting function is not likely to be great. The general administration of public pensions is not necessary inefficient, and assigning the underwriting function to the government agency that administers what remains of the public pension system need not create a bloated bureaucracy. The underwriting function as such need not employ a great many people. There are obvious economies of scale with such aspects of the underwriting function as actuarial analysis and data maintenance, and privatization would entail some duplication of these activities. Finally, the plain vanilla wrapper character of the indexed life annuity implies that the innovation and product differentiation that private sector competition is thought to foster is less of an issue.

The case for privatizing the underwriting function obviously has to be decided on a country by country basis. Countries that wished to develop the life insurance business as part of a general strategy of financial sector development might benefit substantially from privatizing the underwriting function, as well as the investment function. The life insurance industry would have to have reached some minimum level of development to benefit from its enhanced role, however. Moreover, if every aspect of the business were regulated down to the last detail, it is not obvious what advantages privatization would confer.

If the public sector assumes the underwriting function, it would set the terms of annuitization, which would address the problem of premium fluctuations and undesirable premium discrimination. It would not need to provide a guarantee to itself, and its assumption of the underwriting function would be an explicit recognition of an implicit political obligation. In addition, the government can assume (or take back) the inflation risk entailed by indexed life annuities. With a carve-out reform, the quantum of inflation risk it would be assuming would be unchanged. An additional point to bear in mind is that maintaining the underwriting function in the public sector would effectively require that the administrative function remain there as well.

As for the investment function, its assignment to the public sector runs contrary to two generally accepted principles in public finance. First, governments in general have no obvious comparative advantage in financial investment. Second, the investment decisions of a public agency might be seen to be, or could in fact be, vulnerable to politicization. This latter concern will be more relevant for some countries than for others. The Canadian government agency responsible for investing the reserves of the Canada Pension Plan in the financial market has been cited as a counter example to the risk of politicization. In any case, contracting out the investment function may a risky proposition in many countries, simply because financial markets are not sufficiently developed, the financial environment is unstable, and regulation is ineffective.

In the United States and most other OECD countries, contracting out the investment function looks as if it would be workable. Governments and their citizens would have an overriding interest in seeing that the money was invested responsibly. The potentially conflicting goals of efficient investment and safe investment might be reconciled by contracting the investment function out to qualified private financial institutions, while applying strong regulatory guidelines to their activities to minimize investment risk. To ensure an adequate degree of competition without compromising the quality of the investment function, the responsible government agency could ask for bids from a group of institutions that had first been vetted for their accounting and financial control procedures and other relevant attributes. Transparency in accounting would be a *sine qua non*.

Many technical issues would have to be addressed before such a scheme could be successfully launched. The monies transferred from the individual accounts under private management would need to be held by a separate legal entity, and not be part of the general assets of the managing financial institutions. These funds would be held in the name of the responsible public agency, and not in the names of individual account holders (see Burtless (2001) for an illuminating discussion of these and related issues).

MAKING THE VOLUNTARY PRIVATE ANNUITY MARKET MORE EFFICIENT AND RELIABLE

Measures can be taken to make private annuity markets more efficient, and allow them to play a greater role in providing a secure source of income for older people. What should be done clearly depends on the country concerned – and in particular on the role that the public pension is expected to play in providing retirement income, on how developed are its financial markets, and on how sophisticated its regulatory agencies.

The reader is perhaps persuaded by this point that private annuity markets worldwide are not playing the role they might or should play. However, public pensions are waning in importance, and the inhibiting effects of adverse selection or misunderstanding of an annuity's properties can be mitigated. What follows are a series of measures to address what are essentially failures of the private annuity market.

Addressing Informational Failures (Asymmetric Information)

Since annuities are not well understood, there is a case for providing more information about them, provided that the information is comprehensive, reliable, and clear. The basic public policy issue is whether private financial institutions, left to their own devices, will supply reliable information in sufficient quantity. As Chapter 3 has noted, the websites of annuity providers and other institutions in countries like U.S., UK, and Canada do provide a great deal of information.

The case for the public supply of information on financial products (as distinct from the case for the regulation of the private supply of such information) rests on the assumption that the social benefit to additional information exceeds its private benefit. The private financial institution cannot capture all the benefits society gains from the information it disseminates. For example, a potential client may benefit from reading an informative brochure and then take his custom to a business rival.

The advent of the internet has, however, revolutionized the economics of information. The possibility that the information that one seller of annuities provides on its products may increase demand for the products of its rivals remains, but the cost of providing the information has fallen to close to zero at the margin. Anyone with access to the web and a basic understanding of how to search it will not lack for information on annuities (or much else).

But that still leaves some important questions unanswered. The people who need to find out about annuities may not be making the effort. Some varieties of annuities (or other financial products) may be so complex that no amount of public education will make most people able to make an informed choice. It is difficult to make an informed choice about annuities without being reasonably well-informed about other financial instruments. Chapter 5 raised the possibility that a "lack of understanding" may not result from a lack of information, but rather — even in the case of people of normal intelligence — from a propensity to make bad financial choices.

A government wishing to ensure that those of its citizens who were approaching retirement received the information they needed to make a more informed decision could, at comparatively modest expense, design a public website that would set out the basic issues that potential annuitants would have to understand. It would be worthwhile devoting substantial resources to ensuring the website was as easy to navigate as possible. The websites of the Central Provident Fund of Singapore and the Chilean Superintendency, although they were not created solely to provide this kind of public information, could serve as models in certain respects. Depending on the size of the annuity provider or life insurance industry, the website could also serve as a way of both stimulating competition among annuity providers and reducing the costs of search to the potential annuitant.

A detailed treatment of how such a website could be organized and what it should contain would take many pages, and is in any case beyond the book's scope. However, several observations are called for. First, and perhaps most important, the website would have to explain very clearly when the purchase of an annuity was *not* in a person's interest. The website should not be seen as drumming up business for life insurance companies. Second, and related to the first, a decision to annuitize should ideally be taken as a part of an overall retirement financing plan. Third, if the government is going to encourage (or not discourage) the provision of indexed annuities, the website should explain carefully why the initial payments of these instruments are below those of a nominal annuity, and why they can be expected to rise above them.

Setting up and maintaining a website along the lines that the book proposes could go some way to assisting informed choice. However, it also has to be recognized that even in rich countries not everyone has access to the internet, and that access rates will tend to decline with average income levels. Consequently, governments would need to continue to make use of more traditional modes of communication like the mail.

Even the best-designed communications strategy will not obviate the need to regulate the information that private financial institutions provide. Chapter 3 noted that the consumer protection is normally the responsibility of a regional or local government. However, if the financial industry is organized on a national scale, it is worth considering assigning responsibility for the regulation of information to retail customers to the same authority that regulates the insurance business. Assigning this responsibility to a centralized agency would require that it be able to handle efficiently inquiries and complaints from anyone in the country.

Measures to Avoid Systematic Bad Choices (Lessons from Behavioral Finance)

The earlier chapters have noted the shift in employer-provided pensions in the United States and other countries from defined-benefit to defined contributions. Distributions from defined contributions plans are typically lump sum. The same is usually true of tax-favored retirement savings plans – there is generally no requirement to annuitize. Tax-favored saving or retirement plans are normally voluntary; participation in an employer-provided defined-contribution plan may or may not be, although the employee is not, of course, legally bound to work for that particular employer. Evidence of a strong tendency for ill-considered investment choices (i.e. choices during the accumulation phase) by participants in defined contribution plans have led to proposals that employers be encouraged or required to promote conservative asset allocations (mainly cash and bonds) as default choices for their participants. By these means, employees are encouraged, but not obliged to make prudent investment choices.

A similar policy could be implemented for the distribution or payout stage of both employer-provided plans and tax-favored plans. For example, a participant in an employee plan might, unless he or she explicitly chooses otherwise, agree that if he separates from the company with some minimum number of years of service at some threshold age — for example, 60 years — that distributions would take the form of a life annuity that might be single or joint, depending on his family status. The choice could always be revoked.

In light of the growing importance of defined contributions plans provided by the employer, there is a strong case for providing at least a basic education in retirement finances at the work-place. In a number of countries, many larger companies already provide training or seminars along these lines. But there is undoubtedly room to increase the effort. D'Ambrosio (2003) surveys a limited literature on financial education provided by the employer and finds that its main conclusion is that it can increase retirement saving, and potentially alter the way savings are invested. Reporting on a survey of the effects of a program of financial seminars, she finds that it has a substantial impact on the apparent intentions of participants, and a lesser but still positive impact on their actions. In some countries, it would be worth exploring whether it might be possible to make a pension plan's tax-favored status — if it has one — dependent on the plan sponsor's offering basic financial education.

In the case of tax-favored plans, in addition to encouraging a default setting, the government could provide an additional inducement in the form of a preferential rate of tax on distributions taking the form of an annuity. The budgetary cost of such an inducement to annuitization would have to be carefully reckoned. Tax-advantaged retirement saving plans have traditionally been justified on the grounds that they mitigate the distortive effects of income tax on saving, and that saving tends to be insufficient in any case because people are short-sighted. Favorable tax treatment of annuities can be justified for similar reasons — as the book has discussed, problems of control arise with lump-sum distributions that do not arise with annuities.

A further step may be taken, which emphasizes more the "paternalism" in libertarian paternalism than it does the "libertarian". This step involves inviting plan participants to lock into an annuity some years in advance of retirement, under certain conditions, and is discussed below.

Mitigating Adverse Selection

As Chapter 1 discusses, the effects of adverse selection on market size are uncertain, although there is good reason to believe that it reduces demand for annuities by the less well off. The welfare of groups that are on the whole more vulnerable than the population at large would be enhanced if adverse selection is reduced. If Diamond (2004) is right in conjecturing that its persistence reflects an unwillingness of insurance companies to set up a rating system, then the natural growth of the market that aging can be expected to bring in its train may reduce it (although some threshold market size might have to be reached for this to happen). In the United States, a change in the laws that would allow insurance companies to charge African Americans a lower premium than other Americans could have a similar effect. The book makes no judgment about whether this is either likely or desirable from the point of view of social policy.

Another possible remedy is inspired by the study by Palmon and Spivak (2002). They emphasize the origin of adverse selection in the asymmetry of information on the two sides of the market: annuitants have a better idea about their longevity than insurance companies do. However, if the commitment to annuitization can be made early in the annuitant's life, the asymmetry is greatly reduced, if not eliminated. The reason for the reduction is that young people do not normally have a good idea of their conditional life expectancy at the age of retirement. Consequently, any device that can secure a commitment from annuitants well before they are likely to retire might reduce adverse selection.

In principle, for example, participants in an employer-provided defined contributions plan might make a commitment at a relatively early age to annuitize a minimum proportion — for example, 50 percent — of the accumulated balance in their plan when they separate from the company, provided their age exceeds some specified threshold. It would probably be necessary to add the condition that the premium per dollar of regular income could not exceed some specified value.

Such a commitment device would not necessarily eliminate adverse selection. A choice — to commit or not to commit — is still involved, and those who make the commitment might tend to be far-sighted or long-lived people. Nonetheless, it would, in principle reduce the potential role of adverse selection. In addition, the more employees of a company who opted for annuitization — either by choice at the end of the working period or because they had committed to annuitization some years earlier — the better the terms the company could obtain for them in purchasing annuities.

Taxation

Chapter 7 explains that the appropriate tax treatment of annuities, as with any distribution of unearned income, depends on how the principal — the premium – is taxed, and on the model adopted for the taxation of income from capital. Under the classical income tax model, for example, the funding might be from after-tax dollars, which means that the principal component of the income from the annuity should not be taxed. If the funding were deductible from taxable income, both interest and principal should be taxed.

Whatever the tax model, and whatever degree of preferential tax treatment is accorded to annuities, the less complex the tax regime the more popular are the annuities likely to be. One unattractive feature of U.S. taxation is that the effective tax rate on the regular annuity payment increases abruptly once the annuitant outlives the life expectancy that the IRS regulations apply to him or her. In addition to the increasing tax burden, the calculation of the part of the regular payment that should be included in adjusted gross income must be burdensome for many people, and lacking an intuitive explanation.

General Regulatory Issues

The basic issue – what model: direct or indirect control? – is settled for most OECD countries, although some countries still rely on quantitative restrictions on portfolio allocation. Are these systems up to dealing with a much larger voluntary annuity market, and what are the weak links in their regulatory apparatus? If history is any guide, the money that annuitants have entrusted to life insurance companies should be pretty safe. Instances of life insurance company failure in industrialized countries are few, and there is apparently only one instance where annuitants received less than 100 cents on the dollar, and that for a comparatively short time. Nonetheless, the increased complexity of the business of life insurers means that generalizations from past experience are more hazardous than usual. The increased complexity of the business requires increased sophistication on the part of the regulator.

One regulatory improvement that some countries need to consider would be the adoption of a more sophisticated approach to testing for solvency – i.e. the risk-based capital model that Chapter 3 described, supplemented with the use of stress tests and simulations with models. Although not all regulators will wish to rely on a model-based assessment of the riskiness of a portfolio of assets and liabilities, it will be essential that regulators be as adept at the use of modeling techniques as their regulatory charges. A related issue is provisioning, although this cuts both ways. Too lax a requirement can encourage excessively risky funding, while too strict a requirement means that the regulation is tantamount to an onerous tax on the provision of annuities (or on some other life insurance product).

A generous public guarantee for the voluntary annuity market would be as unwise as a guarantee on mandatory annuities. A preferable device for increasing the security of this source of retirement income, which might be feasible for some countries, would be to give annuitants a higher ranking in the pecking order of company creditors in the event of financial distress or bankruptcy. If the regular payments under an annuity contract are indeed bond-like, they might be granted a legal status next to bonds.

This book began with a capsule history of annuities. This remarkable financial instrument has been around in one form or another for many centuries. The fact that the public sectors of all industrialized and many middle-income countries essentially came to monopolize the provision of life annuities is an indirect testimony to the importance of these instruments in providing secure income in retirement.

The grip of public pension systems on the annuity market is now loosening. Perhaps the next chapter in the history of annuities will relate a story of flourishing and well-regulated markets that play a vital role in providing a secure retirement to an aging global population, either as an integral part of individual accounts systems, in much enlarged voluntary markets, or even in a combination of the two.

Appendix 1: The Economics and Financing of Annuities

INTRODUCTION

The text's discussion of the economics of annuities avoids the use of mathematics. This expository device makes the text more readable, but in the eyes of some readers may also diminish the rigor of its arguments. Appendix 1 will use simple models, and in particular a two-period life cycle model to demonstrate that the text's propositions may be rigorously derived. The mathematical demands it makes on the reader do not go much beyond basic calculus. Walliser (2001) is an excellent reference for the economics of annuities.

A TWO-PERIOD MODEL

We assume that potential annuity purchasers may live for as long as two periods. We may think of the first period as working life, and the second as retirement. Everyone lives for at least one period, but some persons die before the second period starts. In the first period, a person earns income, and in the second, if he or she is still alive, must live off his savings from the first period. He may save (i.e. transfer consumption to period two) in one of two ways: by buying a bond, or by buying an annuity. People know they may not survive to the second period.

To begin with, we assume that potential annuitants do not wish to leave a legacy, and that the only uncertainty confronting them is the date of their death. They do not need to plan for unexpected contingencies in the second period, such as ill-health, and the attendant costly medical care. These simplifying assumptions are relaxed subsequently.

People's decisions on how much to consume in the first period and save for the second are based on a "constant relative risk aversion" or CRRA utility function. Equation (A.1.1), where C stands for consumption and U for utility, is the one-period version of the function. The role of the coefficient γ is explained below.

$$U = \frac{C^{1-\gamma} - 1}{1 - \gamma} \qquad \text{(A.1.1)}$$

Economists assume that one of the main influences on how much people will save for old age is their perception of the tradeoff involved in saving more now, and consuming more later. Imagine for the sake of argument that people were indifferent about when consumption takes place: a dollar more in period one (working life) is valued as much as a dollar more in period two (retirement). If this were so, they would have no reason to save. However, people normally prefer eating two hamburgers today and two tomorrow to eating four today and none tomorrow. Even if they can afford to buy four hamburgers today, they will save enough to spread their consumption over two days. Consequently, economists assume that past a certain point, the more that is consumed in period one (and the less that is saved for period two) the greater the cost in welfare. In mathematical terms, the first derivative of Eq. (A.1.1) declines as C increases, which is the case when, as we assume, γ is greater than one:

$$\frac{dU}{dC} = C^{-\gamma} \qquad \text{(A.1.2)}$$

The ratio of the second derivative to the first derivative of U with respect to consumption is a measure of how rapidly marginal utility declines as consumption increases. That ratio is:

$$\frac{d^2U}{dC^2} \bigg/ \frac{dU}{dC} = \frac{-\gamma}{C} \qquad \text{(A.1.3)}$$

The coefficient γ is known as the Arrow-Pratt coefficient of relative risk aversion. As Eq. (A.1.3) shows, at a given level of consumption, the greater the value of γ, the more rapid is the decline in utility for a given decline in consumption, and the less rapid is its increase for a given increase. The greater the value of γ, the greater the loss (or the lesser the gain) in utility from transferring consumption from period one to period two.

In the first period, a person chooses his level of consumption for period one, and then allocates the rest of his income to the purchase of either a simple life annuity, in the amount A or a bond in the amount B. With these assumptions, annuities are effectively one-period bonds that pay the annuitant a gross return of $1 + r_A$, if he survives to the second period, and zero if he does not. Thus, if the value of the annuity purchased is 100 and r_A equals 0.60, the gross rate of return is 1.60 or 160 percent and the annuitant receives 160 in the second period (a high value for the return is chosen because the period over which the annuity would be invested would be several decades). The gross rate of return to a bond is $1 + r_B$.

In making his decision about how much to consume in period one, a person takes into account the probability he will survive to the second period, denoted by p_S (for survival probability). The utility he gains from consumption in the second period is also discounted by a factor β ($0 \le \beta \le 1$) to reflect a natural tendency to discount to some extent the need to provision for the future. (This is usually referred to as the subjective discount factor; the closer β is to one, the lesser the future is discounted.) A person maximizes the sum of the utility he expects to enjoy in the two periods, but discounts period two utility by the factor $\beta \cdot p_S$, as shown in Eq. (A.1.4). In other words, the lesser the probability of survival, and the greater the subjective discount factor (the lesser the value of β), the lesser the weight that second period consumption receives.

$$\text{Max } V = \frac{C_1^{1-\gamma} - 1}{1 - \gamma} + \frac{p_S \cdot \beta(C_2^{1-\gamma} - 1)}{1 - \gamma} \qquad (A.1.4)$$

In the first period, a person makes a decision to maximize V, the sum of the expected utility from consumption in the first and second periods, subject to the following constraints:

$$\begin{aligned} (W - C_1 - A) \cdot (1 + r_B) + A \cdot (1 + r_A) &\ge C_2 \quad \text{or} \\ (W - C_1) \cdot (1 + r_B) + A \cdot (r_A - r_B) &\ge C_2 \end{aligned} \qquad (A.1.5)$$

$$W - C_1 = A + B \qquad (A.1.6)$$

$$A, B \ge 0 \qquad (A.1.7)$$

The term $W - C_1 - A$ is equal to the value of bonds purchased. Equation (A.1.5) states that the gross return from investing in bonds plus the gross return from investing in annuities must be at least as great as second period consumption. Equation (A.1.6) states simply that the sum of the value of annuities and bonds purchased in period one equals total savings in period one. In addition, the value of annuities and bonds purchased cannot be negative (Eq. (A.1.7)).

Equation (A.1.5) can be interpreted as a strict equality, since it is clear that utility would not be maximized if savings plus its return exceeded consumption in the second period. Since we assume that r_A is greater than r_B, no one would hold bonds. This allows us to substitute for C_2 using Eqs. (A.1.5) and (A.1.6) in Eq. (A.1.4), which gives the Eq. (A.1.8).

$$\text{Max } V = \frac{C_1^{1-\gamma} - 1}{1 - \gamma} + \frac{p_S \cdot \beta \cdot [\{(W - C_1) \cdot (1 + r_A)\}^{1-\gamma} - 1]}{1 - \gamma} \qquad \text{(A.1.8)}$$

Differentiating Eq. (A.1.8) with respect to C_1, and setting equal to zero gives:

$$C_1^{-\gamma} + p_S \cdot \beta \cdot \{(W - C_1) \cdot (1 + r_A)\}^{-\gamma} \cdot (-1) \cdot (1 + r_A) = 0 \qquad \text{(A.1.9)}$$

With some rearranging, Eq. (A.1.9) becomes:

$$(W - C_1) / C_1 = (1 + r_A)^{1 - \gamma/\gamma} (p_S \cdot \beta)^{1/\gamma} \qquad \text{(A.1.10)}$$

By inspecting Eq. (A.1.10), we see that increases in the probability of survival p_S, and in the value of the subjective discount factor β both increase the right-hand side. Consequently, increases in these variables require that C_1 decline to increase the left-hand side of Eq. (A.10) to maintain the equality. The decline in C_1 is intuitively justifiable: the greater the probability of survival to period two, the greater the need for saving in period one; and the higher the value of β, the less the future is subjectively discounted. An increase in the annuity interest rate increases consumption in both periods; in addition to making consumption in period two less expensive relative to consumption in period one, it has an income effect that boosts consumption in both periods. With some manipulation, it can be shown that if $p_S \beta (1 + r_A) > 1$, then an increase in γ will shift consumption back from period two to period one, and conversely. The intuition for this result is that when $p_S \beta (1 + r_A) > 1$, consumption will be back loaded ($C_2 > C_1$). In this circumstance, the increase in γ has a more depressing effect on the marginal utility of period two consumption than on period one consumption.

Appendix 1

BEQUESTS, LUMPY EXPENDITURE, AND OTHER COMPLICATIONS

Bequests

The basic result of the simple model is that if annuities have a conditional return (i.e. the return assuming the annuitant survives) that is greater than that of bonds, they will dominate bonds as an investment. No one would buy bonds. However, this result depends on some extreme assumptions and in particular on the assumption that people do not wish to leave a bequest, and are concerned only about their own consumption. We now assume that potential annuitants may wish to leave a bequest (or a gift if they survive) in period two.[1] This bequest motive is introduced by including the variable H, for the size of the bequest (inheritance) in the utility function, as in Eq. (A.1.11), where D is a constant:

$$V = \frac{C_1^{1-\gamma} - 1}{1 - \gamma} + p_S \cdot \beta \frac{C_2^{1-\gamma} - 1}{1 - \gamma} + D \cdot H^\alpha \qquad (A.1.11)$$

Equation (A.1.11) is then maximized, subject to these constraints:

$$W - C_1 = B + A$$
$$H = B(1 + r_B) \qquad (A.1.12)$$
$$C_2 = A(1 + r_A)$$

By substituting for A and B in these three constraints, they can be reduced to one:

$$\left(W - C_1 - \frac{H}{1 + r_B} - \frac{C_2}{1 + r_A} \right) = 0 \qquad (A.1.13)$$

Instead of devoting all his savings to the purchase of an annuity, a person splits them between the purchase of a bond and an annuity. Consumption continues to be financed by an annuity.

The Lagrangian corresponding to Eqs. (A.1.11) and (A.1.13) is:

$$L = V - \lambda \left[W - C_1 - \frac{H}{(1 + r_B)} - \frac{C_2}{(1 + r_A)} \right] \qquad (A.1.14)$$

---

[1] See Jousten (2001), for a richer model which includes constraints on the ability to borrow on the strength of future income.

The first-order conditions are:

$$\frac{\delta L}{\delta C_1} = \frac{\delta V}{\delta C_1} + \lambda = 0$$

$$\frac{\delta L}{\delta C_2} = \frac{\delta V}{\delta C_2} + \frac{\lambda}{(1 + r_A)} = 0 \qquad (A.1.15)$$

$$\frac{\delta L}{\delta H} = \frac{\delta V}{\delta H} + \frac{\lambda}{1 + r_B} = 0$$

These conditions imply the following relationship:

$$\frac{\delta V}{\delta C_1} = \frac{\delta V}{\delta C_2}(1 + r_A) = \frac{\delta V}{\delta H}(1 + r_B) \qquad (A.1.16)$$

The equalities of Eq. (A.1.16) have a straightforward interpretation, which is that the size of the bequest or gift is set so that at the margin the person is indifferent between setting aside another dollar for the bequest; spending another dollar in period one; and spending another dollar plus interest in period two. Turning back to the utility function (A.1.11), it may be seen that the greater the value of D, the coefficient and α, the exponent on the bequest term in the utility function, the lesser the person will devote to consumption in either period one or period two, and the smaller will be the annuity that he will buy. Introducing or enhancing a bequest motive should reduce consumption in both periods.

It may seem paradoxical that a person who wishes to leave a bequest, and possibly a large one, should buy an annuity. One can imagine the heirs worrying about the waste if the annuitant dies prematurely. However, assuming that the utility attached to the bequest declines as it gets larger, an annuitant who is indifferent between allocating one additional dollar to a certain bequest or one dollar to consumption should finance the consumption with a larger annuity, and not a larger bond, because the return to the annuity is higher ($r_A > r_B$). Assuming the person does survive to period two, he maximizes his consumption in that period by annuitizing that part of his wealth which he intends to devote to consumption.

The analysis assumes that the annuitant is concerned with the amount of his estate that will pass with certainty to his heirs, and not with the maximum *possible* value. By choosing not to annuitize any of his wealth, the annuitant maximizes only the value he will leave if he dies prematurely, not the expected value of his estate.

One way of dealing with the risk that the annuitant's premature death will deplete his estate is to buy a certain and life annuity. The option of a certain and life annuity is superficially attractive, because even if the annuitant dies shortly after signing the contract, his estate will continue to receive an income from the annuity for some time. If the annuitant is concerned with the actual size of the bequest, however, and not with the maximum size he might leave if he dies unexpectedly early, it is an inferior option (Brown (2001)).

This conclusion may be derived by making a comparison between an immediate life annuity and the certain and life annuity. In our first model, however, there are only two periods, and it is obvious that investing in a bond as opposed to an annuity reduces either consumption in retirement or the size of the retired person's estate, or both.

The same result holds if we extend life in retirement to T periods. Following Brown, the premium per dollar of a certain and life annuity (PPDCLA) can be decomposed into two components: a fixed interest investment with a maturity of N, where N is the period over which payments are made whether the annuitant survives or not, and a deferred life annuity, with the first payment beginning $N+1$ years from now:

$$\text{PPDCLA} = \sum_{i=1}^{N} \frac{1}{(1 + r_B)^i} + \sum_{i=N+1}^{T} \frac{1}{(1 + r_A)^i} \qquad (A.1.17)$$

The premium per dollar of a life annuity (PPDA) can also be decomposed into two terms of the same length each, where r_A is the annuity's conditional rate of return, which is assumed constant and exceeds the rate of return on fixed-interest securities, r_B:

$$\text{PPDA} = \sum_{i=1}^{N} \frac{1}{(1 + r_A)^i} + \sum_{i=N+1}^{T} \frac{1}{(1 + r_A)^i} \qquad (A.1.18)$$

The second terms of each expression are equal, but the value of the first term of the certain and life annuity exceeds the first term of the life annuity, because $r_B < r_A$.[2] Hence, by buying a certain and life annuity, the annuitant,

---

[2] It is not necessary to assume that both r_A and r_B are constant, and that $r_A > r_B$. If both rates vary, it is enough to assume that $\sum_{i=1}^{N} 1/(1 + r_{Bi}) - \sum_{i=1}^{N} 1/(1 + r_{Ai}) > 0$.

if he survives the first N years, either has to consume less or encroach more on his wealth than he would have had he bought the immediate life annuity.

It may be that some people are targeting the *expected* value of their bequest, and are prepared to tolerate some uncertainty about the actual amount. For example, they may plan their affairs on the assumption that the length of their postretirement life will equal their conditional life expectancy at retirement. The assets they have left at this point are then bequeathed to their heirs. In contrast with the strategy just described, this strategy implies that the size of the bequest will be larger, the shorter the person's postretirement life, and conversely.

In practice, what this strategy would entail is making a bigger investment in bonds, and a smaller investment in annuities, with the idea of maintaining or increasing postretirement consumption by encroaching on the investment in bonds should the person live longer than expected. Using the two-period framework, it can be shown that provided the annuity is actuarially fair, this strategy will not increase consumption. It increases consumption only if the annuity is actuarially unfair, the increase being greater the less actuarially fair the annuity is.

The bequest, H_0, can be expressed as follows, where A_0 is the value of the annuity purchased on the assumption that it will finance all second-period consumption (C_2):

$$H_0 = (W - C_1 - A_0)(1 + r_B) \qquad (A.1.19)$$

Now let us suppose that the retired person wants to ensure that the value of the expected bequest $E(H)$ equals the value given by Eq. (A.1.19):

$$
\begin{aligned}
E(H) &= (W - C_1 - A_0)(1 + r_B) \\
&= (1 - p_S)(W - C_1 - A)(1 + r_B) \\
&\quad + p_S[(W - C_1 - A)(1 + r_B) - C_2 + A(1 + r_A)] \\
&= (W - C_1 - A)(1 + r_B) + p_S(A(1 + r_A) - C_2)
\end{aligned}
\qquad (A.1.20)
$$

Eliminating W and C_1 results in the expression (A.1.21):

$$-A_0(1 + r_B) = -A(1 + r_B) + p_S(A(1 + r_A) - C_2) \qquad (A.1.21)$$

Rearranging, and solving for C_2,

$$C_2 = A(1 + r_A) + (A_0 - A)(1 + r_B)/p_S \qquad (A.1.22)$$

Noting that actuarial fairness implies that $p_S(1 + r_A) = (1 + r_B)$, Eq. (A.1.22) shows that, although the value of the annuity that would be chosen to equate the expected bequest with the certain bequest is not unique, C_2 would be the same, being equal to $A_0 (1 + r_A)$. In other words, second-period consumption cannot be increased even if the retired person is willing to forego certainty, and be content with leaving a bequest with the same *expected* value as he would leave if he wanted to ensure a certain bequest of the same amount. If actuarial fairness does not hold (it cannot in practice, for all the reasons the book has explored), then a decrease in the value of A and an offsetting increase in holdings of bonds for a given level of C_1 either increases C_2 or the expected value of the inheritance. With the difference between the conditional return to the annuity and the return to the bond having declined, the higher conditional return to the annuity is no longer enough to compensate for the possible loss in inheritable wealth if the annuitant dies prematurely.

The intuition behind the result that actuarial fairness achieves no increase in second-period consumption, even if the retired person is prepared to leave a bequest of an uncertain amount, is that buying a smaller annuity and investing in bonds does increase the value of the estate if the person dies relatively young, but at a substantial cost in terms of a reduced bequest if the person does not die young.

Life Insurance

Saving is not the only way to leave a bequest. The same end can be achieved by a combination of term life insurance and an annuity. We make the simplifying assumption that both life insurance and life annuities are issued on actuarially fair terms. That is, if a person has a 20 percent chance of dying in a period, then life insurance for that period will cost 20 cents on the dollar. More generally, the relationship between premium (PR_{LI}) and value of the policy (LI) is given by Eq. (A.1.23), where p_S is the probability of surviving to the next period:

$$PR_{LI} = (1 - p_S) \cdot LI/(1 + r_B) \qquad \text{(A.1.23)}$$

Making a similar assumption for an annuity, the relationship between the premium, A, and the payment AP is given by Eq. (A.1.24), where AP equals $(1 + r_A)A$:

$$A = p_S \cdot AP/(1 + r_B) \qquad \text{(A.1.24)}$$

Given these assumptions, a person can leave a bequest of H dollars by buying term life insurance for $(1-p_S) \cdot H/(1 + r_B)$ dollars, and by buying an annuity that will pay H dollars in period two, if he stays alive, for $H \cdot p_S/(1 + r_B)$ dollars.[3] If he dies before period two, his heirs cash in on the life insurance; if he lives, he has an annuity of equivalent value to give to his heirs. Effectively, term life insurance is like a contingent bond that pays only if the holder dies; as we have seen, the annuity is a contingent bond that pays only when the holder lives. Holding one of each bond, each with a payoff of H in period two can be expected to cost $H/(1 + r_B)$ in period one, assuming costless financial intermediation, since the probability of occurrence of one of the two events must be 100 percent.

This example illustrates how life insurance can be used to offset the impact of involuntary or mandatory annuitization on the size of bequests. How complete the offset is must depend on the terms of the life insurance and the annuity.

Lumpy Expenditure

An annuity is ideally suited to financing the regular, predictable expenses of daily life. However, people need to be prepared to finance irregular and large expenditures, unless these are covered by insurance. In any event, insurance typically does not cover 100 percent of the expenses associated with a contingency. It is difficult to portray this real-life situation in the two-period model. One simple way of doing it is to assume that a person confronts a second source of uncertainty in addition to mortality. Specifically, if he does survive to period two he may face unpredictable contingencies for which he will need a fixed sum of money.

We model the possibility of such nonroutine expenditures by assuming that the probability that a person who lives to period two and has to pay the contingent expenditures is p_L, and the probability that a person who lives to period two but will not have to pay the extra expenditures is p_H. To keep the model simple bequests are dropped. (The variables β and p_S are defined as before.) The expenditure may be thought of as medically necessary expenditure — we assume that there is no trade-off between this and the other expenditure. We also assume that the individual saves at least enough in the first period to cover the medical expenditure, $\bar{M}$, and that the funds saved for this purpose are invested in a bond. This assumption

---

[3] Given the model's assumptions, it is not possible to get insurance for the second period, since the probability of death rises to 100 percent.

is necessary because the model has two periods. Because the medical expenditures can be incurred only if the individual is alive, it would be optimal for him to finance them with an annuity. In real life, relying on an annuity would not be feasible, because the expenditures might be very large in relation to annual income.

The function to be maximized is expressed as Eq. (A.1.25), subject to the constraints expressed by Eq. (A.1.26).

$$V = U(C_1) + \beta p_S[p_H U(C_{2H}) + p_L U(C_{2L})] \qquad (A.1.25)$$

$$
\begin{aligned}
C_{2L} - (1 + r_A) \cdot [(W - C_1 - \bar{M}/(1 + r_B)] = 0 \\
C_{2H} - C_{2L} - \bar{M} = 0
\end{aligned}
\qquad (A.1.26)
$$

The Lagrangian is given by:

$$
\begin{aligned}
L = V - \lambda_1[C_{2L} - (1 + r_A) \cdot [(W - C_1 - \bar{M}/(1 + r_B)] \\
- \lambda_2[C_{2H} - C_{2L} - \bar{M}]
\end{aligned}
\qquad (A.1.27)
$$

The first order conditions are:

$$\frac{\delta U}{\delta C_1} - \lambda_1(1 + r_A) = 0$$

$$\beta p_S p_H \cdot \frac{\delta U}{\delta C_{2H}} - \lambda_2 = 0 \qquad (A.1.28)$$

$$\beta p_S p_L \cdot \frac{\delta U}{\delta C_{2L}} - \lambda_1 + \lambda_2 = 0$$

From the first order conditions it may be seen that:

$$\frac{\delta U/\delta C_1}{1 + r_A} = \beta p_S \left[p_H \cdot \frac{\delta U}{\delta C_{2H}} + p_L \cdot \frac{\delta U}{\delta C_{2L}} \right] \qquad (A.1.29)$$

If $\bar{M}$ is increased, and C_1 is unchanged, then C_{2L} has to decline. C_{2H} declines as well because less period one saving is devoted to purchasing an annuity. Restoring equilibrium requires a decrease in C_1 and C_{2L}, and C_{2H}. More generally, the more a person has to put aside for unpredictable but necessary expenditures in period two, the less he will (or should) consume in either period.

Competing Assets: Residential Investment

The home competes with the annuity as an investment for the older person. For many reasons, the competition is an unequal one. Someone who already owns a home or who has the capital to finance the purchase of one makes a choice between owning and renting. That choice is undoubtedly influenced by much more than dollars and cents. However, even if we assume that pride of ownership plays no role in the decision, it is relatively straightforward to show that the favored tax treatment that home ownership enjoys in many countries will tip the scales in favor of buying.

Demonstrating this proposition in a way that does justice to all aspects of the housing market would be very involved. However, the basic idea can be illustrated by a simple two-period model, for which we assume that the rate of interest r that the homeowner pays on his mortgage is the same as the rate that the landlord pays for his funds.

The homeowner who sells his property at retirement can use the proceeds of the sale (V_0) to defray a stream of rental payments R assumed to be made in the first period. The value of his net outlays (PVO_{HO}) is given by:

$$PVO_{HO} = -V_0 + R \qquad (A.1.30)$$

If PVO_{HO} is greater than the value of net outlays associated with home ownership, then owning is preferable to renting. In economic terms, the homeowner is a landlord who rents to himself, and the purchase of a house is an investment like any other.

Assuming that the landlord pays tax at the rate t on his net income including capital gains, the discounted present value of the net outflows (PVO_{LL}) the landlord incurs when he invests in and rents out a property during period one and then sells it in period two for the amount V_1 may be expressed as:[4]

$$PVO_{LL} = V_0 - (1 - t)(R - C) + (t(V_1 - V_0) - V_1)/(1 + r) \qquad (A.1.31)$$

---

[4] This formulation assumes that interest costs are not deductible and they are not included in the maintenance costs represented by the variable C. Mortgage interest deductibility, which in countries like the United States benefits both investor and owner occupier, would lower the gross rent the investor would have to charge to earn a given after-tax rate of return, but would not alter the relative advantage of owning relative to renting.

If PVO_{LL} equals zero, so that the landlord earns an after-tax rate of return of r, then the value of rental payments will be:

$$R = C + V_0/(1 - t) + (t(V_1 - V_0) - V_1)/(1 - t)(1 + r) \qquad (A.1.32)$$

This allows us to express the present value of the homeowner turned renter's net outlays as:

$$\begin{aligned} PVO_{HO} &= C + [(1 + r)tV_0 + (t(V_1 - V_0) - V_1)]/(1 - t)(1 + r) \\ &= C + \frac{rtV_0 - (1 - t)V_1}{(1 + r)(1 - t)} \end{aligned}$$

$$(A.1.33)$$

Had the homeowner hung on to the house, selling it in the second period and incurring the same maintenance costs, his net outlay would have been:

$$PVO'_{HO} = C - V_1/(1 + r) \qquad (A.1.34)$$

The difference between PVO_{HO} and PVO'_{HO} is positive, and is given by:

$$PVO_{HO} - PVO'_{HO} = \frac{rtV_0}{(1 - t)(1 + r)} \qquad (A.1.35)$$

The difference stems entirely from the tax exemption enjoyed by the imputed rental income (and in this case capital gains) of a homeowner and varies with the rate of tax, t.

Competing Assets: Risky Financial Assets

The earlier analysis assumed that the annuitant faced a choice between annuities and bonds, and that the contingent rate of return of the annuity exceeded the yield of the bond. This section uses a simple model to show how the demand for annuities might be affected by this sort of competition from a risky asset with a higher rate of return.

To keep the model as simple as possible, it is assumed that the risky asset yields a high return, r_H with probability p_H, and a low return of r_L with probability $(1 - p_H)$ or p_L. Using again a more general form of the utility function, the function to be maximized can be expressed as follows, where the symbols β and p_S stand again for the discount factor and survival probability, and C^H and C^L stand for consumption in the high and low return states.

$$V = U(C_1) + \beta p_S[p_H \cdot U(C_2^H) + p_L \cdot U(C_2^L)] \tag{A.1.36}$$

This expression is maximized subject to the following constraints, where W stands again for initial wealth, A for the value of annuity purchased, and r_A for its return, which is assumed to lie in between the low and high returns of the risky asset:

$$(W - C_1 - A)(1 + r_H) + A(1 + r_A) = C_2^H \text{ and} \tag{A.1.37a}$$

$$(W - C_1 - A)(1 + r_L) + A(1 + r_A) = C_2^L \tag{A.1.37b}$$

Solving for the variable A in Eq. (A.1.37b) and substituting for A in Eq. (A.1.37a), after some manipulation, yields:

$$(W - C_1)(1 + r_A) - (r_A - r_H)/(r_L - r_H)C_2^L$$
$$- (r_L - r_A)/(r_L - r_H)C_2^H = 0 \tag{A.1.38}$$

There are two additional inequality constraints, to take account of the fact that the quantity of the risky asset and the annuity cannot be less than zero (and if the constraint is satisfied exactly for one or the other, it must not be for the other):

$$C_2^L - (W - C_1)(1 + r_L) \geq 0$$
$$C_2^H - (W - C_1)(1 + r_A) \geq 0 \tag{A.1.39}$$

The Lagrangian is then:

$$L = V + \lambda_1[(W - C_1)(1 + r_A) - (r_A - r_H)/(r_L - r_H)C_2^L$$
$$-(r_L - r_A)/(r_L - r_H)C_2^H]$$
$$+ \lambda_2[C_2^L - (W - C_1)(1 + r_L)] + \lambda_3[C_2^H - (W - C_1)(1 + r_A)] \tag{A.1.40}$$

Assuming that some amount of both the risky asset and the annuity will be held, the second and third constraints will not be binding, and λ_2 and λ_3 are both equal to zero. Then, the first order conditions for a constrained maximum are:

$$\frac{\delta L}{\delta C_1} = U'(C_1) - \lambda_1(1 + r_A) = 0$$

$$\frac{\delta L}{\delta C_2^H} = \beta p_S \cdot p_H U'(C_2^H) - \lambda_1(r_L - r_A)/(r_L - r_H) = 0 \qquad (A.1.41)$$

$$\frac{\delta L}{\delta C_2^L} = \beta p_S \cdot p_L U'(C_2^L) - \lambda_1(r_A - r_H)/(r_L - r_H) = 0$$

It is then straightforward to derive Eq. (A.1.42) from the second and third necessary conditions, which combined with the first condition, yields Eq. (A.1.43)

$$\beta p_S(p_L U'(C_2^L) + p_H U'(C_2^H)) = \lambda_1 \qquad (A.1.42)$$

$$U'(C_1)/(1 + r_A) = \beta p_S(p_L U'(C_2^L) + p_H U'(C_2^H)) \qquad (A.1.43)$$

Equation (A.1.43) has a straightforward interpretation, which is that the utility at the margin from an extra unit of consumption in the first period should equal the expected utility of consumption in the second period discounted by the rate of return to the annuity. An increase in the probability of a high return should increase the share of saving devoted to the risky asset. Assuming consumption in the first period does not decline, that implies a reduction in the size of the annuity. It may be shown that Eq. (A.1.43) continues to hold if no saving is devoted to the risky asset, but does not hold if all of it is devoted to the risky asset.

Competition from the Public Pension System

The introduction of a public pension changes the budget constraint (for simplicity, we revert to the first model, and ignore bequests and lumpy expenditure). We assume that in period one a person pays a tax, $\check{T}$, and in period two, if he is still alive, receives a pension S, equal to $\check{T}(1 + r_S)$, where r_S is the implicit conditional return of the public pension system. With these assumptions, the optimization problem may be formulated as equations (A.1.44) to (A.1.47).

$$\text{Max } V = (C_1^{1-\gamma} - 1)/(1 - \gamma) + p_S \cdot \beta \cdot (C_2^{1-\gamma} - 1)/(1 - \gamma) \quad \text{(A.1.44)}$$

Subject to:

$$(W - C_1 - \check{T} - A) \cdot (1 + r_B) + S + A \cdot (1 + r_A) \geq C_2$$

$$\text{or } (W - C_1 - \check{T}) \cdot (1 + r_B) + \check{T} \cdot (1 + r_S) + A \cdot (r_A - r_B) \geq C_2 \quad \text{(A.1.45)}$$

$$W - C_1 - \check{T} = A + B \quad \text{(A.1.46)}$$

$$A, B \geq 0 \quad \text{(A.1.47)}$$

It is useful to express the implicit rate of return to the payroll tax contribution as $r_S = r_A + r_\Delta$, where r_Δ may take any value. If r_Δ equals zero, so that there is no difference between the conditional return to buying an annuity and the return to the state system, the addition of the public pension makes no difference to the result as long as $\check{T}$ is less than or equal to the value of the annuity that would have been purchased without a public pension.

Re-expressing (A.1.45), assuming that r_S equals r_A,

$$(W - C_1) \cdot (1 + r_B) + (A + \check{T}) \cdot (r_A - r_B) \geq C_2 \quad \text{(A.1.48)}$$

By comparing Eq. (A.1.5) with (A.1.45), it can be seen that if the value of A that maximizes V without the public pension is greater than $\check{T}$, then the value of the annuity $\bar{A}$ that maximizes V with the public pension will be $A - \check{T}$. In this particular case, the inclusion of a public pension has no effect on the distribution of consumption between periods or on welfare, but it leads to a one-for-one substitution of an annuity provided by the state for the private annuity. Thus, the addition of a public pension imposes no additional effective constraint.

When the rate of return to the public pension is less than the return to an annuity, as it may well be for many participants of public pension plans, the difference can be thought of as a tax, with the contribution as the base. If $\check{T}$ is constant, as we assume in this model, then lowering the rate of return to the public pension is tantamount to imposing a lump-sum tax of $r_\Delta \cdot \check{T}$ on wealth, or lowering wealth from W to $(W - r_\Delta \cdot \check{T})$. This will reduce consumption in both periods (by comparison with the situation in which r_S equals r_A), and will reduce the value of the annuity purchased.

If $\check{T}$ is sufficiently large, then the constraint preventing the value of the annuity from being negative will become binding and no annuity will be purchased. Even if the implicit rate of return to the state system equals the return to the annuity, the annuitant's welfare will be reduced by comparison with the state of the world where there was no public pension. If we respect a person's decision regarding the amount of his wealth to annuitize, then it follows that a public pension of this size entails overannuitization.

A desire to leave a bequest, the need to provide for unexpected expenditure, and the competition from the public pension can all reduce the demand for annuities, but these are not the only influences that can have that effect. Adverse selection is another important influence. Before discussing it, we will explore the cost side of the annuity market, or more generally the conditions under which they are supplied. Earlier it was noted that the conditional return to an annuity should be higher than the return on a bond, because an annuity was a contingent bond. We will now use the two-period model to analyze the relationship between r_B and r_A. Given the importance of interest rates and their term structure in the pricing of annuities, the exposition then adopts a multi-year model to capture some key features of annuity supply that the two-period model cannot handle well.

THE COST AND FUNDING OF ANNUITIES

The exposition will make the standard simplifying assumption that financial markets are perfect. This means that financial intermediation is costless (there are no commissions or sales charges, or other costs of doing business) so that borrowing and lending rates are equal. It is also assumed that an insurance company, when it sells an annuity for A invests the proceeds in bonds yielding the return r_B. In practice, insurance companies can fund annuities by investing in other financial instruments, a possibility we consider further below. The one-period probability of survival is p_S, as before, and is known to the insurance company. The insurance company is assumed to be risk neutral, which means that it is indifferent between an expected return of x percent and a certain return of x percent.

Given these assumptions, the following relationship (introduced in the section on life insurance) holds, where AP, which equals $A(1 + r_A)$, is the payment conditional on annuitants' survival:

$$A(1 + r_B) = p_S \cdot \text{AP} \qquad (\text{A.1.49})$$

As an example, suppose A equals 100, r_B equals 0.05 and p_S equals 0.5. Then r_A equals 1.10, or 110 percent. This high yield reflects the assumed survival probability of 50 percent, which implies that, for every two annuitants, only one on average lives to receive an annuity. For each pair of annuitants, the insurance company can invest 2 times 100 dollars at a rate of interest of 5 percent, allowing it to make a payout of 210 dollars to the survivor of each pair.

If the probability that one individual survives to period two is independent of the survival probabilities of other individuals (i.e. the survivals of individuals to period two are independent events), then the assumptions of risk neutrality will not be necessary for Eq. (A.1.49) to hold, at least approximately. The larger the group of annuitants on an insurance company's books, the lower the risk that it will underestimate the *average* life expectancy of its group. The law of large numbers (or a version of it) applies.[5]

We now assume that period two, the retirement period, is composed of many years. However, the exposition assumes initially that future rates of interest are known with certainty and that the only uncertainty insurance companies face is the timing of the death of individual annuitants. The longest available maturity in the bond market is at least as long as the maximum number of years an annuitant can survive in retirement.

Given these assumptions, an insurance company, provided it has enough policyholders, can predict with great accuracy the proportion of a group of them of a particular age buying an annuity that will live for a given number of years in postretirement. For example, using the estimates of Table 2.1, it could project that 1.6 percent of the men who annuitize at age 65 in 2005 will not survive to age 66; that 1.8 percent of those who survive to age 66 will not survive to age 67; that 2.0 percent of those who survive to age 67 will not survive to age 68; and so on.

Armed with this information, the insurance company then acquires a portfolio of bonds that maximizes its rate of return. In fact, because future interest rates are known with certainty, the insurance company will be indifferent as to the maturity structure of its portfolio. It has no interest-rate risk to contend with, and there is no possibility of profits from arbitrage.

---

[5] If the life expectancy of a single annuitant is x, where x is a random variable, and the variance of that life expectancy is var(x), then the variance of the average life expectancy of a cohort with n members will be var(x)/n, which approaches zero as n grows arbitrarily large.

If we relax the implausible assumption that interest rates are perfectly predictable but retain all the others, it remains the case that the insurance company can insulate itself from interest-rate fluctuations by structuring its portfolio so that it never has to sell bonds before they mature, or reinvest maturing bonds at an unpredictable interest rate. For a group of annuitants who are all of the same age (say 65 years) the insurance company faces a stream of expected future annuity payment obligations AP_1, AP_2, $AP_3, \ldots, AP_{35}$ (the subscript denotes the year that the payment is due), assuming that no annuitant lives beyond the age of 100. For a group of life annuities paying a fixed nominal regular payment, it will be the case that:

$$AP_1 > AP_2 > AP_3 \cdots > AP_{35} \qquad (A.1.50)$$

The insurance company acquires bonds of different maturities $(B_1, B_2, \ldots, B_{35})$ so that the following relationships hold, assuming that interest is paid only once a year for simplicity, and that r_i is the rate of interest on a bond that matures in i years after annuitization:

$$(1 + r_{35}) \cdot B_{35} = AP_{35}$$

$$(1 + r_{34}) \cdot B_{34} + r_{35}B_{35} = AP_{34}$$

$$(1 + r_{33}) \cdot B_{33} + r_{34}B_{34} + r_{35}B_{35} = AP_{33}$$

and so on, to

$$(1 + r_1) \cdot B_1 + \sum_{2}^{35} r_i B_i = AP_1 \qquad (A.1.51)$$

Consequently, provided the range of the maturity spectrum is long enough, and has no gaps, it would be possible for an insurance company to match its annuity liabilities perfectly by choosing an appropriately structured bond portfolio.

If the bonds are zero-coupon — so that the interest is not paid regularly but instead accumulates until the bond matures — the formula is less cumbersome. With zero-coupon bonds, the insurance company, if it wishes to avoid the risk of losses from selling bonds before they mature or reinvesting the proceeds of maturing bonds at unexpectedly low interest rates, will buy bonds of maturity i to fund the expenses on surviving annuitants i years after annuitization. The current (discounted) value of bonds maturing in i years (DB_i) will be given by Eq. (A.1.52):

$$DB_i = AP_i/(1 + r_i)^i \tag{A.1.52}$$

Generalizing the formula for the premium, PR, for a stream of payments AP_1, AP_2, ..., AP_{35} can be expressed as follows:

$$PR = \sum_{i=1}^{35} DB_i = \sum_{i=1}^{35} \frac{AP_i}{(1 + r_i)^i} \tag{A.1.53}$$

Since AP_i equals the constant regular payment if all annuitants survived, represented by Y, times the probability of survival to year i post annuitization, p_{Si}, Eq. (A.1.53) can be expressed as

$$PR = \sum_{i=1}^{35} \frac{p_{Si} Y}{(1 + r_i)^i} \tag{A.1.54}$$

With no interest-rate uncertainty, it is not possible to earn a higher return by holding long-term bonds to fund short-term obligations, even if they pay a higher rate of interest than short-term bonds. This can be most easily illustrated with zero-coupon bonds. Suppose that the initial value of a zero-coupon bond with a maturity of 5 years is given by I_{05}. The rate of interest denoted by r_{ij} is the average annual return on a bond issued in period i and maturing in period j. Arbitrage implies that $(1 + r_{0N})^N$ must equal $(1 + r_{01})(1 + r_{12}) \cdots (1 + r_{(N-1)N})$. The five-year interest rate, r_{05}, is assumed to be higher than the three-year interest rate, r_{03}, which implies that:

$$(1 + r_{05})^3 > (1 + r_{01})(1 + r_{12})(1 + r_{23}) \tag{A.1.55}$$

The return from holding the five-year bond for three years, selling it, and investing the proceeds in two one year-bonds should be equal to the return from holding the five-year bond to maturity, taking into account the proportional capital gain or loss, g, when the five-year bond is sold before maturity:

$$I_{05}(1 + r_{05})^3 \cdot (1 + g) \cdot (1 + r_{34}) \cdot (1 + r_{45}) = I_{05}(1 + r_{05})^5$$

or

$$(1 + g) \cdot (1 + r_{05})^3 = (1 + r_{01})(1 + r_{12})(1 + r_{23}) \qquad \text{(A.1.56)}$$

As Eq. (A.1.56) implies, the basic arbitrage condition requires that g be negative — that there be a capital loss — when the interest rate on five-year bonds exceeds the interest rate on three-year bonds. It may be seen that the loss will vary inversely with the ratio of $(1 + r_{03})$ to $(1 + r_{05})$.

RELAXING THE ASSUMPTIONS

Nonmatching Receipts and Payments

Chapter 2 discussed the problems entailed by nonmatching receipts and payments, and referred to immunization strategies that sought to match the *duration* of the stream of payments with the stream of receipts. A standard definition of duration is the Macaulay or M duration. The M duration of a bond making a stream of payments $P_1, P_2, \ldots, P_N$ is defined as follows, where B is the current value of the bond and r is the (assumed constant) rate of interest: $M = \frac{1}{B} t \sum_{t=1}^{N} P_t / (1 + r)^t$. De la Granville (2001, p. 75) states: "Duration has a neat physical interpretation. As a weighted average (the sum of the discounted value of the payments equals B, the value of the bond), it is none other than a center of gravity."

There is one special case, in which a stream of payments and receipts will be perfectly immunized by ensuring that the duration of the stream of receipts equals the duration of the payments. To demonstrate, we assume that payments (L_i) and receipts (A_i) are made over a period of T years, so that i takes a value from 1 to T. Let N_i be net receipts in year i, so that $N_i = A_i - L_i$. The present discounted value of payments and receipts are assumed to be equal at the initial position of the yield curve. Then the present discounted value of net receipts (S), which equals zero, is expressed as Eq. (A.1.57), where r_i is the discount rate for net receipts in year i.

$$S = N_1(1 + r_1)^{-1} + N_2(1 + r_2)^{-2} + \cdots + N_T(1 + r_T)^{-T} \qquad \text{(A.1.57)}$$

A parallel shift of the yield curve of amount δ entails a change in the surplus — S_δ is the new surplus — as expressed by Eq. (A.1.58).

$$S_\delta = N_1(1 + r_1)^{-1}(1 + \delta)^{-1} + N_2(1 + r_2)^{-2}(1 + \delta)^{-2}$$
$$+ \cdots + N_T(1 + r_T)^{-T}(1 + \delta)^{-T} \qquad \text{(A.1.58)}$$

By taking the derivative of S_δ at $\delta = 0$, and setting the derivative equal to zero, it is possible to determine the conditions under which a small shift in the yield curve has no impact on the value of the surplus (Eq. (A.1.59)):

$$\frac{dS_\delta}{d\delta} = N_1(1 + r_1)^{-1}(-1)(1 + \delta)^{-2} + N_2(1 + r_2)^{-2}(-2)(1 + \delta)^{-3}$$

$$+ \cdots + N_T(1 + r_T)^{-T}(-T)(1 + \delta)^{-T-1}$$

$$= (1 + \delta)^{-1}(-1) \sum_{t=1}^{T} t \cdot N_t(1 + r_t)^{-t}(1 + \delta)^{-t}$$

$$(A.1.59)$$

Evaluated at $\delta = 0$, Eq. (A.1.59) can be re-expressed as Eq. (A.1.60):

$$\frac{dS_\delta}{d\delta} = (-1) \sum_{t=1}^{T} t \cdot N_t(1 + r_t)^{-t} \quad \text{or}$$

$$(-1) \sum_{t=1}^{T} t \cdot (A_t - L_t)(1 + r_t)^{-t}$$

$$(A.1.60)$$

It may be seen that this expression will always equal zero when receipts and payments are perfectly matched, but also when they are not perfectly matched, provided that the M duration of receipts equals the M duration of payments. It may be shown, however, that the second derivative of Eq. (A.1.60) is positive, which means that an equal shift in the yield curve would not only not reduce the surplus, but would increase it over some interval.[6]

It will not be generally possible to immunize a stream of net receipts against a nonuniform shift in the term structure of interest rates. We can show this by assuming that the shift at each maturity is not uniform, but is instead a function of δ that is continuous but can take any form. Specifically, we assume that for maturities of one year, the shift is not δ but $a(\delta)$; for maturities of two years $b(\delta)$, and so forth. When $\delta = 0$, $a(\delta)$, $b(\delta), \ldots, \tau(\delta)$ equal zero. The value of the surplus after a shift of amount δ

---

[6] The second derivative of Eq. (A.1.58) has two terms: the summation term times $(-1)(-1)(1+\partial)^{-1}$ which is positive, and a team equal to the product of $(-1)(1+\partial)^{-1}$ and a sum of terms, all of which are negative, so that this product is positive.

is then given by Eq. (A.1.61):

$$S_\delta = N_1(1 + r_1)^{-1}(1 + a(\delta))^{-1} + N_2(1 + r_2)^{-2}(1 + b(\delta))^{-2}$$
$$+ \cdots + N_T(1 + r_T)^{-T}(1 + \tau(\delta))^{-T} \tag{A.1.61}$$

The derivative of this expression is given by Eq. (A.1.62). By inspection, unless the pattern of the shift is known in advance, it will not be possible to structure the maturity profile of net receipts so that the derivative will equal zero.

$$\frac{dS_\delta}{d\delta} = N_1(1 + r_1)^{-1}(-1)(1 + a(\delta))^{-2}a'(\delta)$$
$$+ N_2(1 + r_2)^{-2}(-2)(1 + b(\delta))^{-3}b'(\delta) + \cdots \tag{A.1.62}$$
$$+ N_T(1 + r_T)^{-T}(-T)(1 + \tau(\delta))^{-T-1}\tau'(\delta)$$

Funding with a Risky Asset

An insurance company may be able to offer cheaper annuities by funding them with a combination of bonds and other instruments. However, this strategy will increase the risks of default on annuity payments and loss to the insurer.

To analyze the consequences of a mixed portfolio strategy, we assume that annuitants may be treated like they were the holders of the debt of a financial corporation that finances its operations with a mix of debt and equity, and invests its assets in a safe low-yielding instrument like a government bond and another security with an uncertain but higher expected return. The mean and variance of the return of the risky asset, which is a random variable r_E, are μ_E and σ_E, respectively. As before, the return to the bond is r_B. We assume that the corporation's only liabilities are its annuity contracts, and that the cost of this capital is $r_{\bar{a}}$. The proportion of its assets in the risky asset is e, and in the safe asset is b or $(1-e)$. The ratio of annuity debt to assets is a, and the return to the annuity is $r_{\bar{a}}$.

Ignoring the opportunity cost of the corporation's equity, and normalizing the value of its assets to one, the gross return to the corporation in period two, R, is:

$$R = [e(1 + r_E) + b(1 + r_B) - a(1 + r_{\bar{a}})] \tag{A.1.63}$$

The expected return, μ_R, is:

$$\mu_R = [e(1 + \mu_E) + (1 - e) \cdot (1 + r_B) - a(1 + r_{\bar{a}})] \tag{A.1.64}$$

The expected return as a ratio of corporate equity is:

$$\frac{\mu_R}{1 - a} = \frac{[e(1 + \mu_E) + (1 - e) \cdot (1 + r_B) - a(1 + r_{\bar{a}})]}{1 - a} \tag{A.1.65}$$

For given values of the other variables, the expected return varies with the share of the risky asset in the portfolio, because μ_E exceeds r_B. The higher return comes at a cost. The variance of the return is given by:

$$\sigma_R = \text{var}(e(1 + r_E) + (1 - e) \cdot (1 + r_B) - a(1 + r_{\bar{a}})) \quad \text{or}$$

$$\sigma_R = e^2 \text{var}(r_E) \tag{A.1.66}$$

The ratio of the variance to the mean return, which is a measure of the riskiness of the financing and investment strategy, varies positively with e:

$$\frac{\sigma_R}{\mu_R} = \frac{e^2 \text{var}(r_E)}{[e(\mu_E - r_B) + (1 + r_B) - a(1 + r_{\bar{a}})]} \tag{A.1.67}$$

The ratio varies positively with a, because for a given asset allocation, the claim of annuitants on the gross return increases when a increases. The model is a simple illustration of how the risk of poor stock market performance to annuitants can be reduced by adequate provisioning (i.e. increasing the ratio of corporate equity to annuity liabilities). Conversely, increasing leverage by reducing that ratio increases the expected return, but also increases the risk to the insurance company of loss and default. The condition for default is shown below (r_E can be negative).

$$(1 - a) + b(1 + r_B) + e(1 + r_E) - a(1 + r_{\bar{a}}) < 0 \tag{A.1.68}$$

The ratio of the variance of the left-hand side of Eq. (A.1.68) to its mean is:

$$\frac{e^2 \text{var}(r_E)}{(1 - a) + (1 + r_B) + e(\mu_E - r_B) - a(1 + r_{\bar{a}})} \tag{A.1.69}$$

Equation (A.1.69) shows that for a given allocation of assets, the risk of default declines as *a* declines.

The two-period model of the annuity provider may also be used to illustrate the consequences of uncertainty regarding the survival rates of annuitants, by making the variable $r_{\bar{a}}$ stochastic (and symbolized by $\tilde{r}_{\bar{a}}$). This change is assumed not to affect the expected rate of return (the expected value of $\tilde{r}_{\bar{a}}$ is set equal to $r_{\bar{a}}$). Assuming that the random variable $\tilde{r}_{\bar{a}}$ is independent of the value of r_E, the variance of μ_R may be expressed as:

$$\sigma_R = \text{var}\left(e(1 + r_E) + (1 - e) \cdot (1 + r_B) - a(1 + \tilde{r}_{\bar{a}})\right)$$
$$= e^2 \text{var}(r_E) + a^2 \text{var}(\tilde{r}_{\bar{a}})$$

(A.1.70)

This is a simple illustration of the extra risk entailed by the uncertain longevity of annuitants.

In a world where the only random variable is the date of death of individuals, annuity pricing should be straightforward. There is no doubt about what the discount rate should be. Things become more complicated when asset returns are stochastic. An insurance company with annuities backed entirely by bonds is in an analogous position to a corporation that invests in projects with a certain rate of return (we assume that the company is financed in part by equity). If it shifts part of its portfolio from bonds to stocks, its expected return goes up, but does that mean it can charge a lower premium per dollar of regular annuity payment? Charging a lower premium – which would be the equivalent of offering a higher interest rate on bonds – would depress the value of the company's equity below that of a company with the same mix of risky and safe assets and the same gearing ratio (ratio of debt to equity) but paying the market rate of interest on its debt.

This situation would create an opportunity for arbitrage. If bonds and annuities are similarly structured, an insurance company would be saddling itself with unduly costly debt were it to follow such a strategy. Taking into account the cost of the insurance business and the survival probabilities of annuitants, as long as the risk of default on annuity payments is minimal, annuity premiums should be closely related to government bond rates for given mortality rates.

If we allow for the realistic possibility of default on annuities, the relationship between the rates of return on the benchmark safe asset, government debt, and annuities can be less tight. Corporations have different degrees of creditworthiness, and holders of their debt are presumably willing to trade off a higher risk of default for a higher expected return. Whether annuitants are willing to make a similar tradeoff is uncertain.

ADVERSE SELECTION

The exposition has so far made no distinction between the life expectancy of the population at large and the life expectancy of the sub-population of annuitants. In fact, and as the introduction points out, life insurers discovered early on that annuitants on average live longer than the population at large. As Chapter 1 discusses, this entails a problem for the annuities market. The problem does not result from systematic differences in longevity per se. The life expectancy of women is higher than the life expectancy of men, and accordingly female annuitants pay a higher premium than male annuitants do. However, the higher premium they pay is actuarially fair.

Women are usually readily distinguishable from men, so the average woman is not being overcharged (at least not relative to the average man). We can imagine that blue-eyed men and women might have greater life expectancies than men and women with brown, gray and green eyes, and there could be four sets of premiums. Blue-eyed women might pay quite a bit more than gray-eyed men, but the extra cost would reflect the greater longevity of the former group.

Adverse selection in annuity markets arises when a class or classes of people have a life expectancy significantly different from the population mean, but there are no obvious markers to identify them as different. It usually results from asymmetric information. In the case of life annuities, annuitants would have a better idea of their life expectancy than the insurance company would. Unlike the imaginary world where eye color and sex are all that matters for annuity pricing, there are not many signs the insurance company can exploit to assign potential annuitants to many different classes of longevity.

To illustrate how adverse selection might affect the market for annuities, we assume that there are two classes of annuitants, who can live for a maximum of M years after annuitization, with survival probabilities P_{S1i} and P_{S2i}, where i is a time subscript. We assume that P_{S1i} is greater than P_{S2i} for all i, $0 < i < M$. The number of each group of annuitants is N_j, where j takes the value 1 or 2. Although the whole group pays the same premium per dollar (PPD), it is useful to assume that the regular payment members of each group receives differs, with $AP_1 > AP_2$. The average premium the first group pays, PR_1 exceeds PR_2.

In a perfectly competitive market, the following expression holds:

$$PR_1 \cdot N_1 + PR_2 \cdot N_2 = AP_1 \cdot N_1 \sum_{i=1}^{M} \frac{P_{S1i}}{(1+r_i)^i} + AP_2 \cdot N_2 \sum_{i=1}^{M} \frac{P_{S2i}}{(1+r_i)^i}$$

(A.1.71)

Equation (A.1.72) for the premium per dollar follows from Eq. (A.1.71):

$$PPD = \omega_1 \sum_{i=1}^{M} \frac{P_{S1i}}{(1+r_i)^i} + \omega_2 \sum_{i=1}^{M} \frac{P_{S2i}}{(1+r_i)^i}$$

(A.1.72)

A load factor may be introduced into the model by multiplying the RHS of Eq. (A.1.72) by a coefficient, F, that takes a value greater than one, as shown in Eq. (A.1.73). The higher the F, the greater the load factor and the premium per dollar. The weights, ω_i, in Eqs. (A.1.72) and (A.1.73) are equal to the regular payments received by each group upon annuitization, expressed as a share of the total.

$$PPD_F = F \left[\omega_1 \sum_{i=1}^{M} \frac{P_{1i}}{(1+r_i)^i} + \omega_2 \sum_{i=1}^{M} \frac{P_{2i}}{(1+r_i)^i} \right]$$

(A.1.73)

Equation (A.1.73) demonstrates the intuitive result that the premium per dollar for a market with two classes of annuitants will be a weighted average of the premiums each group would pay if they alone constituted the market, with the weight for each group depending on their share of the market, as measured by share of regular payment. The larger the group of short-lived annuitants, and the higher the average payment the group received, the better their terms (the lower the premium per dollar).

Equation (A.1.73) also makes clear that the greater is the difference between the survival probabilities of the two groups, the greater will be the difference between the premium established in the market and the actuarially fair premium for short-lived persons, other things equal. In turn, the greater this difference, the fewer the number of short-lived people wishing to buy an annuity, and the more expensive the annuity. In an extreme case, short-lived people might not participate in the market at all.

Equation (A.1.73) can also be used to derive a simple estimate of the impact of the introduction of individual accounts and mandatory annuitization on the premium per dollar, given certain simplifying assumptions, and making group one the voluntary annuitants and group two the mandatory annuitants. In particular, we assume that the size of the two populations is known, the average payment demanded by the voluntary annuitants is known and unchanged, and the aggregate premium paid by group two annuitants is known (and equal, for example, to the balance in their accounts). By expressing PR_1 in terms of AP_2 and substituting in Eq. (A.1.71), the premium per dollar post reform may be derived.

AN ASIDE ON THE TIMING OF ANNUITIZATION

The exposition has thus far assumed that the decision to buy an annuity centered on its value, and not the timing of its purchase. It is possible, however, that a retired person may gain from delaying annuitization (or annuitizing in installments). The premium per dollar of annuity payment does decline with the age of the annuitant. Perhaps it might make sense to purchase some fixed-term securities at age 65, and delay the purchase of an annuity to age 70 or 75, if the extra return at these later ages makes up for the lower return earned initially from investing in bonds.

To explore this possibility, it is assumed that retirement – period two in the earlier model – is divided into two sub-periods, and that it is possible to buy annuities for each of the sub-periods (for convenience, they will be referred to as periods) as well as an annuity for the whole retirement period. Financial intermediation is again assumed to be costless. The probability of surviving to the first retirement period, using the terminology of Chapter 1, is denoted as $1/(1+\varphi_1)$, and the conditional probability of surviving to the second, having survived to the first is $1/(1+\varphi_2)$. Assuming actuarial fairness, the PPD of annuity payment (Z) for a two-period annuity can be expressed as Eq. (A.1.74), where r_{01} and r_{12} are the one-period interest rates:

$$Z = \frac{1}{(1+r_{01})(1+\varphi_1)} + \frac{1}{(1+r_{01})(1+r_{12})(1+\varphi_1)(1+\varphi_2)} \quad \text{(A.1.74)}$$

For a premium of Z dollars, an annuitant obtains one dollar of income in each of the two periods. An annuitant who buys a one-period annuity instead consumes one dollar and survives to the second retirement period will be able to be able to consume the amount C_2, as shown in Eq. (A.1.75).

C_2 equals one dollar, the same amount that the annuitant would have been able to consume had he purchased a two-year annuity.

$$C_2 = (Z(1 + r_{01})(1 + \varphi_1) - 1)(1 + r_{12})(1 + \varphi_2) = 1 \qquad \text{(A.1.75)}$$

This result may be generalized to N periods, and shows that, given the special assumptions that underlie the exposition, replacing longer with short-duration annuities does not change an annuitant's consumption possibilities. If lump-sum transactions costs are introduced, however, frequent annuity purchases can be shown to reduce an annuitant's expected consumption.

Now suppose that the annuitant had purchased a one-period bond, intending to wait until the premium per dollar dropped, rather than purchasing a series of annuities, or one annuity. Because the return to the bond is less than the conditional return to the one-period annuity, there is less to invest in a second-period annuity than there would have been had the initial investment been in a one-period annuity. However, we have shown that there is no advantage to buying one-period annuities.

Given the assumption of predictable interest rates, if the conditional rate of return to the annuity exceeds the rate of return to a bond in each period, delaying annuitization reduces second-period consumption. Even if annuities are not actuarially fair, the annuitant who invests Z dollars in a one-period bond will be able to consume less in period two than he would have had he purchased a two-period annuity. This may be seen by interpreting $1 + \varphi_1$ and $1 + \varphi_2$ not as the inverses of the one-period survival probabilities, but as the ratios of the conditional rates of return of the one-period annuities to one-period bonds.

THE INSURANCE VALUE OF ANNUITIES

In principle, it is possible to self-insure against longevity risk by making a highly conservative assumption regarding one's maximum lifespan, and investing in a set of bonds with maturities encompassing the entire range up to that maximum lifespan, if they exist. However, the risk-pooling properties of an annuity allow an annuitant to obtain a higher rate of return, as Chapter 1 explains. This is true whether or not the rate of return to the annuity is actuarially fair. The MW ratio does not have to equal or even be very close to one for annuities to provide longevity insurance.

The model of the demand for annuities, which is based on the maximization of expected utility, can be used to give an indication of the gains that annuitization bestows. The basic idea is that an assumption is made about the form of the utility function, and utility is then maximized given assumptions about the conditional rate of return to annuities (r_A in the model), survival probabilities, and the subjective rate of discount. Then the exercise is repeated using the rate of interest on standard securities (r_B in the model), which is lower than r_A. The extra wealth required to compensate for the unavailability of annuities − the additional wealth that is needed to equalize utility levels − may then be calculated.

What follows is a relatively simple model of this type of calculation. The reader can consult Brown (2001) and Mitchell et al. (2001) for a model with more realistic assumptions. The presentation assumes that the utility function is logarithmic, which means that the coefficient of relative risk aversion is 1, which is relatively low. For ease of exposition, it is also assumed that the one-period survival probability, p_S, and the discount rate, β, are constant (varying survival probabilities can be easily introduced). The utility function takes the form of Eq. (A.1.76):

$$U = \ln C_1 + p_S\beta \ln C_2 + p_S^2\beta^2 \ln C_3 + \cdots + p_S^{N-1}\beta^{N-1}\ln C_N \quad (A.1.76)$$

Utility is maximized subject to the wealth constraint, which assumes that the conditional rate of interest of annuities, which may have a term of one or more periods up to N, the maximum lifespan in retirement, is constant and equal to $r_{A:}$

$$W = \sum_{i=1}^{N} \frac{C_i}{(1+r_A)^{i-1}} \quad (A.1.77)$$

A necessary condition for maximization is

$$\frac{\delta U}{\delta C_n} = (1+r_A)\frac{\delta U}{\delta C_{n+1}},$$
$$\text{for } n = 1, 2, 3, \ldots, N-1 \quad (A.1.78)$$

which may be re-expressed as:

$$1/C_n \cdot (p_S\beta)^n = (1+r_A)/C_{n+1} \cdot (p_S\beta)^{n+1} \quad \text{or}$$
$$C_{n+1} = C_n(1+r_A)p_S\beta \quad (A.1.79)$$

By successive substitutions for C_2, C_3, C_4, etc. the utility function may be re-expressed as follows:

$$U = \ln C_1 + p_S\beta(\ln C_1(1 + r_A)p_S\beta) + (p_S\beta)^2(\ln C_1((1 + r_A)p_S\beta)^2) + \cdots$$
$$+ (p_S\beta)^{N-1}(\ln C_1((1 + r_A)p_S\beta)^{N-1})$$

(A.1.80)

After some rearranging:

$$U = \ln C_1 \sum_{i=0}^{N-1} (p_S\beta)^i + \sum_{i=0}^{N-1} (p_S\beta)^i \ln\{[(1 + r_A)p_S\beta]^i\}$$

(A.1.81)

By using the wealth constraint and the necessary condition for maximization, we derive the following:

$$W = C_1 + C_1 \cdot p_S\beta + C_1 \cdot (p_S\beta)^2 + \cdots + C_1 \cdot (p_S\beta)^{N-1}$$

(A.1.82)

Given values for p_S, β, N, and W, we can solve for C_1. With a value for r_A, we can solve for U. Assuming that $W = \$1,000,000$; $r_A = 0.07$; $p_S = 0.97$, $\beta = 0.98$, and $N = 35$, first-period consumption is $\$59,503$. Assuming now that annuities are not available, and that the rate of return on the alternative financial instrument is 0.055, it can be shown that first-period consumption has to increase by 18.6 percent to achieve the same level of utility. The form of the utility function implies that wealth is proportional to first-period consumption, so wealth has to increase by 18.6 percent as well to achieve the same level of utility. Consumption is more frontloaded when annuities are not available, because the return to saving declines.

Appendix 2: Aging and its Impact on Pension Systems

A PARABLE

The nineteenth century economists were accustomed to illustrating their arguments with stories about a "Robinson Crusoe" economy – a barter economy with only one inhabitant. The basics of the economics of aging can be illustrated in a similar way, although the economy's population must be greater than one since it must span at least three generations. Imagine a small island economy, Arcadia, organized like a collective. Arcadia has for some time had a static population with a stable demographic pyramid – the two dependency ratios have each been constant for some time. In addition, there is positive gross but zero net investment, so the stock of capital (fishing boats, nets, tools, and the like), like the supply of labor has also been constant for some time.

One day, two momentous trends emerge: Arcadia's birth rate drops, and the life expectancy of its elders (i.e. their life expectancy at the time they stop working) increases. If the Arcadians are prescient, they will realize that in about 15 years the labor supply will begin to fall, assuming that retirement continues to begin at the accustomed age, because the number of new entrants to the Arcadian labor force does not match the number of retirees leaving it. They should also notice, perhaps more quickly, that the total amount of time their society needs to devote to the care and upbringing of children (to provide the traditional standard of care and upbringing per child) will decline. The caregivers have more time on their hands. If the increase in the elderly dependency ratio is sufficiently great, Arcadia will have an aging problem. The island has too many elderly people to support (although there are fewer children to care for and educate).

What should the citizens of Arcadia do? Suppose for the sake of argument that Arcadia, traditional society though it is, has a simple system of national accounts that is extremely progressive, and treats the value of the labor devoted to the care and education of children as investment. (We sidestep the problem of placing a value on human capital investment.) They would then have noticed – actually, they could have noticed even without a system of national accounts – that investment, and specifically the quantity of investment in human capital, was declining. Arcadia might then have tried to ensure that the time previously devoted to child care and education was devoted to some other form of investment, or that the quantity or quality of care per child was increased. The decline in the quantity of human capital formation can be partly compensated by increases in the quality of child care (or in the time devoted to caring for each child) and in nonhuman capital formation.

The Arcadians do not take these steps. We assume that the effect of the decline in the number of children to feed and care for is overwhelmed by the effect of the greater numbers of the elderly, who do not increase the length of their working life. As a result, there must initially be a decline in consumption per head, at least initially, since there are more mouths to feed, and once the impact of the declining birth rate on the labor force makes itself felt, fewer hands to feed them. This impact can be offset over time, however, by reducing average consumption further and building up the capital stock.

Suppose that the demographic shift results in a new static steady state (the drop in the birth rate is compensated by the drop in the death rate), and that the demographic pyramid has a narrower base. If the Arcadians want to raise consumption per capita to the level it had reached before the demographic shift, they could do so by increasing the resources devoted to investment, and restraining consumption. They can adopt a Stalinist approach to accumulation, which entails severe privations that must be shared in some way by the elders and the young. Alternatively, they can follow a more gradualist approach. If diminishing returns to capital do not set in too quickly, the consumption levels of former days can be restored at some higher capital–labor ratio. Clearly, the sooner the problem is recognized and a solution to it adopted, the easier will be the period of transition to the old consumption levels.

The basic lessons of this simple story are not changed by making it dynamic. Suppose that the economy had been in a state of steady growth; that the consumption per capita of both the working generation and older people had been growing at the same rate as productivity; and that the rate of growth of productivity was unaffected by aging. If the change in the elderly dependency ratio is sufficiently great, and consumption per capita continues to grow at its former rate, total consumption will now grow more rapidly than output, implying that the saving rate declines. As a result, the growth of the capital stock would decline below the sum of the rate of growth of productivity and the labor force, and output growth would slow.

If we assume now that the Arcadian elders receive some transferable title to consumption when they stop working, so that they are not simply supported by their families, then it is possible to speak meaningfully of differences in generational saving rates. The aging problem will be aggravated if, as the simple version of the life cycle hypothesis assumes, older people save less than the working generation. If the share of older people in the population grows; if their saving rate and that of the working generation are both constants; and if the ratio of their average income to that of the working generation does not change, then the aggregate saving rate must fall. It may fall even if the average income of older people declines.

The parable of Arcadia is based on a small collective economy without financial institutions. The aging problem in such an economy is not reflected in financial disequilibria, but more directly, in physical shortages — too few workers, too little consumption to distribute across generations. In an economy with financial institutions, the problem shows up in a different way. A falling birth rate eventually creates problems for social security systems, because payroll tax collections fall short of public pension obligations, but the decisions of married couples regarding the number of children they have entails no consequences for their support in old age: if anything, since children are not expected to pay their parents back, with interest, for the cost of their care and upbringing, having fewer children can increase the retirement savings of the parents. In a small collective, however, the investment character of the time and resources devoted to childcare should be more obvious. Modern financial institutions break the link between the individual decision and the collective result.

The institution of money alone is not the root of the aging problem. Financial institutions did not spring into being after the Second World War, although financial products for households in the advanced economies have become considerably more sophisticated since then, and allow households much easier access to credit. The costs that parents incur in raising children have been rising in most countries for some time, in large part because the opportunity cost of childcare has risen as the workforce opportunities for women — typically the primary caregiver if not the only caregiver — have risen. In the advanced economies, the period of a child's dependency has been prolonged by the increase in the length of formal schooling, which also increases the upfront cost of children, and of course birth control methods have become more reliable. In sum, the private costs to families of rearing children have risen while the private benefits have not increased. Seen in this light, it is not surprising that birthrates have tended to decline with economic development.

REAL WORLD AGING PROBLEMS

The demographic assumptions of the dynamic version of the Arcadian parable are a reasonable approximation to the trends that have been evident for some time in industrialized countries and many emerging market economies. Unless immigration rates increase greatly, the growth of the labor force in the industrialized economies is bound to remain low or slow down (barring dramatic changes in the labor force participation rate, the increase in the labor force over the next twenty years is already in the pipeline). Meanwhile, the share of older people in the population will grow. Among the largest advanced countries, America's position is the most manageable. Its labor force growth is buoyed by continued large flows of immigrants and its birth rate has not fallen by as much as birth rates in European countries. Its population is not as old, and is not aging as rapidly as Europe's.

Aging sows the seeds of a generational conflict over resources. As in the parable, both old and young cannot continue to consume as much as they did previously, and the basic question is how the necessary decline in consumption will be distributed across generations. Any number of technical solutions to this problem can be advanced. Depending on a country's political institutions, and especially on the distribution of political power between young and old, some of them may be nonstarters politically. Speaking rather broadly, there are three classes of technical solutions: changes to the parameters of the existing public pension system (parametric reform of the existing system); more radical reform of the public pension system, such as the introduction of an individual accounts system; and fiscal consolidation, or changes to the tax system and expenditure programs that achieve the same ends – e.g. an increase in the saving rate – as the first two approaches. A reform may combine elements from each of the three classes of solutions: an individual accounts reform may be combined with a parametric reform of the existing system that, for example, increases the standard retirement age gradually over time, and with measures to reduce the size of the fiscal deficit excluding the public pension system, to facilitate the financing of that system.

Depending on how labor market, investment, and saving decisions are affected by changes to the tax system, these reforms can achieve their effects with little impact on gross domestic product (GDP). They simply lower the income of different generations to ensure that demand for consumer goods equals the share of GDP available for consumption. This might entail safeguarding the income of the current generation of retirees, and placing the burden on current working generations. It might entail imposing a large part of the necessary adjustment on the current generation of retirees, although this strategy would not be politically viable in most countries.

There is an alternative, however, as the Arcadian parable implied, which is to increase the rate of investment. This too involves a decline in consumption. With a fully employed economy, short of increasing the external current account deficit, more investment means less consumption, if additional external borrowing is ruled out. However, if the rate of return to the investment is sufficiently high, this strategy may make the intergenerational tradeoff less acute.

MACROECONOMIC ASPECTS OF AN INDIVIDUAL ACCOUNTS REFORM

A parametric reform of a public pension system may be undertaken for reasons that have nothing to do with population aging. As three examples, pension reform might seek to increase the minimum pension; to rectify unequal treatment of men and women at retirement; or to eliminate incentives for early retirement created by the existing system. Similarly, there are many possible reasons for wanting to introduce an individual accounts component to a public pension system, or even to supplant the old system completely. This book is particularly concerned with the security of retirement income, and that security will depend crucially on the impact of an individual accounts reform on saving. Advocates of individual accounts reforms have usually stressed this aspect above others. They have also argued that a system of individual accounts will make labor markets function more efficiently, since they reduce or eliminate the distortive impact of payroll taxation on labor supply.[1]

In fact, depending on how it is introduced, an individual accounts reform can either increase aggregate saving, decrease it, or leave it

[1] For further discussion of this point as it applies to the United States, see Diamond and Orszag (2004, pp. 46, 48–49, 161). Barr (2001) and Orszag and Stiglitz (2001) discuss the macroeconomic impacts of an individual accounts reform in some detail. Heller (2003) addresses the long-run fiscal implications of population aging.

unchanged. As an example of a reform that leaves saving unchanged, consider a "carve-out" reform. Assume further that the expected rate of return to the contributions to the accounts is exactly equal to the implicit return these contributions would have earned had they gone to finance the public pension. Put more precisely, the expected present discounted value of the annuity that the individual accounts will finance for the average member of a given age cohort is exactly equal to the expected present discounted value of the decline in the public pension that is entailed by the diversion of the payroll tax.

The reform will increase the budget deficit as it is conventionally measured, since payroll tax collections will decline, but pension payments will not decline, at least not initially. Nonetheless, unless the change in the reported deficit changes the behavior of consumers and investors, there is no effect on the macroeconomy. Saving is unaffected, because the recorded saving of the private sector will increase to offset exactly the increased public sector deficit.[2]

Given these assumptions, for an individual accounts reform to increase aggregate saving, it has to stimulate an additional increase in private sector saving, or be accompanied by a change in the stance of fiscal policy that increases public sector saving – for example, a reduction in the size of some government expenditure programs, or tax increases. In sum, if an individual accounts reform is to increase the resources available for future generations, consumption today – either public or private sector consumption – must decline below what it otherwise would have been. There is no free lunch.

---

[2] Mackenzie et al. (2003) analyze this particular case in more depth. Kotlikoff (1986) has argued that the conventional accounting classification of payroll contributions as a tax is seriously misleading. He maintains that they are better thought of as borrowing, on the grounds that contributing to a public pension program creates an obligation on the part of the government to pay a future benefit. This obligation is sometimes termed implicit or soft public debt.

Glossary

Accrual factor – the rate at which a pension increases with the period of service under a defined benefits plan. For example, a pension will increase by 2 percent of final salary for the first 25 years of plan service, and 1.5 percent up to 35 years of service.

Actuarial fairness – the property of an insurance arrangement where the expected value of the payments made if an insured event occurs equals the cost of the insurance. An immediate life annuity would normally be described as actuarially fair if the premium equals the expected value of the future payments discounted at a risk-free interest rate. In practice, insurance can never be consistently actuarially fair because it is not costless.

Actuarial balance – see funded plan.

Adverse selection – a phenomenon that is thought to affect most insurance markets to some degree. It occurs when the insured has a higher probability than the population at large of experiencing the contingency for which the insurance policy is written. For example, life insurance policy-holders have a higher mortality rate than does the general population. Adverse selection implies that insurance rates or premiums will be higher than they would be if the insured population was a representative sample of the general population.

Annuity – a financial instrument that in return for a consideration pays the purchaser (the annuitant) a stream of payments over a period specified by the contract; sometimes refers simply to a stream of payments made to a beneficiary under a legal settlement or inheritance. Annuities can assume many forms. See Table 1.1.

Asymmetric information – the state of a market in which one side (the buyer or the seller) has more relevant information than the other.

In the case of life insurance and annuities, asymmetric information obtains because the buyer is presumed to know more about his mortality or longevity risk than the seller.

Conditional life expectancy – the expected number of additional years of life at a given age, or life expectancy conditional on reaching the given age. Life expectancy at birth is often simply referred to life expectancy.

Defined benefits pension plan – a pension plan where the benefit paid to plan participants is determined by the terms of the plan. Typically, a defined benefits plan determines the pension benefit on the basis of the number of years of participation and a participant's salary history. In a typical plan, the pension will be a percentage of the participant's salary over a period of a year or more at the end of the contributory period. The percentage will be determined by an accrual factor (see accrual factor).

Defined contributions pension plan – a pension plan under which the contribution made to the plan by its participants is determined by the terms of the plan. The terms of the benefit are not defined under the plan.

Funded plan – a pension plan where the plan's reserves are maintained at a level that is sufficient to finance the pensions expected to be paid to current members after taking into account the members' contributions. In determining the value of the reserve, the plan needs to make an assumption about the period over which the plan will operate and the number of individuals it will cover. One common approach with private sector plans is the closed group method, where the calculations include only those who are now plan members.

Hybrid plan – a pension plan that normally takes the legal form of a defined benefits plan, but has features of a defined contributions plan. Typically, the employer bears the risk of sub-par investment performance, but the benefit is defined (in the case of cash balance plans) as an account balance.

Implicit rate of return of a public pension plan – The implicit rate of return of a public pension system is normally defined as that rate of return that would equalize the discounted value of a particular age cohort's expected benefits with the discounted value of present value of their expected payroll tax contributions and employers' contributions made on their behalf.

Life table – a table giving mortality rates for a whole population or sub-population. Life tables are made up from period life tables and cohort tables. Period tables show for a given year (e.g. the year 2000) the risk of dying for persons at all ages in the following year. A cohort table shows the risk of dying for a cohort (group) of people born in the same year at different ages. Thus, a period table shows the risk that some one of a given age (50, 55, 60, 65, 70, ...) in the year 2000 will not live to the year 2001. A cohort take shows the risk that a person born in 1950 and alive in 2000 will not live to 2001; or alive in 2005 and will not live to 2006.

Longevity bonds – see survivor bonds.

Mathematical reserves – see technical reserves.

Moral hazard – a risk thought to infect all insurance markets to some degree, because being insured reduces the disincentive the insured party has to engage in or avoid risky behavior. For example, insured drivers are more likely to speed; insured home owners are less cautious about locking their doors. The difference between moral hazard and adverse selection is that adverse selection does not entail a change of behavior.

Notional defined contribution system – despite its name, a pension system that is not actually funded, but where the pension is determined by the value of contributions plus a notional interest rate. The interest rate may be fixed in nominal or real terms, or may be a function of some market interest rate.

Pay-as-you-go plan (PAYG plan) – the typical form of a public pension plan, where a payroll tax levied on the current working generation finances the pensions paid to the previous generation.

Pensionable base – that part of the compensation of a member of an employer-provided or public pension plan that is used to determine typically both contributions and pension.

Reinsurance – the insurance provided to insurance companies by specialist reinsurers, allowing the insured companies to lay off part of the risk they assume when they underwrite a policy.

Replacement rate – the ratio of the pension to a worker's salary, usually averaged over a period at the end of his or her working life.

Survivor bonds (also known as longevity bonds) – a proposed new type of government bond, with coupons whose value would vary over time with the proportion of a birth cohort aged a specific number of years when the bond was issued who were still alive at the time of the coupon payment.

Technical reserves — the reserves held to back the liabilities that an insurance company incurs when it contracts to insure policyholders.

Term life insurance — insurance where the premium varies over time with the mortality risk of the policy holder. The premium per dollar of insurance increases with the policy holder's age.

Yield curve — the relationship between the interest rate on a bond and its maturity. Typically, the yield curve slopes upward: a 10 year bond pays a higher rate of interest than a 2 year bond. The yield curve is said to be inverted when the opposite obtains.

References

American Academy of Actuaries (2002). *Fair Valuation of Insurance Liabilities: Principles and Methods.* Public Policy Monograph, September. http://www.actuary.org.

Ameriks, J., Veres, R. and Warshawsky, M. J. (2001). Making retirement income last a lifetime. *Journal of Financial Planning*, December. http://www.fpanet.org/journal/articles/2001_Issues/jfp1201.cfm.

Anusec, Z., O'Keefe, P. and Madzarevic-Sujster, S. (2003). Pension Reform in Croatia. Social Protection Discussion Paper 0304. Washington: World Bank. http://wbln018.worldbank.org/HDnet.

Association of British Insurers (2005). The Pension Annuity Market: Further Research into Supply and Constraints. http://www.abi.org.uk.

Atkinson, D. B. and Dallas, J. W. (2000). *Life Insurance Products and Finance: Charting a Clear Course.* Schaumburg, Illinois: Society of Actuaries.

Augusztinovics, M., Gál, R. I., Matits, A., Máté, L., Simonivits, A. and Stahl, J. (2002). The Hungarian pension system before and after the reform of 1998. In *Pension Reform in Central and Eastern Europe: Volume 1*, ed. E. Fultz. Budapest: International Labor Office, pp. 25–94.

Austen, J. (1811). *Sense and Sensibility.* New York: Everyman's, 1992.

Baeza, S. and Manubens, R. (1988). *Sistema privado de pensiones en Chile.* Centro de Estudios Públicos. Santiago de Chile.

Banks, J. and Emerson, C. (1999). UK annuitants. *Institute for Fiscal Studies, Briefing Note No. 5*, December. http://www.ifs.org.uk.

Barr, N. (2001). *The Welfare State as Piggy Bank: Information, Risk, Uncertainty and the Role of the State.* Oxford: Oxford University Press.

Benartzi, S. and Thaler, R. H. (2001). Naïve diversification strategies in defined contribution saving plans. *American Economic Review*, **91**, 79–98.

Bernstein, P. L. (1996). *Against the Gods: The Remarkable Story of Risk.* New York: John Wiley and Sons.

Blake, D. (1999). Annuity markets: problems and solutions. *The Geneva Papers on Risk and Insurance – Issues and Practice*, **24**, 358–75.

Blake, D. and Burrows, W. (2001). Survivor bonds: Helping to hedge mortality risk. *Journal of Risk and Insurance*, **68**, 339–48.

Bodie, Z. (2001). Financial engineering and social security reform. In *Risk Aspects of Investment-Based Social Security Reform*, eds. J. Y. Campbell and M. Feldstein. Chicago: University of Chicago.

Brown, J. R. (1999). Are the elderly really over-annuitized? New evidence on life insurance and bequests. NBER Working Paper 7193. Cambridge, Massachusetts: National Bureau of Economic Research. http://www.nber.org/papers/W7193.

— (2001). Redistribution and insurance: Mandatory annuitization with mortality heterogeneity. CRR Working Paper 2001–02. Boston: Center for Retirement Research, Boston College. http://www.bc.edu/centers/crr/wp_2001-02shtml.

Brown, J. R., Mitchell, O. S. and Warshawsky, M. J. (2001a). The role of real annuities and indexed bonds in an individual accounts retirement program. In *The Role of Annuity Markets in Financing Retirement*. Cambridge, Massachusetts: MIT Press, pp. 107–52.

Brown, J. R., Mitchell, O. S., Poterba, J. M. and Warshawsky, M. J. (2001b). *The Role of Annuity Markets in Financing Retirement*. Cambridge, Massachusetts: MIT Press.

Burtless, G. (2001). International evidence on the desirability of individual retirement accounts in public pension systems. Testimony for the Subcommittee on Social Security, Committee on Ways and Means. U.S. House of Representatives. July. http://www.brook.edu/views/testimony/burtless/20010731.htm.

— (2004). Social norms, rules of thumb, and retirement: Evidence for rationality in retirement planning. CSED Working Paper No. 37. The Brookings Institution — The Johns Hopkins University Center on Social and Economic Dynamics. November. http://www.brookings.edu/es/dynamics/papers/csed37.htm.

Cardinale, M. (2004). The Long-Run Relationship between Pension Liabilities and Asset Prices: A Cointegrating Approach. Presented to the Staple Inn Actuarial Society, May 4, 2004. http://www.sias.org.uk/papers.

Cardinale, M., Findlater, A. and Orszag, M. (2002). Paying out pensions: a review of international annuities markets. Watson Wyatt Research Report 2002-RU07. http://watsonwyatt.com.

Chlon, A. (2002). The Polish pension reform of 1999. In *Pension reform in Central and Eastern Europe: Volume I*, ed. E. Fultz. Budapest: International Labor Office, pp. 95–205.

Clark, G. L. (2003). Pension fund governance: Moral imperatives, state regulation, and the market. Paper presented at World Bank Conference: Contractual savings conference: Regulatory and supervisory issues in private pensions. November 3–7.

Clark, R. (2003). Pension plan options: preferences, choices and the distribution of benefits. Pension Research Council Working Paper. 2003–24. rider.wharton.upenn.edu/~prc/PRC/WP/WP2003-24.pdf.

Cohen, L. C., Steuerle, E. and Carasso, A. (2001). Social security redistribution by education, race, and income: How much and why? Paper prepared for the Third Annual Conference of the Retirement Research Consortium: Making hard choices about retirement. Washington.

References   237

D'Ambrosio, M. (2003). Ignorance is not bliss: The importance of financial education. Paper presented at World Bank Conference: Contractual Savings Conference: Regulatory and supervisory issues in private pensions. November 3–7.

Das, U., Davies, N. and Podpiera, R. (2003). Insurance and issues in financial soundness. International Monetary Fund Working Paper 03/138. Washington: International Monetary Fund. http://www.imf.org/external/pubs/ft/wp/2004/wp03138.pdf.

Davidoff, T., Brown, J. and Diamond, P. A. (2005). Annuities and individual welfare. *American Economic Review*, **95**, 1573–90.

Davis, E. Phillip (2001). Portfolio regulation of life insurance companies and pension funds. Discussion paper PI-0101. London: The Pensions Institute, Birkbeck College, University of London. http://www.pensions-institute.org/workingpapers/wp0101.pdf.

De la Granville, O. (2001). *Bond pricing and portfolio analysis: Protecting investors in the long run.* Cambridge: MIT Press.

Del Guercio, D. (1996). The distorting effect of the prudent-man laws on institutional equity investments. *Journal of Financial Economics*, **40**, 31–62.

Devesa-Carpio, J. E. and Vidal-Meliá, C. (sp). (2002). The reformed pension systems in Latin America. Pension reform primer. World Bank, Washington. http://www.socsec.org/research.asp?pubid=669.

Diamond, P. A. and Valdéz-Prieto, S. (1994). Social Security Reforms. In *The Chilean Economy: Policy Lessons and Challenges*, eds. B. R. Bosworth, R. Dornbusch and R. Labán. Washington: Brookings Institution.

Diamond, P. A. (2004). Social Security. *American Economic Review*, **94**, 1–24.

Diamond, P. A. and Orszag, P. A. (2004). *Saving Social Security: A Balanced Approach.* Washington DC: Brookings Institution Press.

Dickens, C. (1839). *Nicholas Nickelby.* New York: Penguin, 1999.

Dickens, C. (1854). *Hard Times.* New York: Modern Library, 2001.

Doyle, S., Mitchell, O. S. and Piggott, J. (2001). Annuity values in defined contributions systems: The case of Australia and Singapore. NBER Working Paper 8091. Cambridge, Massachusetts: National Bureau of Economic Research. http://www.nber.org/papers/W8091.

Doyle, S. and Piggott, J. (2002). Mandatory annuity design in developing countries. Pension Primer Series. Washington: World Bank. http://wbln0018.worldbank.org/HDnet.

Dus, I., Maurer, R. and Mitchell, O. S. (2004). Betting on death and capital markets in retirement: A shortfall risk analysis of life annuities versus phased withdrawal plans. NBER Working Paper 11271. Cambridge, Massachusetts: National Bureau of Economic Research. http://www.nber.org/papers/w11271.

Dynan, K. E., Skinner, J. and Zeldes, S. (2002). The importance of bequests and life-cycle saving in capital accumulation: A new answer. *American Economic Review*, **92**, 274–8.

Engen, E. M., Gale, W. G. and Uccello, C. E. (1999). The adequacy of household saving. *Brookings Papers on Economic Activity*, **2**, 65–187.

Ernst and Young (2004). Equity release – a thing of the past or the future? *Financial Services Brief* (Winter). www.ey.com\global\download.nsf\Bermuda\Financial_Services_Brief_Winter_2004.

Eschtruth, A. D. and Long C. Tran. (2001). A primer on reverse mortgages. *Just the Facts on Retirement Issues.* Center for Retirement Research, Boston College. http://www.bc.edu/centers/crr/jtf_3.shtml.

Favreault, M., Sammartino, F. J. and Steuerle, C. E., eds. (2002). *Social Security and the Family.* Washington: Urban Institute Press.

Feldstein, M. and Samwick, A. (2000). Allocating payroll tax revenue to personal retirement accounts to maintain social security benefits and the payroll tax rate. National Bureau of Economic Research Working Paper 7767. http://www.nber.org/papers/w7767.

Ferguson, N. (2001). *The Cash Nexus: Money and Power in the Modern World 1700–2000.* New York: Basic Books.

Financial Services Authority (2003). *Enhanced capital requirements and individual capital assessments for life insurers. Consultation paper 195.*

— (2005). FSA Factsheet – Raising money from your home. http://www.fsa.gov.uk/consumer/pdfs/raise_home.pdf.

Finkelstein, A. and Poterba, J. (1999). Selection effects in the market for individual annuities: New evidence from the United Kingdom. NBER Working Paper 7168. Cambridge, Massachusetts: National Bureau of Economic Research. http://www.nber.org/papers/W7168.

Finkelstein, A. and Poterba, J. (2000). Adverse selection in insurance markets: Policyholder evidence from the U.K. annuity market. NBER Working Paper 8045. Cambridge, Massachusetts: National Bureau of Economic Research. http://www.nber.org/papers/W8045.

Gale, W. G. and Slemrod, J. (2001). Overview. In *Rethinking estate and gift taxation,* eds. W. G. Gale, J. R. Hines, Jr. and J. Slemrod, pp. 1–64. Washington: Brookings Institution Press.

Gale, W. G. and Orszag, P. R. (2003). Private pensions: issues and options. In *Agenda for the Nation,* eds. H. Aaron, J. Lindsay and P. Nivola. Washington: Brookings Institution Press.

García, S. J. A. (1988). Mercado de Renta Vitalicia y Bono de Reconocimiento. Período 1985–2000. In *Sistema privado de pensiones en Chile,* eds. B. Sergio and R. Manubens. Santiago de Chile: Centro de Estudios Públicos.

Garcia, G. G. H. (2000). *Deposit insurance: Actual and good practices,* International Monetary Fund Occasional Paper 197. Washington: International Monetary Fund.

Gardner, J. and Orszag, M. (2004). Individual Choice and Financial Education in OECD Countries. Presentation at the OECD/INPRS Conference on Private Pensions. Manila. March 30–April 1. http://www.oecd.org\dataoecd\37\1331078626.pdf.

General Accounting Office (1999). Social Security Reform: Implications of Private Annuities for Individual Accounts, GAO/HEHS-99-160.

Greenblatt, S. (2004). *Will in the World: How Shakespeare Became Shakespeare.* New York: Norton.

Greenwood, M. (1940). A statistical mare's nest? *Journal of the Royal Statistical Society.* **103,** 246–8.

Gustman, A. L. et al. (1997). Pension and social security wealth in the health and retirement study. NBER Working Paper 5912. Cambridge, Massachusetts: National Bureau of Economic Research. http://www.nber.org/papers/W5912.

Hacker, I. (1976). *The Emergence of Probability*. Cambridge: Cambridge University Press.

Heller, P. S. (2003). *Who will pay? Coping with Aging Societies, Climate Change and other Long-Term Fiscal Challenges*. Washington: International Monetary Fund.

Holzmann, R. (1997). Pension reform, financial market development and economic growth: Preliminary evidence from Chile. *Staff Papers*, International Monetary Fund, **44** (2), pp. 149–78.

Holzmann, R. and Stiglitz, J. E., eds. (2001). *New Ideas about Old Age Security: Toward Sustainable Pension Systems in the 21st Century*. Washington: World Bank.

Holzman, R. and Hinz, R. (2005) *Old Age Income Support in the 21st Century: An International Perspective on Pension Systems and Reform*. Washington: World Bank.

Impavido, G., Thorburn, C. and Wadsworth, M. (2004) A conceptual framework for retirement products: Risk sharing arrangements between providers and retirees. WPS 3208. World Bank, Washington. http://wbln0018.worldbank.org/html/FinancialSectorWeb.nsf/(attachmentweb)/3208/$FILE/3208.pdf.

International Association of Insurance Supervisors (2002). *Principles on Capital Adequacy and Solvency*. http://www.iaisweb.org/133_358_ENU_HTML.asp.

— (2005). *Toward a Common Structure and Common Standards for the Assessment of Insurer Solvency*. http://www.iaisweb.org/051021_Framework_paper.pdf.

International Monetary Fund (2004a). *Global Financial Stability Report: Market Developments and Issues*, April. Washington: International Monetary Fund.

— (2004b). *World Economic Outlook: The Global Demographic Transition*.

— (2005). *Global Financial Stability Report: Market Developments and Issues*. April.

Jack, F. (1912). *An Introduction to the History of Life Assurance*. London: PS King and Son(s).

James, E. and Vittas, D. (2000). Annuities markets in comparative perspective: Do consumers get their money's-worth? World Bank Policy Research Working Paper No. 2493. http://ssrn.com.abstract=632563.

James, E. and Song, X. (2002). Annuities markets around the world: Money's worth and risk intermediation. http://papers.ssrn.com/abstract=287375.

James, E., Smallhout, J. and Vittas, D. (2001). Administrative Costs and the Organization of Individual Accounts Systems: A Comparative Perspective. In *New Ideas about Old Age Security: Toward Sustainable Pension Systems in the 21st Century*. Washington: World Bank, pp. 254–307.

James, M. (1947). *The Metropolitan Life: A Study in Business Growth*. New York: Viking.

Jousten, A. (2001). Life-cycle modeling of bequests and their impact on annuity valuation. *Journal of Public Economics*, **79**, 149–77.

Keynes, J. M. (1936). *The General Theory of Employment, Interest and Money*. Royal Economic Society. London: MacMillan, 1973.

King, J. (2004). Securities companies, investment funds and pension funds. In *Taxing the Financial Sector*, ed. H. Zee. Washington: International Monetary Fund.

Kotlikoff, L. J. and Spivak, A. (1981). The family as an incomplete annuities market. *The Journal of Political Economy*, **89**, 372–91.

Kotlikoff, L. J. (1986). Deficit delusion. *The Public Interest*, 84 (summer), pp. 53–65.

Kristensen, J. F. and Yew-Lee, A. (2002). The Singapore Insurance Market. http://www.irmi.com/Expert/Articles/2002/Kristensen09.aspx.

Kritzer, B. E. (2001/2002). Social security reform in Central and Eastern Europe: Variations on a Latin American theme. *Social Security Bulletin*, **64** (4).

Larraín, G. R. (2004). *Renta vitalicias y jubilación anticipada*. Paper presented at a seminar: Ley de rentas vitalicias: Las nuevas reglas en juevo. AIPEP, Chile. http://www.safp.cl/_communicados/site/pags/20040812173546.html.

Lee, R. (2003). The demographic transition: Three centuries of fundamental change. *Journal of Economic Perspectives*, **17**, 167–90.

Lowenstein, R. (2000). *When Genius Failed: The Rise and Fall of Long-term Capital Management*. New York: Random House.

Mackenzie, G. A. (1995). Reforming Latin America's old-age pension systems. *Finance and Development*, **32** (1), 10–13.

Mackenzie, G. A., Gerson, P. and Cuevas, A. (1997). *Pensions and saving*. IMF Occasional Paper 153. Washington: International Monetary Fund.

Mackenzie, G. A., Gerson, P., Cuevas, A. and Heller, P. S. (2003). The fiscal impact of pension reform. *Journal of Budgeting and Finance*, **23**, 115–27.

Mackenzie, G. A. and Schrager, A. (2004). Can the private annuity market provide secure retirement income? International Monetary Fund Working Paper 04/230. http://www.imf.org/external/pubs/ft/wp/2004/wp04230.pdf.

McCarthy, D., Mitchell, O. S. and Piggott, J. (2002). Asset rich and cash poor: Retirement provision and housing policy in Singapore. *Journal of Pension Economics and Finance*, **1**, 197–222.

Malkiel, B. G. (1999). *A Random Walk Down Wall Street*. New York: Norton.

Milevsky, M. A. and Young, V. R. (2002). Optimal asset allocation and the real option to delay annuitization: It's not now or never. Birkbeck College, The Pensions Institute, London. Discussion paper PI-0211. www.pensions-institute.org/workingpapers/wp0211.pdf.

Mitchell, O. S., Poterba, J., Warshawsky, M. J. and Brown, J. R. (2001). New evidence on the money's-worth of individual annuities. In *The Role of Annuity Markets in Financing Retirement*. Cambridge, Massachusetts: MIT Press, pp. 71–106.

Mitchell, O. S. and Piggott, J. (2003). Housing equity and senior security. Paper prepared for presentation at the Tokyo, Japan September 10, 2003 International Forum on the System for security economic stability for seniors and the improvement of housing in Japan, August. http://www.esri.go.jp/prj-rc/forum/030910/kitcho1-e.pdf.

Mitchell, O. S. and Utkus, S. (2004). Lessons from behavioral finance for retirement plan design. In *Pension Design and Structure: New Lessons from Behavioral Finance*, eds. O. S. Mitchell and S. P. Utkus. Oxford University Press.

Muir, M. and Waller, R. (2003). Twin peaks: the enhanced capital requirement for realistic basis life firms. Presented to Staple Inn Actuarial Society, November 5. www.sias.org.uk/papers/twinpeaks.pdf.

Munnell, A. H., Sass, S. A. and Soto, M. (2005). Yikes! How to think about risk? Issues in brief. No. 27. Center for Retirement Research, Boston College, Boston. http://www.bc.edu/centers/crr/ib_27.shtml.

Murthi, M., Orszag, J. M. and Orszag, P. R. (2001). Administrative costs under a decentralized approach to individual accounts: Lessons from the United Kingdom. In *New Ideas about Old Age Security: Toward Sustainable Pension Systems in the 21st Century*. Washington: World Bank, pp. 308–35.

Organization for Economic Cooperation and Development.(1999). *OECD Economic survey Australia*. Paris: Organization for Economic Cooperation and Development.

— (2001). *OECD Economic survey Australia*. Paris: Organization for Economic Cooperation and Development.

— (2002). *Financial market trends*. Paris: Organization for Economic Cooperation and Development.

— (2004). *Tax-favored Retirement Savings Plans: A Review of Budgetary Implications and Policy Issues*. Annex 1: Tables and figures. ECO/CPE/WPI(2004)4/ANNI. Economics Department. Economic Policy Committee.

Orszag, M. J. (2000). Annuities: The Problems. Paper presented at NAPF Annual Conference, May 11–12, 2000. http://www.econ.bbk.ac.uk/wp/ewp/ewp0007.pdf.

Orszag, P. R. and Stiglitz, J. E. (2001). Rethinking pension reform: Ten myths about social security systems. In *New Ideas about Old Age Security: Toward Sustainable Pension Systems in the 21st Century*. Washington: World Bank, pp. 17–56.

Palacios, R. and Rofman, R. (2001). Annuity markets and benefit design in multipillar pension schemes: Experience and lessons from four Latin American countries. Pension Primer Series. Washington: World Bank.

Palmer, E. (2000). The Swedish pension reform model: framework and issues. World Bank Discussion Paper Series. No. 0012. http://siteresources.worldbank.org/SOCIALPROTECTION/Resources/SP-Discussion-papers/Pensions-DP/0012.pdf

Palmon, O. and Spivak, A. (2002). Adverse selection and the market for annuities. Bank of Israel. Research Paper. August 19, 2002. http://www.boi.gov.il/deptdata/neumim/neum133e.pdf.

Penner, R. and Cove, E. (2002). Women and individual accounts. In *Social Security and the Family*. Washington: Urban Institute Press, pp. 229–70.

Perun, P. (2002). Multiple choices: Property rights and individual accounts. In *Social Security and the Family*. Washington: Urban Institute Press, pp. 271–94.

Pinker, S. (2002). *The Blank Slate*. New York: Norton.

Pinsky, R. (1994). *Dante's Inferno: A New Verse Translation*. New York: Ferrar, Strauss and Giroux.

Posner, R. A. (1995). *Aging and Old Age*. Chicago and London: University of Chicago Press.

Poterba, J. M. (2001). A Brief History of Annuity Markets. In *The Role of Annuity Markets in Financing Retirement*. Cambridge, Massachusetts: MIT Press, pp. 23–56.

— (2005). Annuities in early modern Europe. In *The Origins of Value: The Financial Innovations that Created Modern Capital Markets*, eds. W. N. Goetzmann and K. G. Rouwenhorst. New York: Oxford University Press, pp. 207–24.

Reno, V. P., Graetz, M. J., Apfel, K. S., Lavery, J. and Hill, C., eds. (2005). *Uncharted Waters: Paying Benefits from Individual Accounts in Federal Retirement Policy.* Study panel final report, January. Washington DC: National Academy of Social Insurance.

Rocha, R. and Thorburn, G. (2006). *Developing the Market for Retirement Products: The Case of Chile.* Washington: The World Bank 2006.

Saas, S. (2004). Reforming the Australian Retirement System: Mandating Individual Accounts. Center for Retirement Research, Boston College, Boston. April. http://www.bc.edu.centers/crr/dummy/gib_2.shtml.

SAFJP (Superintendencia de Administradoras de Fondos de Jubilaciones y Pensiones) (2004). *El régimen de capitalización a nueve años de la reforma previsional.* http://safjp.gov.ar.

Samwick, A. A. (1999). Social security reform in the United States. *National Tax Journal*, **52**, 819–42.

Schwartz, B. (2004). *The Paradox of Choice.* New York: Harper Collins, Echo.

Shiller, R. (2000). *Irrational Exuberance.* Princeton: Princeton University Press.

Singh, M. and Kong, J. (2005). Insurance companies in emerging markets. International Monetary Fund Working Paper 05/88. http://www.imf.org/external/pubs/ft/wp/2005/wp0588.pdf.

Smith, A. (1789). *An Inquiry into the Nature and Cause of the Wealth of Nations.* 5th edn. Modern Library edition. New York: The Modern Library, 1994.

Social Security Administration (Various dates). Social security programs throughout the world. http://www.ssa.gov/policy/docs/progdesc/ssptw.

Stark, J. and Curry, C. (2002). Reforming annuities: Big bang or softly, softly? *Insurance Trends.* January. http://www.abi.org.uk/.

Sunstein, C. and Thaler, R. (2003). Paternalistic liberalism is not an oxymoron. *University of Chicago Law Review.*

Superintendency of Pension Companies (Superintendencia de Administradoras de Fondos de Pensiones, or SAFP) (2002). *The Chilean Pension System.* http://www.safp.cl.

TIAA-CREF (2004). How annuities can reduce retirement income risk. *TIAA-CREF Quarterly.* (Winter). http://www.tiaa-crefinstitute.org. Accessed on November 1, 2004.

Taylor, R. (2004). The economics of annuities. *Geneva Papers on Risk and Insurance*, **29**, 115–27.

Thompson, J. (2003). Risk-based supervision of the insurance corporation, an introduction. Paper presented at World Bank Conference: Contractual Savings Conference: Regulatory and supervisory issues in private pensions. November 3–7.

Thompson, L. H. (1998). *Older and Wiser: The Economics of Public Pensions.* Washington: Urban Institute Press.

Thompson, L. H. and Carasso, A. (2002). Social security and the treatment of families: How does the U.S. compare to other developed countries? In *Social Security and the Family*. Washington: Urban Institute Press, pp. 123–76.

United Nations, Population Division, Economic and Social Affairs Department (2003a). *World Population Prospects: the 2002 Revision. Highlights.*

— (2003b). *World Population Prospects: the 2002 Revision. Vol. III: Analytical Report.*

United Kingdom Pensions Commission (2004). *Pensions: Challenges and Choices: The First Report of the Pensions Commission.*

Walliser, J. (1998). Social Security Privatization and the Annuities Market. Congressional Budget Office. http://www.cbo.gov/showdoc.cfm?index=348&sequence=0.

— (2000). Adverse selection in the annuities market and the impact of privatizing social security. *Scandinavian Journal of Economics*, **102**, 373–93.

— (2001). Regulation of withdrawals in individual account systems. In *New Ideas about Old Age Security: Toward Sustainable Pension Systems in the 21st Century*. Washington: World Bank.

Warner, J. T. and Pleeter, S. (2001). The personal discount rate: Evidence from military downsizing programs. *American Economic Review*, **91**, 33–53.

Warshawsky, M. J. (2001). Private Annuity Markets in the United States: 1919–1984. In *The Role of Annuity Markets in Financing Retirement*. Cambridge, Massachusetts: MIT Press, pp. 57–70.

Yaari, M. E. (1965). Uncertain lifetime, life insurance, and the theory of the consumer. *Review of Economic Studies*, **32**, 137–50.

Index

actuarial fairness, 31, 201, 202
adverse selection, 41, 142, 190, 191, 219
aging, 6, 8, 145, 225–30
allocated annuities (Australia), 26
annuities
  guarantees on, *see* guarantees
  history of, 1
  group purchases, 182
  inhibitions on demand for, 31–43
  investment alternatives to
    residential investment, 205–6
    risky financial assets, 206–8
    tax-favored competing assets,
      34–5
  role in mitigating shortfall risk in
    retirement, 53–5
  taxation of, *see* taxation of annuity
    income,
  theoretical superiority of, 28–31
  varieties, 22
annuitization
  deferred, 52, 167
  extent of, 140–7
  individual preferences and, 144–5
  mandatory, *see* mandatory
    annuitization
annuity pricing and premiums, 43–5,
  72
annuity provision/supply, 142
  actuarial function, 142
  administrative function, 142
  cost of supplying, 75–7
    administrative, 75–6
    marketing, 75–6

  reserving, 77
  investment function, 142
anti-discrimination law (U.S.), 43
appeals process under mandatory
  annuitization, 145
Arrow–Pratt coefficient of risk aversion, 195
asymmetric information, 82, 142, 187

bad choices, 140, 189
  insights of behavioral finance into,
    140, 189
  measures to avoid, 189–90
bankruptcy, *see* life insurance
  companies,
bequest, 31, 198, 199
  accidental, 32, 33
  altruistic, 33
  deliberate, 32
  exchange, 33
  expected value of, 201, 202
  motives for, 32
  premature death and, 199, 200
  size of, 198, 199
behavioral finance, 140

Central Provident Fund (CPF)
  (Singapore), 25, 188
Chilean Pensions Superintendency, 188
compulsory participation in public
  pension plans, 138, 139
consumer education, 84
contingent security, 29
corporate transparency, 86
CRRA utility function, 194

debt management office (U.K.), 64
declining (income replacement)
    schedule, 147
defined benefit pension plan, 10–2
defined contribution plan, 11
demographic transition, 6
discount rate, 68
distributions from individual accounts,
    178
    after retirement, 146–7, 149–54
    form of annuity, 179–80
    share of account balance to be
        annuitized, 178–9
    before retirement, 147–9

efficiency of private annuity market, 187
employer-provided pension plan, 138–9
European Investment Bank, 70
Exemption from mandatory
    annuitization, 147
expected capitalized value, 168
expected rate of return, 65, 217
expected value, 33

framing effect and choice among
    alternatives, 140

government regulation, rationale for,
    143
group purchase of annuities, 182
guarantees
    on individual account balance, 154–6
    on regular annuity payment, 170–2
guaranteed annuity options (GAOS)
    (U.K.), 101

immunization of life insurance
    company portfolios, 63, 214–16
indexed annuity, 27, 149, 151
indexed bonds, 62
indexed debt, 62
individual accounts reform and
    population aging, 229–30
individual capital assessment (ICA)
    (U.K. regulatory system), 102
individual capital guidance (ICG)
    (U.K. regulatory system), 102

inflation and impact on real value of
    annuity payment, 149
insurance value of annuities, 49, 221
interest rate fluctuations, 165
international association of insurance
    supervisors (IAIS), 96
internet, 188
investment in residence, 184 *see*
    annuities, investment alternatives
    to
IRA (U.S.), 35, 139

liabilities of life insurance companies,
    63, 67
liberalized withdrawal from individual
    accounts, 144, 149
libertarian paternalism, 139–41
life annuities, 5
life insurance companies 202
    accounting procedures, 85
    actuarial assumptions, 85
    capital adequacy, 85, 96
    corporate governance, 85
    failure of, 103–4
    financial difficulties of, 171
    funding practices of, 85
    guarantees on annuity
        payments, 85
    insolvency procedures, 85, 94
    investment practices, 85
    pricing practices, 85
    qualifications of staff, 85
    regulatory change and, 85–6
    reserve adequacy, 96, 98
life tables, 73
    cohort life table, 73
    period life table, 73
life-cycle saver, 136
long-term insurance capital
    requirement (LTICR)
    (U.K. regulatory
    framework), 100, 101
lump-sum withdrawal, 152, 203

Macaulay duration, 214
mandatory annuitization, 41, 137, 144
maturity spectrum of a bond portfolio,
    62, 63

maturity structure of a bond portfolio, 211–4
minimum capital requirement, 100
money's worth ratio, 45, 47, 48
moral hazard, 43
mortality rate, 72
MW ratio *see* money's worth ratio,

non-matching payments and receipts, 214

occupational pension plan, *see* employer-provided pension plan,
OECD (Organization for Economic Cooperation and Development), 35, 92

parametric reform of public pension systems, 228
  impact on GDP, 229
paternalism, 137
PAYG (pay as you go), 124, 159
payout, 189
pension reform (*see also* reforms), 8–10, 24
phased withdrawal from individual accounts, 152
PPD (premium per dollar), 219–21
precautionary expenditure, 31
premium differentiation, 167, 182
  by health status, 182
  by sex/gender, 182
premium level, 163
premium variability, 165, 166
preservation age (Australia), 26
private annuity markets, 6, 21
  Australia, 26–7
  Chile, 24–5
  France, 27
  Germany, 27
  Israel, 27
  Italy, 27
  Japan, 27
  Singapore, 25–6
  Switzerland, 25
  United Kingdom, 24
  United States, 23–4

private annuity provision, 66, 141, 163, 175, 181, 185
  premium variability, 181
  educational programs for, 175
  exemptions to mandatory annuitization under, 176
  guarantees, administration of, 176
  notification system for, 176
  regulation of eligibility annuity providers, 176
  advantages of, 185
prudent person rule, 85–7
public pension system, 5, 38–40, 208–10

quantitative restrictions on insurance company portfolios, 92
  advantages, 91
  defects, 87

realistic liabilities (U.K. regulatory system), 100
reforms, 106, 164
  Argentina, 119
  Bolivia, 119
  Chile, 106–19
    AFP (administrador de fondo de pensión), 107, 118
    brokers, 116
    contribution rate, 108
    deferred annuity, 117
    guaranteed annuities, 112
    immediate life annuity, 112
    indexed instruments, 109
    limits on holdings of AFPs, 110
    mortality table, 116
    MW ratio, 116
    programmed withdrawal, 112
    recognition bond (bono de reconocimiento), 111–2
    regulation of investments, 110
    retirement pension, 112
      early retirement, 112, 117
      regular retirement, 112
    SAFP (superintendencia de administradores de fundo de pensiones), 107, 118
    UF (Unidad de fomento), 109

reforms (*cont.*)
Colombia, 119
Costa Rica, 119
Croatia, 125
El Salvador, 119
Estonia, 124
Europe, 124
Hungary, 124, 125
Kazakhstan, 124
Mexico, 119
Peru, 119
Poland, 124
United Kingdom, 24
Uruguay, 119
regulation of life insurance companies, 81, 85–7
direct approach, 86
of discount rate, 122
indirect approach, 87
mixed approach, 91
prudent person rule and, 87
rationale for, 82
regulation of withdrawals, 138
regulatory agency, 98
regulatory issues, general aspects of in design of reform, 192
regulatory peak (U.K. regulatory system), 99–101
reserve measurement system, 65
resilience capital requirement (RCR) (U.K. regulatory system), 100
retirement planning, 135
reverse mortgage, 36
bequest motive and, 37
impact on demand for annuities, 38
market in United Kingdom, 36
market in United States, 36
risk, 60
business risk, 59, 61
capital risk, 60
credit risk, 59, 60
investment risk, 59, 60
interest risk, 60
liquidity risk, 59, 60
mortality risk, 59
aggregate, 59, 96

select, 59, 70–2
persistency risk, 101
risk capital margin (RCM) (U.K. regulatory system), 101
risky assets, 206
Roman law and capitalization of annuity income, 1–6
RRSP (Canada), 139

self-control, problems of, 135
shortfall risk in retirement, 54
single premium immediate life annuity (SPIA), 21, 28
social safety net, 154, 180
account guarantees, 180
disability benefits, 180
family benefits, 180
redistributive concerns, 180
social solidarity, 168
state second pension (U.K.), 24
subjective discount factor, 196
superannuation guarantee (Australia), 26
survival probability, 196, 220
survivor bonds, 71

taxation of annuity income, 172–4, 191
and classical model of income taxation, 192
in OECD member countries, 172
tax-favored competing assets, *see* annuities, investment alternatives to 34
teacher's insurance company TIAA-CREF, 71
temporary annuity, 72
term life insurance, 70
transparent accounting, 85
treasury inflation protected securities (TIPS), 27
twin peaks regulatory approach of the U.K., 99, 102
two-period life-cycle model, 194

U.K. financial service authority (FSA), 99
U.S. social security, 154

variable annuity, 149, 151
variance of return, 217,
    218
voluntary annuitant, 164

withdrawal rules for individual
    accounts, 134

with-profit insurance capital
    component (WPICC) (U.K.
    regulatory system), 101

yield curve, 65

zero-coupon bonds, 212, 213

Printed in the United States
By Bookmasters